CECIL COUNTY
LIBRARY
park Ave.
MD 21921

THE DAY THE EARTH CAVED IN

THE DAY THE EARTH CAVED IN

AN AMERICAN MINING TRAGEDY

Joan Quigley

RANDOM HOUSE NEW YORK

Copyright © 2007 by Joan Quigley

All rights reserved.

Published in the United States by Random House, an imprint of
The Random House Publishing Group, a division of Random House, Inc., New York.

Random House and colophon are registered trademarks of Random House, Inc.

ISBN 978-1-4000-6180-8

Library of Congress Cataloging-in-Publication Data

Quigley, Joan.
The day the earth caved in: an American mining tragedy / Joan Quigley
p. cm.
Includes bibliographical references.
ISBN-13: 978-1-4000-6180-8
1. Mine fires—Pennsylvania—Centralia. 2. Mine fires—Social aspects—Pennsylvania—Centralia.
3. Mine gases—Pennsylvania—Centralia. 4. Coal mines and mining—Pennsylvania—Centralia.
5. Centralia (Pa.)—History. 6. Centralia (Pa.)—Social conditions. I. Title.

TN315.Q54 2007
363.37'9—dc22 2006051047

Printed in the United States of America on acid-free paper

www.atrandom.com

246897531

First Edition

For my maternal grandmother,
Mildred Holland Reifke

And Robert

Double, double, toil and trouble;
Fire burn and cauldron bubble.

Macbeth, Act IV, Scene 1

CONTENTS

CENTRALIA, PENNSYLVANIA

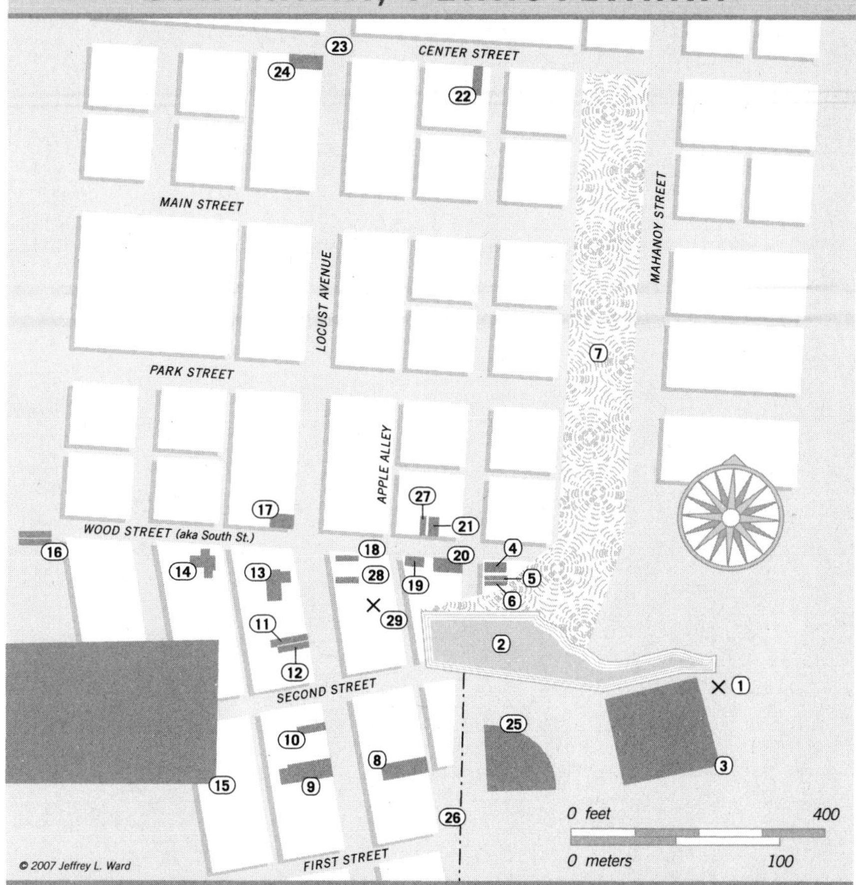

Key to Locations

1. *Centralia Dump*
2. *The 1969 Trench*
3. *Odd Fellows Cemetery*
4. *Annie Donahue Ryan's home*
5. *Birsters' home*
6. *Michael and Anna Fowler Laughlin homestead*
7. *Fly-ash barrier*
8. *St. Ignatius School*
9. *St. Ignatius Church*
10. *Catharene and Peacho Jurgill's home*
11. *Dave Lamb's home*
12. *Oakums' home*
13. *John Coddington's gas station*
14. *Terrence Burge's home*
15. *St. Ignatius Cemetery*
16. *Chapmans' home*
17. *Tony Andrade's home*
18. *Kanes' home*
19. *Helen Womer's home*
20. *Mary Lou Gaughan's home*
21. *Nance Maloney's home*
22. *Quigley homestead*
23. *The Four Corners*
24. *The Speed Spot*
25. *St. Ignatius baseball field*
26. *Centralia borough line*
27. *Flo Domboski's home*
28. *Carrie Wolfgang's home*
29. *Todd Domboski's cave-in*

PROLOGUE

Into the Fire

Todd Domboski broke into a run. From the front porch of his mother's row house, he cut across Apple Alley and into the yard behind his grandmother's home. Every weekday, he traveled the same route on his way to St. Ignatius School, where he was in seventh grade. Perched near the crest of Locust Mountain, the one-story brick school boasted a baseball diamond in back, a magnet for local enthusiasts. To the east, it looked out over the Odd Fellows Cemetery and, farther east, the hills and ridges of the Appalachians. From his grandmother's slender backyard, flecked with trees and birdhouses, Todd could see into the well-maintained yards of her next-door neighbors, including Harry Kleman's lawn, dotted with miniature wooden windmills. In the woods behind their property, Todd and his friends built forts, shot BB guns, and rode motorbikes. Uptown in Centralia, Pennsylvania, that's what boys did for fun.

Minutes earlier, Todd's grandmother, Carrie Wolfgang, had glanced out the bay window in her living room, gazing out onto South Locust Avenue, the main north-south corridor through town. Just beyond her front porch, Centralia descended into a valley, one mile long and six blocks across, lined with about five hundred homes, most of them twelve-foot-wide wooden row houses. Just wide enough at street level for one window and a front door, they pressed against each other like kernels of corn, housing the town's one thousand or so residents, many of whom had lived in the same homes all their lives. Pickup trucks and sedans lined the curb, two- and four-door models in 1970s hues such as sea-foam green and metallic blue. At the opposite end of town, near the crest of Aristes Mountain, the turquoise onion-shaped dome of St. Mary's Church towered over black mounds of coal waste, refuse from strip-mining in the 1930s and underground operations dating back to the Civil War.

On this sunny Saturday morning—Valentine's Day 1981—when Carrie peered out the window she spotted a cluster of officials across the street, men in suits and overcoats leaving Tony and Mary Andrade's house, next door to John Coddington's Amoco station. Curious, she phoned her daughter, Flo Domboski, a garment worker who lived around the corner on Wood Street. Flo dispatched Todd, her twelve-year-old son, to investigate.

Meanwhile, Carrie's sixteen-year-old grandson, Erik Wolfgang, crouched over Todd's motorcycle in the backyard. Erik, who had been staying with Carrie while his parents enjoyed a midwinter cruise, was trying—without success—to fix a flat tire. When Todd darted past, Erik called out, asking for help. Todd stopped to watch while Erik strained to rig a hot patch, gluing a rubber strip over the hole and heating the adhesive with a match.

A few yards away, Todd noticed a wisp of smoke floating from the ground, like a smoldering match buried under damp leaves. In Centralia, where an abandoned coal mine beneath the town had been burning for nineteen years, tiny fissures often punched through the topsoil, trailing bands of sulfurous steam—especially in Todd's neighborhood, where an old tunnel from the burning mine sliced underneath Wood Street's south side, below the Gaughans' and Womers' backyards. On a regular basis, Todd watched his neighbor across the street, Carl Womer, pack sinkholes in his yard, filling them with ashes from a coal stove.

Todd stood there, convinced he and Erik had ignited a fire with their matches and glue. And now, on a day otherwise consigned to roses, chocolate, and construction paper hearts, loomed the prospect of torching their granny's yard—and being held responsible. Todd skirted the edges of her metal shed, crammed with patio furniture and lawn mowers, and crept over for a closer look. Erik, with his back to his cousin, focused on the decommissioned tire. Todd, a thin preadolescent boy with long legs and large feet into which his frame hadn't grown, paused near the puff of smoke to brush away dead leaves. The ground, still saturated from a deluge that had pummeled Columbia County three days earlier, gave way beneath him.

Todd started sinking—first to his knees. He tried to pull himself out but plunged even deeper until he was submerged to his waist. He placed his hands on the ground next to his hips and tried to push out, like someone who had fallen into a frozen pond. But his hands disappeared into the slime, as if he had slipped them into his pockets. The soggy earth kept melting, sucking him in and burying him—to his sternum, his neck, his chin. In a split second, Todd plummeted all the way underground, into a cavity as wide as his chest, a column of hot sticky mud moistened by emissions from the mine fire.

This is it, he thought. *I'm going to die.*

Steam rolled up from beneath his feet, thick and sulfurous. Vapors lapped at his face and clung to his nostrils, reeking like rotten eggs. Every time Todd wrestled for a foothold, the earth collapsed, tugging him down still farther. Below him, gases from the mine fire gushed skyward, fanned by oxygen from the opening over his head. They made a howling sound like the roar of a tornado.

Still foundering, Todd jammed his back into the damp soil. He dug his feet in, too, hoping to break his downward slide.

I've got to get out of here, he thought. *Now.*

Flailing, Todd grabbed at the moist dirt. He latched onto a cluster of tree roots, finally stopping his descent. Clutching the roots, with his back and feet wedged into the ooze, he screamed for help.

Erik heard Todd's cries and looked up. A plume of steam poured from the ground just a few yards from his grandmother's shed—a funnel so dense motorists could spot it four miles away, on the highway outside Mount Carmel. Erik sprinted over and dropped to his stomach. Peering into the hole, two feet wide and swirling with hot white vapors, he could barely discern the outlines of Todd's orange hat, about six feet down. Erik knew he couldn't reach him.

"Put your hand up!" Erik yelled. "Put your hand up!"

Still pressing his feet and back into the muck to keep from sliding farther down, Todd clutched at the roots with one hand and lifted the other, straining toward Erik. With Todd extending his arm as high as he could, Erik stretched down, about three feet, into the hole. Their hands met in the middle. Erik grabbed Todd's wrist, locking his grip. With a heave, he plucked Todd from the ground like a fresh onion, forty-five seconds after the earth had first begun to swallow him.

Back on dry land, Todd's hooded nylon parka and jeans were caked with sticky, warm mud. Otherwise, he had escaped unscathed. The steam hadn't singed his hair or his clothing. He didn't have any burns. The round-faced parochial student, schooled by the nuns, thought God had saved him.

The boys, numb with shock, dashed into their grandmother's house. Todd raced straight to the sink, a cast-iron behemoth with separate hot and cold water faucets. He opened the cold spigot and started gulping, not bothering with a glass. Carrie found her grandsons in the kitchen and demanded an explanation of the smoke—now billowing from the ground—in her backyard. Erik told her what had happened.

Carrie sent them across the street to the Andrades' to alert the officials who had gathered there. Erik ran over and explained to the mine inspector and the men in suits: Todd had fallen into a hole in his grandmother's backyard. Todd, still coated with dirt, approached Locust Avenue, where workers had drilled into the pavement and installed a series of metal pipes to vent steam from the mine fire. Even after his rescue, however, he hovered near his grandmother's front porch, reluctant to cross the street, afraid it, too, might open underneath him. A reporter for the Shenandoah *Evening Herald* snapped Todd's photograph: arms and legs tense with fear, his half-open mouth turned down at the corners, fighting back tears.

THE TOWN of Centralia sits in a 484-square-mile region of northeastern Pennsylvania honeycombed with vast deposits of anthracite coal. That coal was formed from the carbon of ferns and plants when prehistoric swamps submerged beneath the earth's crust and metamorphosed, under intense pressure and heat, into sedimentary layers of rock and shale. The greater the force generated by the folding layers, the higher the carbon content, and hence the quality, of the coal. On a scale from peat, which hails from swampy bogs, to pure carbon, anthracite falls at the latter end of the spectrum. Bituminous coal, the kind scooped from shallow seams in West Virginia and western Pennsylvania, is somewhere in the middle. Anthracite, so hard and shiny locals dubbed it the black diamond, shatters like glass when it breaks.

Situated at the northern tip of the Appalachian coalfield, which runs from Pennsylvania to Alabama, the anthracite coal region stretches from Forest City in the north to just short of Harrisburg in the south. From a geological perspective, the region consists of four contiguous fields, aligned with the ridges and valleys of the Appalachians: the Northern, the Eastern Middle, the Western Middle, and the Southern. Centralia occupies the center of the Western Middle Field, a thirty-four-mile-long, four-mile-wide strip of rolling terrain hemmed in to the far west and north by the Susquehanna River. During the mountain-building Permian period, the Western Middle Field's coal deposits contorted into flat, deep basins with steep sides that dive under the ridges in V-shaped layers, like graduated upside-down buckets. All around Centralia, anthracite coal seams plunge underground at 33- to 45-degree angles to the surface, bottom out two thousand to three thousand feet below ground, and surge back upward several miles away, often in the next coal town. For the quality and quantity of its deposits, an early mining official observed, the Centralia basin was unsurpassed anywhere in the state.

For millions of years, the area's anthracite lay buried in inaccessible coal seams. After the War of 1812, however, when Philadelphia entrepreneurs developed an anthracite-fired furnace, the industry sprang to life. Financiers such as Stephen Girard, John Biddle, and Lloyd Wharton invested in mineral-rich coal lands. And, like colonial barons, they siphoned profits from the third-world region that generated them, routing the revenue back to New York and Philadelphia.

In the mid- and late nineteenth century, fourteen mines opened in and around Centralia, each employing up to several hundred men and boys—some as young as nine years old—to unearth, process, and haul anthracite. By 1890, Centralia boasted more than twenty-five hundred residents, most of whom had emigrated from Ireland, Wales, Germany, and, to an increasing extent, southern and eastern Europe. By day, they blasted through coal seams hundreds of feet underground. At night, they crammed into row homes erected on top of the mines. The United Mine Workers of America, which helped organize the anthracite coalfields after labor unrest rocked the region in 1902, maintained three locals in Centralia alone, with a combined membership of more than one thousand miners.

After the 1929 stock market crash, however, one of the town's main employers, the Lehigh Valley Coal Company, folded and never recovered. The regional economy, like the industry that created it, sank into a prolonged decline. Out-of-work miners scraped by on income from bootleg coal holes scattered across property owned by their former employers. Coal companies leased their land to strip miners, who deployed steam shovels into coal seams at the easy-to-reach surface. Where mountains had once stood, laced with pines, birch trees, and mountain laurel, the strip miners left behind piles of black waste, often towering several stories high, and hollowed-out basins, some as long as football fields.

After a brief resurgence during World War II, the industry collapsed for good in the 1950s. Across the coal region, cash-strapped local governments—deprived of their principal source of tax revenue and employment—couldn't afford municipal landfills. Residents dragged their trash—lumber, furniture, petrochemicals—to stripping pits, hollowed-out caverns where bulldozers and high-powered steam shovels had once pawed into the earth for anthracite, like demolishing a cake's layers to reveal the icing between them. Garbage heaped atop exposed coal seams ignited, setting fire to abandoned underground workings. By 1954, fires raged in seven inactive anthracite mines. One mine fire in Laurel Run, near Wilkes-Barre, had been smoldering since 1915.

Just before Memorial Day in 1962, a fire broke out at a garbage dump on Centralia's southeastern edge, near the Odd Fellows Cemetery. The landfill sat atop an abandoned strip-mining pit, a hollowed-out bowl about fifty feet deep and seventy-five feet wide, where an independent contractor had stripped the Buck Mountain vein—a seven-foot-wide coal seam—in the 1930s. The trash fire swept down the Buck vein and into the defunct Centralia Colliery, abandoned by the Lehigh Valley Coal Company in 1931. As the fire reached the underground tunnels, laden with millions of tons of anthracite, it blazed through the coal like molten lava, spewing methane, carbon dioxide, and carbon monoxide. For years, the mine fire kept burning, defying the government's repeated efforts to bring it under control by digging it out, starving it of oxygen, and pumping noncombustible powder into the workings.

Yet well into 1980, most Centralia residents largely ignored the fire. In a town with a nine-thousand-dollar median annual income, about half the national average, many were preoccupied with working, raising children, and paying bills, or, for older widows and retired miners, stretching Social Security checks and finding rides to doctors' appointments. Of course, Centralians saw steam chugging from the vent pipes in Todd Domboski's neighborhood. They smelled sulfurous fumes there, too, especially on humid summer days when a milky haze coated the mountains, trapping vapors near the surface. Lingering over beers at the American Legion or chatting with neighbors at the post office, they griped about contractors who managed to get rich—by local standards—bilking taxpayers on the government's ill-fated projects.

Still, most Centralians felt safe, particularly ex-miners on the opposite end of town who knew the coal seams lay hundreds of feet below ground—and below their row houses. Even many of Todd's Wood Street and Locust Avenue neighbors assumed the fire smoldered out in the woods on the borough's eastern edge, near the dump. Mine fires were part of life in the anthracite region, like church picnics, minstrel shows, and high school football games. No one really knew the Centralia fire's precise location or how far it had spread, so it remained easy to ignore.

Like their parents, grandparents, and great-grandparents before them, Centralians filed in to Mass on Sunday. The Irish Catholics gathered at St. Ignatius, whose modest white steeple dominated the Locust Avenue hilltop, just up the street from Carrie Wolfgang's house. The descendants of Ukrainian immigrants congregated on the hill that marked the town's northern frontier, climbing the winding road to St. Mary's. Men and women who couldn't find work in the region commuted to state government jobs in Harrisburg, more than an hour away. Ex-miners and their widows lunched on oven-fried fish at the senior center, swapped gossip over porch railings, and bought cigarettes at John Coddington's store for sixty-five cents a pack.

Even the local media had wearied of the underground fire, now closing in on its second decade. The week before Todd fell, even the most banal news pouring off the AP wire seemed more pressing. Polish Defense Minister Wojciech Jaruzelski, newly installed as premier, dispatched a deputy to meet with an independent union leader, Solidarity's Lech Walesa, hoping to obtain a ninety-day moratorium against labor strikes and stave off intervention by Soviet troops massed near Poland's border. Three weeks after taking the oath of office, President Ronald Reagan met with cabinet officials and his budget director, David Stockman, to finalize the federal budget. They gutted $26 billion in Interior Department programs and rent subsidies for the poor and elderly and increased defense spending by the same amount, to a total of $220 billion. And in a Philadelphia trial court, a coal company executive testified that the state's proposed strip-mining regulations, designed to bring Pennsylvania into compliance with federal legislation enacted four years earlier, would devastate the industry.

AFTER SEVERAL DAYS of unpredictable weather, ranging from unseasonably warm breezes to snow flurries and subfreezing temperatures,

February 14 dawned clear and mild in Centralia, with temperatures forecast to reach the low forties. The youth auxiliary of St. Ignatius readied the teen club, located in the old Episcopal church, for a Valentine's dance that evening, featuring music by Audio-Feedback. At the Lynch-Gugie-Cheppa-Liptock Post No. 608 of the American Legion on West Park Street, where residents had buried a time capsule in 1966 to honor the town's centennial, members were gearing up for Whitey's Polka Band, the star attraction at its Valentine's dance that evening.

Meanwhile, down at the municipal building, a squat 1970s structure topped by solar heating panels, federal, state, and local officials and a handful of residents gathered for a morning meeting with Centralia's new congressman, James Nelligan, a silver-haired Wilkes-Barre Republican who had ridden Reagan's coattails into office. Nelligan, flush with victory, had conferred with Interior Department Secretary James G. Watt about the mine fire in January. Before joining Reagan's administration, Watt had headed the Mountain States Legal Foundation, defending western mining, timber, and cattle industries in court and advancing their legislative agenda. And Watt, an avowed foe of federal spending projects, particularly if they harmed the coal industry, had asked the freshman congressman what Centralians wanted the federal government to do.

Inside the municipal building, Nelligan pressured Centralia's mayor, John Wondoloski, and the members of its part-time borough council for guidance about solutions, including relocating the town. Wondoloski, who still eked out a living in the strip mines, favored making the county government decide. The borough councilmen, who earned twenty dollars per month for their services, balked at shouldering responsibility for the town's fate. They knew that Centralians—when they even paused to think about it—did not agree about the mine fire. Roughly half the borough opposed measures, including relocation, designed to provide relief. Exasperated, Nelligan suggested a referendum, letting the borough's citizens determine their fate.

After the meeting, Nelligan and the officials ventured up South Locust Avenue to the Andrades' house. Ed Narcavage, a state mine inspector with the frame and belly of an aging high school fullback, briefed them on the fundamentals. During the previous month, the Andrades' carbon monoxide monitor had sounded seven times, signaling a buildup higher than 35 parts per million, the governmental safety threshold. One week earlier, the state health department had declared the home unsafe for habitation. But without financial help from the government—which had not materialized—the Andrades were reluctant to move, even temporarily. So Narcavage, who lugged his thirty-pound gas detection equipment into about a dozen houses in that neighborhood every day, testing for carbon monoxide and methane, knew their house well.

While officials huddled outside the Andrades', Nelligan spotted figures running in the yard across the street, where a column of smoke belched from the ground. Moments later, Erik ran over to them. Narcavage thought someone had died.

State Senator Edward Helfrick, a local coal magnate, grabbed an aide and told him to call Governor Richard J. Thornburgh.

CARRIE WOLFGANG picked up the phone and dialed her daughter, Flo, who was upstairs in Todd's bedroom installing wood paneling. "Get over here," Carrie said. "Todd fell in a hole with water or something and he's awfully dirty."

Strolling up Apple Alley, thinking her son had splashed in a puddle, Flo noticed steam billowing from Carrie's backyard. A crowd had already gathered, neighbors and politicians alike, gaping down at the hole, speculating about how deep it was, and wondering how Todd had escaped. As Flo walked up to her mother's house, the bystanders called out to her. He fell in over there, they said.

Realizing what had happened, Flo panicked. She found Todd and tried to hug him, but he pushed her away and said he was okay. Pete Wysochansky, a volunteer fireman, drove up in the town's ambulance and started hooking Todd to an oxygen tank. Mayor Wondoloski, who had a daughter Todd's age, told Flo to take her son to Ashland State

General Hospital, two miles away, to have him tested for carbon monoxide poisoning.

Helen Womer, a plump fifty-two-year-old bank teller with oversized glasses and a helmet of curly gray hair, raced over from her house next door, about 150 feet from where Todd fell. Earlier that morning, she had appeared at the meeting in borough hall, saying she vehemently opposed relocating the community because it simply was not necessary.

Cover that up, she said to the throngs of people at the opening. There's no fire in there.

Womer, a lifelong Centralia resident whose husband plugged sinkholes in their yard, knew the mine fire had smoldered under her neighborhood for years. This new subsidence in Carrie Wolfgang's backyard frightened her, however, and not for the reasons it alarmed so many others. This cave-in, which had just nearly swallowed her twelve-year-old neighbor, might prove irresistible to news-media outsiders. Once they started poking around, interviewing neighbors and shooting footage of the steam pipes, officials would bow to the pressure. Womer, who lived closer to the fire's leading edge than virtually anyone else in town, didn't want the government stirred into action. If it was, it might revive a plan to control the fire by digging a massive trench through the neighborhood, one that promised to burrow through her living room.

Womer zeroed in on Flo.

You keep this quiet, Womer said. We don't need any publicity.

Flo didn't answer. She turned and walked away, more concerned about getting her son to the hospital than about pacifying Helen Womer. Never one to mince words, though, Flo knew she wouldn't keep her mouth shut.

Flo had now crossed an invisible threshold in her head—one from which she could not turn back. Nineteen years earlier, the government could have dug out the fire for a pittance, a mere thirty thousand dollars. But the politicians had never wangled enough money to do the job right, and the mine fire had kept on burning. Now she had almost lost her son because the bureaucrats still couldn't decide what to do: put out the fire or the people who lived there. She knew she'd do everything she could to keep this in the news. She needed to sell her house and get out.

Narcavage, the mine inspector, borrowed a ladder from the American Legion and laid it across the crater. He eased out onto the wooden rungs, braving a sulfurous curtain of steam, and dangled a thermometer into the void. At the opening, the temperature hovered around 280 degrees. When he tried to take a carbon monoxide reading with his portable monitor, which registered from zero to 30 parts per million, the needle raced to the end of the dial. By the time he erected a slatted wooden snow fence around the cave-in to keep anyone else from falling in, local reporters and television crews had converged on the scene, elbowing the mine inspector aside.

Across the street, outside Chrissie Oakum's house, a cluster of young parents gathered to talk on the sidewalk. Tom Larkin, a beefy short-order cook and fifth-generation Centralian with thinning salt-and-pepper hair and a mustache, chatted with Congressman Nelligan while steam vented from a pipe at Coddington's station down the block and across the street in Carrie's yard. Larkin, a former peace activist who had marched on the Washington, D.C., mall in the late 1960s to protest the Vietnam War, told Nelligan it was the federal government's responsibility to put the fire out. Meanwhile, Larkin knew that the presence of the news media, and their interest in the mine fire, gave Centralia residents unprecedented leverage. In those cameras and notebooks lay the opportunity to make the government do something about the fire—and save the town before someone died.

Later that afternoon, Narcavage saw Todd seated on his grandmother's back porch, worn out from repeating his story. The mine inspector, the only other person in Centralia who had come as close as Todd to the cave-in, feeling its heat and breathing its sulfur-laden fumes, asked the boy how he felt. Todd said he was scared. In fact, he was terrified, convinced another hole would open beneath him, sucking him in all over again.

That evening, in the bedroom his mother hadn't finished paneling, Todd couldn't sleep. After surviving a plunge into the ground over the mine fire and feeling the hot mud press against his chest, he couldn't even stand to have a blanket cover him.

As Valentine's Day settled into evening in Centralia, Catharene Jurgill ducked into a meeting at a neighbor's house on South Locust Avenue, about two blocks from the bedroom where Todd Domboski lay awake. Catharene, a nineteen-year-old housewife four months pregnant with her second child, had grown up in Ringtown, an agricultural village just a few miles to the north, picking tomatoes and gathering chicken eggs and earning 4-H Club ribbons for cooking and sewing. A former Girl Scout and cheerleader with wavy brown hair and large hazel eyes, she had married her boyfriend, Leon Jurgill, Jr., in October 1978, a few months after finishing high school. Hours after their wedding, they moved into a row home next to St. Ignatius Convent, just a few doors from the church.

Catharene had heard about the mine fire as a student in Ringtown, which shared a school district with half of Centralia. When she settled in to her new home and learned the fire had been blazing since she was one year old, she started pressing her neighbors for information. That afternoon, when Todd dropped into his grandmother's backyard, she realized she no longer had the luxury of idle curiosity. Carrie Wolfgang's house sat just down the block from the Jurgills', on a route Catharene walked every day, with her one-and-a-half-year-old daughter in a stroller. She knew she had to protect her family.

Looking around the room, Catharene recognized the dozen or so neighbors who had gathered, mostly young parents who lived nearby, on the 100 and 200 blocks of South Locust Avenue: Mary Theresa Gasperetti, a waitress and mother of two; Eleanor O'Hearn, a bank teller and mother with two sons at St. Ignatius School; and Dave Lamb, a father of two who owned a motorcycle shop called the Speed Spot at Locust Avenue and Center Street, the main intersection in town. The mine fire no longer felt like a distant nuisance to them, burning out in the woods near the dump somewhere. That afternoon, it had invaded their neighborhood, drawing in one of their own. Now, they feared, they couldn't let their children play outside. They didn't even feel safe inside their houses, which hugged the same network of mine workings as Carrie Wolfgang's backyard.

What they would learn over the next few days, as test results trickled back from a West Virginia federal laboratory, would confirm Ed Narcavage's initial suspicions: The temperature inside the hole had measured 160 degrees Fahrenheit, and the carbon monoxide level had registered 1,154 parts per million, more than thirty times the federal government's recommended exposure threshold, and 96 percent—a mere 46 parts per million shy—of the concentration deemed immediately threatening to life and health. If Todd had remained trapped just a few minutes longer, he would have died. The doctors and nurses who examined him in the emergency room couldn't fathom how he had escaped without so much as a steam burn.

For weeks, people in Centralia marveled that Todd hadn't been killed by carbon monoxide poisoning. That he had saved himself by clinging to a tree root, with his cousin's help, was a virtual miracle. Those forty-five seconds Todd spent inside the cave-in shook the town like a minor earthquake, jolting residents out of nineteen years of paralysis and denial.

In the late nineteenth century, my great-grandfather James Quigley raised seven children in a row home at East Center and Wood streets in Centralia, in a neighborhood called the Swamp. My grandmother Helen Laughlin Quigley grew up a few blocks uphill on Wood Street, in a tree-lined enclave a few hundred feet from the strip mine that became the dump. My great-aunt Kate Quigley taught first grade in Centralia's public school for thirty-seven years, educating generations of immigrant children and their siblings. When she died in 1940, the school board passed a resolution closing classrooms for her funeral at

St. Ignatius. Her younger sister, Annie, a seamstress, operated a dry cleaner's out of the family homestead into the late 1960s.

My grandfather, also named James, was born in Centralia in 1881. After third grade, he quit school to work as a breaker boy, the entry-level rung on the mine labor hierarchy. For the next five years or so, he crouched over chutes in an aboveground processing hub, logging ten hours a day, six days a week, picking out pieces of slate and refuse as the coal swept past on its way to waiting railroad cars. For his efforts, he pocketed about forty cents a day. Still, he belonged to a lucky minority—he stayed alive, avoided injuries, and rose into management's ranks. In his early thirties, he snared the position of fire boss, an official whose expertise supplanted the proverbial coal mine canary, descending into the workings alone every morning to ensure that flammable gases, such as methane, had not accumulated in the mine overnight. At forty-three, he replaced his older brother as foreman at an eight-hundred-employee Mount Carmel colliery, promoting the mine's safety, efficiency, and profitability.

In 1926, after taking night school and correspondence courses in engineering and calculus, my grandfather passed the state mine inspector's exam, won an appointment from the governor, and began touring mines in his district. Inside the workings, he tested for toxic gases, scouted for hazardous working conditions, and investigated fatal accidents. Day after day, he enforced state safety laws designed to temper the industry's profit motives and keep miners alive.

As a state employee with a middle-class salary, my grandfather also sent each of his three children to college, a feat many of the region's residents still struggle to achieve today. My father, a World War II Army Air Corps pilot, received the Distinguished Flying Cross and two Air Medals in the China-Burma-India theater, air-dropping supplies to General Joseph W. Stilwell's troops, who were fighting to open the Burma Road. After the war, he earned a Phi Beta Kappa key at Bucknell University and moved to New Haven, where the G.I. Bill funded his studies at Yale Law School. Three years later, he moved to Cleveland, joining several Yale law alumni—and at least one other Air

Corps pilot—at Squire Sanders & Dempsey. His older brother, my uncle Jim, graduated from Villanova and Dickinson Law School and served two terms in the U.S. Congress, representing a district near Harrisburg.

Over the years and decades, my father specialized in litigation and labor law, representing management for corporations such as Union Carbide and General Electric. He joined corporate and philanthropic boards, strengthening his ties to the community. He enrolled my brothers and me in private schools, relegating our doctrinal edification to CCD classes every Sunday. And during my freshman year at Princeton, he escorted me—to my mortification—down the Union Club's red-carpeted stairs in a post-Christmas debutante cotillion sprinkled with the female progeny of some of Cleveland's oldest families.

When I was growing up, a suburban child of the seventies in Danskins and Topsiders, my dad rarely spoke of his Quigley forebears or his father's experience as a breaker boy. He didn't talk much about his work or military service either. Like many of his peers from the so-called Greatest Generation, he considered himself lucky to be alive. Perhaps because of his reticence, I always wondered about my Quigley ancestors, especially the grandfather I never knew. One of his mine safety lanterns, a six-inch metal canister sheathed in a wire mesh screen, lay in the kitchen junk drawer with pencils, emery boards, and binder clips. A black-and-white photo of him—clad in shirtsleeves and seated at his desk with mining treatises—sat on the antique desk in my father's book-lined study. By all other accounts, he remained a mystery.

In some respects, so did my father, the ex-pilot who navigated cargo planes in the Himalayas during the war and retained traces of solidarity with the coal region long after. He relished visiting former neighbors, who still called him Tommy, when he returned for brief stays. He ate sticky buns and pretzels, followed the Phillies, attended Mass every Sunday and holy day, and for the most part, at least until the Reagan era, voted for Democrats.

Throughout my childhood, we piled into our wood-paneled Ford

Country Squire and drove across northeastern Ohio and western and central Pennsylvania to Mount Carmel, my father's hometown, where we visited my grandmother in her Chestnut Street row home. Weather permitting, my brothers and I played in a park near her house for hours, climbing on a cannon that had rained firepower on a distant conflict. From the park, we gazed out on the surrounding landscape. Like Centralia, Mount Carmel sat in a coal-rich basin, encircled by the Appalachians. The vista from the cannon supplied me with one of my most vivid childhood memories of the region: black mounds of coal waste, shorn of vegetation. These tar-colored heaps, mountains turned inside out and stripped of their latent anthracite, did not look like anything I had ever seen before.

In May 2000, I took a leave of absence from my government-lawyer job in Washington, D.C., and started knocking on doors in Centralia. All but a dozen or so houses had been torn down a decade earlier, leaving about as many residents, known locally as the holdouts. Grass grew in the vacant lots like playing fields, and the remaining row homes, now uncoupled, relied on brick support columns to keep from falling over. At the main intersection in the valley, the Speed Spot stood forsaken and alone, its display windows cluttered with motorcycle parts and racing trophies. A single row house, with green Astroturf sheathing the front steps and a Notre Dame Fighting Irish sticker in the parlor window, remained on South Locust Avenue, where scores of families once lived. Just beyond the chain-link fence surrounding St. Ignatius Cemetery, steam trickled from a former stripping pit ringed by charred trees and littered with garbage and branches.

Helen Womer's red-shingled house still graced Wood Street, an oasis of propriety surrounded by overgrown lots where black-eyed Susans and Queen Anne's lace sprouted with abandon. One afternoon in late July, I swung by and rapped on her front door. No one answered. A few days later, I called her from a pay phone outside a Turkey Hill Minit Markit in Mount Carmel. She said she wouldn't cooperate with anyone who was trying to make a buck off Centralia and peppered me with questions for thirty minutes, until I exhausted my supply of quarters and the phone company severed the connection.

Two months later, I climbed her front steps again, a legal pad at my side, and knocked. Helen appeared at the screen door and stood behind it, pointedly breaking with coal region hospitality by not coming out on the porch or inviting me in. She looked younger than I expected, with her blue flowered T-shirt and curly gray hair. I introduced myself. She glanced at my notepad. It was a bad time, she said, her voice brisk and authoritative. I asked if I could come back. She said no.

I tried another tack: Father Anthony McGinley, an eighty-year-old priest confined to a Danville nursing home, where he cuddled a velour blanket and watched televised Mass, had told me to appeal to her vanity, saying she was the best source. She smiled slightly, nodding in agreement. Then she said no again. It was very painful, she said.

"I know," I said, nodding my head, trying to project empathy.

"You couldn't know—unless you lived through it."

I wanted to argue with her as I stood on her steps near the three plastic deer pretend-grazing on her lawn. I wanted to tell her that after dozens of interviews, I had a pretty good sense of how the mine fire had polarized her ex-neighbors. I wanted to tell her that I, too, had family from Centralia, several generations of Quigleys and Laughlins buried across Locust Avenue in St. Ignatius Cemetery.

Eventually, the narrative spilled out from every corner. In its details, it reveals the legacy of an environmental catastrophe, its human tolls and triumphs, its corporate greed and indifference, its governmental lapses and neglect. In its historic sweep, it stands as a cautionary tale—timeless and time-bound—in a country divided by class and religion, buffeted by corporate misconduct, and dismantling its environmental protection laws. This is the story of a dying coal town ensnared in the Reagan Revolution's afterbirth, of a small community rent by one of the mining industry's worst disasters, and of the irreplaceable bond of home.

BOOM TO BUST

PART ONE

CHAPTER ONE

Powder Keg

Mary Lou Gaughan grabbed some Windex and paper towels and stepped onto her front porch. Overhead, beyond her red and white aluminum awning, the sun shone down on Wood Street, bathing her neighbors' row homes in late-spring warmth. Summer, at long last, beckoned.

Across town, similar routines unfolded, especially among neighbors who, like her, tackled chores left unfinished from Easter week: a litany of tasks inherited from immigrant mothers and grandmothers. Mattresses had to be flipped, linoleum polished, spring curtains hung. Outside, winter grime had to be wiped from front doors, a shine buffed onto parlor windows, and sidewalks swept free of leaves. Years earlier, when collieries spewed coal dust across the borough and women waged an almost daily battle against black silt, these tasks sprang from practicality and pride, cued, like the Resurrection, to the promise of rebirth. Now, with three days remaining until May 30 and scores of residents slated to converge on the borough for Memorial Day 1962, those who remained honored tradition and burnished appearances, unfurling American flags and draping them from porch railings and banisters.

For many, a separate ritual awaited in the borough's cemeteries, one for each religious denomination: Catholic, Protestant, Greek Catholic, and Russian Orthodox. In front of ancestral graves, they planted rows of red geraniums or purple, white, and pink petunias. Others tendered bouquets of yellow or red roses or, for the Irish, a wicker basket of green carnations. Still others tended to landscaping like groundskeepers, plucking weeds and mowing strips of grass the size of twin mattresses. Even before the mines closed, few Centralians risked the stigma of an untended family plot.

Back on Wood Street, Mary Lou, a thirty-four-year-old garment worker with fair skin, pale blue eyes, and short curly brown hair, leaned into the concrete porch of her ranch-style house, coaxing a gleam from her three side-by-side parlor windows. On the inside, just a few inches from the glass, a Blessed Virgin statue presided over the center, as in a Renaissance triptych, garbed in white robes and gazing toward the sidewalk. Behind Mary Lou, a few feet away, her husband, Tony, a thirty-eight-year-old mine worker with Buddy Holly glasses and slicked-back hair, assumed his Sunday posture. Nestled in his rocking patio chair, he faced Locust Avenue, surveying his neighbors next door, where he grew up, and across the street.

A row of four wood frame houses loomed to his right, buttressed by Nance Maloney's two-story home, with its flat roof. A white picket fence demarcated her yard like rickrack trim stitched to the hem of a dress. Nance's father, Jack McGinley, had owned a bar and hotel, a saloon awash in Depression-era bootleg whiskey. To Mary Lou, he projected the aura of the elite, lavishing his wealth on the parish and his daughter, from fur stoles to a college education. Down at the opposite end of the row, where Fran Jurgill lived, A-line eaves jutted over third-floor attic windows, like a child's rendering of mountain peaks.

At the end of the next block, Wood Street spilled onto Locust Avenue. Cars and trucks rumbled past, gunning for church, the other end of town, or destinations over the mountains, from Ashland to Bloomsburg and beyond. Behind Tony, over Mary Lou's left shoulder, stood the row of houses—two halves of a duplex, called half-doubles, and an unattached single home—built and colonized by Michael and Anna Fowler Laughlin.

The dump's on fire! she heard a voice cry.

Mary Lou glanced over toward Annie Donahue Ryan's house, with its white wooden porch railings and façade of red shingles. In Annie's backyard, a dirt path meandered into the woods east of town, a thicket of huckleberry and laurel bushes called the picnic grounds. Careering down the trail, just outside Annie's chain-link fence, Mary Lou spotted Frank Jurgill, Jr., a fifteen-year-old who lived across the street.

The dump's on fire! he said again.

Tony and Mary Lou, who knew Frank played in the woods behind the Ryans' home, still couldn't decipher what he was saying.

Frank reached their house, winded and gasping for air.

The dump's on fire, he said.

Mary Lou dropped her paper towels and flew down the steps. For generations, women in the coal region had raced to the colliery at the first word of an accident, praying their husbands and sons had escaped. Even now, after most of the mines had closed, the instinct to gather at a disaster site lingered, as if encoded in the collective DNA. When a fire engine rolled down a Centralia street, men, women, and children streamed out their front doors, some falling in behind it.

In front of Annie Ryan's house, Mary Lou swerved right, onto the gravel pavement that mapmakers and bill collectors called Wood Street. With Tony lagging, she sped past the Laughlin half-doubles, their façades shrouded with dark green shingles. At the far end of their row, she rounded the corner and peered across a grassy field to the southeast, the same vista she overlooked from her back porch. The Odd Fellows Cemetery lay straight ahead, enclosed behind a wrought-iron fence. St. Ignatius baseball field unfolded to her right, a grassy expanse next to the school. Now, to the left of the cemetery, she saw white smoke curling from the stripping pit that doubled as the town's dump. One of the borough's fire trucks, a red pumper with an open cab and running boards along the sides, lumbered toward the cemetery, where the burial grounds abutted the landfill.

From their corner lot, Mary Lou and Tony patrolled Wood Street like beat cops, attuned to its rhythms and nuances. In the evenings, she knew, Jim Laughlin sauntered toward Locust Avenue, attired in a gray cardigan and sport coat. Three nights a week at 10:30 P.M., when Mary Lou heard high heels clicking on the sidewalk, she knew Annie Ryan had just returned from bingo in Mount Carmel, wearing a silk dress and pearls. Now, as she dashed along a hard dirt footpath strewn with tar paper, siding, floorboards, and oil drums, she wondered how the fire was started, and by whom. She and Tony hadn't seen anyone heading up toward the dump—but someone could have gone around the back way.

Outside the Odd Fellows Cemetery, just a few hundred feet from her home, Mary Lou came to a stop. The fire truck had parked along the cemetery fence, near the northeast corner. About twenty-five feet away lay the dump, a five-story ravine flecked with large gray rocks and sandy brown dirt. Clumps of slate and light brown rock encircled the rim, tossed aside in the quest for anthracite. Small trees sprouted from the banks, almost three decades after the last stripping contractor fled, with the Buck vein forsaken and exposed at the base. Five volunteer firemen, well tutored in emergency response and dump fires, had dragged a rubber hose from the truck to the edge.

For years, household detritus had accumulated atop the coal seam at the base of the pit, creating a three-story repository of the borough's castoffs: sofas, cardboard, newspapers, braided rugs, kerosene cans. Under the borough's official policy, residents could pay one of two commercial haulers to drive their refuse to the landfill. Unofficially, if residents could tote it there themselves, they could chuck it. Either way, the site lured dumpers, rats, and amateur marksmen, including Tony and Mary Lou, who climbed down inside with a .22-caliber rifle, lined a log with beer and soda bottles and Mason jars, and shot them.

Now, though, as the firefighters sprayed water onto the garbage, about fifteen feet beneath their feet, white smoke drifted up, twirling like funnel clouds. About a dozen spectators hovered outside the cemetery, spurred into action by the fire truck. Hanging around to critique the operation, they swapped information, sharing what they knew. Someone had flung hot ashes from a Heatrola, a coal-burning stove, onto the heap, but the flames were out, Mary Lou overheard one bystander say. In Centralia, where the dumps flared so frequently that the fire company had trouble mustering volunteers to respond, especially to an old Mammoth stripping pit on the borough's west side, news of yet another outburst failed to excite.

About twenty minutes later, Mary Lou retraced her steps and strolled home, back to her windows.

FOR YEARS, Centralia's volunteer fire company had fashioned a spring ritual out of torching the borough's dumps, after the snow melted and the rubbish dried, to banish odors, kill bacteria, and fend off vermin. During Holy Week, firemen crisscrossed the pit with gasoline, matches, and paper, setting the litter on fire. A few volunteers tarried nearby with .22 rifles, nailing rats as they scurried to the surface. Later that afternoon or early the next day, firefighters circled back with a tanker truck and hoses to drench the blaze. Clomping around in boots and gloves, they dissected their handiwork, ensuring the landfill no longer smoldered.

The firefighters, however, did not proctor the landfill alone. The trustees of the Odd Fellows Cemetery, whose northern perimeter ran within a few feet of the dump, also policed conditions in the disposal area, a neighbor they tolerated but did not embrace. As May 30 approached, ensuring a host of downwind visitors, the president of the Protestant burial grounds lobbied for relief: He asked the fire department to clean the dump, meaning torch the top layer, before the holiday. Borough council, the secretary jotted in the May meeting minutes, received the suggestion very favorably.

Before the firemen could incinerate the dump, though, someone else beat them to it. On Saturday, May 26, one of the borough's approved dumping days, a commercial hauler named Curly Stasulevich heaved a load of refuse into the pit, including hot ashes from a coal-burning stove. In and of itself, his act did not embody negligence or malfeasance so much as routine. Across town, residents left their coal stove ashes out for collection in galvanized steel tubs, often while the residue still radiated heat. The haulers heaved their loads into the dump, where the ashes landed atop layers of discards prone to combustion, from paper to gasoline. Across Centralia and the coal region, where similar practices prevailed, the dumps flared on a regular basis, as often as once a week.

The next morning, when the firefighters descended on the landfill with a pumper and a crew of five and Mary Lou trotted over to investigate, they found themselves battling a garbage flare-up. As Mary Lou heard, they thought they had extinguished the flames. Later in the day, when the firemen realized the blaze still raged, they dispatched a bulldozer to root around the landfill, exposing the fire, while they doused the burning garbage with water from the pumper.

Still, two days elapsed before the fire company clamped a hose to a hydrant, several hundred feet away on Locust Avenue, and dragged the line to the landfill. Even then, as white steam and smoke trailed from the waste and the scent of burning wood, plastic, and paper hung in the air, one of the firemen drafted two teenage boys to man the hose. About an hour later, when darkness fell, the teenagers dragged a Naugahyde ottoman out of the dump, placed it at the brink, draped the hose over the stool, and went home, leaving the nozzle aiming moisture onto the heap. The next morning, Wednesday, May 30, a pool of water had formed at the base, six inches deep in some spots. But across the pit a few days later, steam rippled from the high wall, a clifflike face of exposed rock and anthracite left over from strip mining, soaring seventy-five feet above the coal seam.

CENTRALIA OFFICIALS knew they had a problem as soon as they saw the steam. The state, which licensed the landfill, required the borough to crown the dump with clay every day, imposing a nonflammable barricade between the junk at the top and the carbon-dense rock at the bottom: a conglomerate that hadn't quite metamorphosed into anthracite but still conducted heat. In a depressed coal town, however, where the general fund boasted $2,300, resources to ensure compliance had proven scarce. Borough officials added clay when they could, but not every day, and the fire took off, searing through the muck and swill at the surface, piercing whatever clay lay underneath, and igniting the rock, with its high carbon content. In the hours and days after the blaze erupted, it surged around the pit to the northeast, coursing through the rock like a dynamite fuse and homing in on the Buck vein.

As far back as the mid-nineteenth century, colliery officials knew they had to attack a mine fire immediately. Mining treatises, keyed to the state's foreman's examination, devoted pages to the topic. For decades, so long as operators exploited their coal region wealth, they undertook whatever measures were necessary to trounce an underground inferno, including flooding the mine and gouging out the coal seam. Borough officials, who didn't want to highlight conditions at the dump by asking for help, kept their predicament quiet, like a family secret, and dealt with it themselves. Still, word of the fire reached Harrisburg later that month. A mining engineer and state contractor who lived on Troutwine Street alerted the commonwealth's top mining official, who dispatched a memo to an investigator, admonishing him to speak to borough council. The investigator, who was on vacation, said the blaze had been extinguished; the borough hired a bulldozer to disperse the refuse.

But the fire wasn't out. From the vein at the landfill's foundation, it had plunged almost two hundred feet along the Buck outcrop into Centralia Colliery's abandoned workings. Even a cursory glance at a mine map suggested where it would head next. From a wooded ridge about seventeen hundred feet east of Locust Avenue, the outcrop ran west on two fronts, hugging opposite sides of Locust Mountain. Viewed from above, it looked like a wishbone, with the spine facing east and the open-ended prongs, called dips, pointing west. The south dip veered behind St. Ignatius ballfield and away from the borough, toward Ashland and Mount Carmel. The north dip, which the dump straddled and the blaze now consumed, coursed from the Odd Fellows Cemetery toward Wood Street, where Mary Lou lived. From her backyard, it extended under Locust Avenue and around St. Ignatius Cemetery.

The blaze, by now a full-fledged mine fire, also proved impossible to conceal. Vapors spurted from rock fissures along its route, marking its path like runway lights. Fumes wafted across Locust Avenue and into St. Ignatius Church, about nine hundred feet from the landfill. The borough closed the dump until further notice, rerouting haulers to Ashland and Mount Carmel.

For Mary Lou, who maintained a scrapbook of newspaper photographs devoted to President Kennedy and his clan, the site acquired the aura of a news event, like a plane crash in her backyard. In July, she stood at the dump's edge with a camera, memorializing the geysers of steam. Later, she tucked her snapshots into a leather-bound scrapbook: white clouds teeming from the pit. Next to the black-and-white images, she pasted two photographs of her two-year-old son, Tony, and his older sister, Patricia, perched atop a bulldozer outside the Laughlin homestead.

In late July, borough officials conceded the obvious: The fire raged out of control. In a letter to the Lehigh Valley Coal Company, they notified Centralia Colliery's long-absent landlord about a mine fire on its property. A second letter, signed by Centralia's mayor, council president, and council secretary, informed the state. Borough officials, who knew when and how the fire had started, fudged the cause and start date, blaming spontaneous combustion.

State and federal mining officials descended on the landfill the next day, corroborating the worst. The blaze, with its sixty-day head start, had penetrated the Buck vein. Now they had to isolate the fire and uproot the burning seam, like wresting a mole from its underground lair. A few days later, they unveiled their strategy: Strip along the high wall, about two hundred feet east and more than fifty feet below the surface, to the slate underneath the coal; then scoop out the smoldering rock, squelch the blaze, and replenish the site with nonflammable fill. They estimated the cost at thirty thousand dollars.

As mining engineers, the officials knew they had to hustle. As public servants, though, they had to maneuver within Congress's 1954 mandates, including a $500,000 annual spending cap for all mine reclamation projects nationwide. As an upstart, Centralia had to compete against several long-running initiatives, including twenty-three anthracite mine fires, for a slice of the largesse. The 1954 law also restricted the federal government, if it participated, to underwriting half the tab. A separate party, either the state or one of the coal companies, had to finance the rest.

Under the statutory scheme, however, the federal government had little recourse if a coal company invoked financial hardship. Lawmakers had carved an adversity opt-out into the legislative text, empowering the Interior Department secretary, whose agency oversaw the program, to scrutinize a property owner's evidence of fiscal distress and devise a long-term payment plan. In Centralia, where six operators retained an interest in the landfill area's mining rights as owners, lessees, or sub-lessees, any such review, with its inherent delays, was not an option. Each coal company remained free to plead poverty, dodge liability, and externalize the toll of its collapse onto the commonwealth. Under the statute, they knew, federal authorities could require the state to participate.

Federal and state officials convened a Centralia summit on August 6. On the dirt road leading to the Odd Fellows Cemetery, near the stripping pit's southern periphery, borough councilmen mingled with industry emissaries from the Lehigh Valley Coal Company and the Susquehanna Coal Company, which leased the dump's mineral rights from Lehigh Valley. Officials, eager to wring cash from the operators, said the fire had to be suppressed right away. The blaze already menaced the Odd Fellows Cemetery and St. Ignatius school, playground, and church. If they failed to gain control, the fire would march west toward town, jeopardizing nearby homes. The proposed excavation represented their best hope, but federal funding for the project remained in doubt. At best, three months would elapse before any worker clocked a shift. Given the stakes, Charles Kuebler, an official with the federal Bureau of Mines, asked the coal companies to pool their capital so contractors could begin immediately. At issue, if they split the bill: fifteen thousand dollars apiece.

The operators balked. It wasn't their fire and it wasn't their fault, they said. Someone else would have to fix it. Eight months after Lehigh Valley Coal had reported $3.8 million in assets, including $55,000 in cash, they rebuffed Kuebler's overture, saying they didn't have the money. Under the circumstances, with the coal companies and federal government clinging to the sidelines, the state shouldered the project alone.

On August 22, as the fire approached its three-month anniversary, the first real excavation began. At the brim, near the Odd Fellows Cemetery, a local contractor deployed a dragline shovel with an eighty-foot boom and 2.5-yard bucket, the size of a pickup truck's flatbed. From the surface, operators chased the seam underground and to the northwest, toward the Laughlin homestead and Mary Lou's backyard. For sixteen hours a day, from seven A.M. until eleven P.M., two shifts of workers drilled, blasted, and pawed into the burning rock, extracting about a hundred cubic yards per hour. Their shovel, with tines like bear claws and an engine that roared like an airplane on take-off, could plunder to a depth of ninety feet.

The deeper they burrowed, though, the more they primed the inferno, feeding it with oxygen. At night, the rock glimmered: a reddish glow, coated with hot ashes. By late October, the fire had barreled ahead of the trench, stampeding through the workings faster than they could root it out. At the eleven-month mark, in April 1963, the blaze had propagated along two fronts, sweeping about 700 feet east of the inauguration point and about 130 feet north of the outcrop. A revised method, stuffing the mine workings with scraps from a Centralia Colliery slush bank, had flopped. The expense of digging it out had sky-rocketed almost tenfold, to $296,000. Commonwealth officials, who were saddled with more pressing mine fires in more populated towns, did nothing. The state, after one more ill-fated attempt in July 1963, had squandered more than $106,000 in Centralia, and the fire just kept burning.

Centralia residents, meanwhile, geared up for the town's 1966 centennial, a three-day burst of civic pride over July Fourth weekend, with fireworks, band concerts, and three parades, including one for pets. More than ten thousand revelers braved hundred-degree heat for the events, including a ceremony outside the Legion to bury a time capsule, a child's burial vault donated by Stutz Funeral Home. Sealed inside, to be unearthed at the town's 150-year mark in 2016, were a Bible, lumps of coal, a miner's carbide lamp, and a chronological recitation of borough history penned by Annie Quigley. The centennial souvenir booklet, spanning more than a hundred years of local lore and more than sixty pages of ads and photographs, did not mention the mine fire.

ALMOST SEVEN YEARS after the blaze's inception, on May 5, 1969, work began on a long-delayed federal-state venture, originally conceived as a $2.2 million trench. Officials had scrambled after learning that the fire, now consuming an estimated nine acres, would cost about $4.5 million to excavate, more than twice their allotted budget under the Appalachian Regional Development Act, a Great Society push to reverse Appalachian poverty. Federal engineers, who had already earmarked $8.5 million for digging out mine fires in Wilkes-Barre and Scranton, scoured Pennsylvania's bituminous region for inspiration, hoping to leverage their Centralia allocation—accomplishing more for less—by scrapping the trench and swiping technology from the soft-coal fields, where coal seams—and mine fires—ran flat and shallow under the surface.

In the end, officials settled on injecting the Centralia workings with fly ash, a granular waste product belched by bituminous-fired power plants, like talcum powder, laced with arsenic and heavy metals. If their technique worked—and no engineer had braved this approach in the anthracite region—they would snuff the fire from above by starving it of oxygen, rather than eradicating it from below with the more time-honored and expensive approach of dynamite and power shovels.

On paper, they envisioned a noncombustible underground wedge between the fire and the borough, measuring 10 feet high, 150 feet wide, and 1,100 feet long: the fly-ash barrier.

MARY LOU's neighbor Janet Birster woke up early. Upstairs, her husband, Bill, lay sleeping. Their half-double was the next house over, across the alley and about seventy-five feet from Mary Lou's front porch, between the old Laughlin homestead, where Janet's great-grandparents Michael and Anna Fowler Laughlin had lived, and her cousin Annie Ryan's home.

For almost two weeks, workers in hard hats and flannel shirts had stationed drilling rigs and tanker trucks a few hundred feet from Janet's backyard, sinking tubelike openings into the mine tunnels and plugging them with fly ash. In the interim, she and her children battled nausea, headaches, and difficulty breathing. In the homestead next door, her mother, Marion Laughlin, a widow who worked downstairs from Mary Lou at Legion Dress, had similar symptoms, from headaches to vomiting and shortness of breath. Matches and candles had extinguished inside her home without explanation. The smell of sulfur, like rotten eggs, had permeated her kitchen.

Now, though, around five A.M. on Sunday, May 18, 1969, Janet peeked inside the birdcage. Their new canary, the one Bill had brought home the day before, lay under the perch, sprawled on its back. From the dining room, where the cage sat atop a buffet table, Janet filed back upstairs and woke Bill.

Honey, the bird's asleep, she said.

That's what they do, he said. They tuck their heads under their wings and snooze.

His description, though, did not mesh with the scene downstairs.

Well, ours is lying on its back with its feet up in the air, she said.

With that, Bill grasped the canary's fate: not napping. But he was a state highway worker, not a miner. The dump lay about five hundred feet southeast of their back porch, and he had no reason to think the bird's death stemmed from anything other than natural causes, even though the Laughlin row sat closer to the landfill, on a straight northwesterly path, than any other homes in the community—and only about one hundred feet from the Buck outcrop. A year and a half earlier, when officials scoured their homes for carbon monoxide, they found none—though they had discovered slight oxygen shortages and twice the normal level of carbon dioxide.

Still, Janet's mother, a miner's daughter from Ashland, had started fretting about mine fire gases seeping into their home, especially carbon monoxide: tasteless, colorless, odorless, and virtually impossible to detect without specialized equipment. Without warning, it could overtake them at night, hijacking the oxygen in their bloodstream and causing fatal respiratory failure. They had inherited their homes from the Laughlin clan, however, and could not afford to leave.

Later that day, out in the yard, Bill spotted Tony Gaughan and relayed the canary news. Get the hell out of there, Tony said. Bill, who had grown up in nearby Locust Gap as the eighth of fifteen children, did not lose his composure. Even if mine fire gases were percolating in the home, officials said to keep the windows open and they'd be fine.

Down in the cellar, a room the size of a storage shed with a dirt floor dating back almost a hundred years, Bill crouched in front of the hot water heater and struck a match. After a flicker, the flame expired. Unfazed, he tromped upstairs to the dining room and lit a newspaper. A flame about a foot high jumped from the newsprint. He crept into the kitchen and down into the basement, one stair at a time. On the third step, the flare disappeared, as if someone had blown it off the paper.

Bill called a mine inspector in Mount Carmel, who drove over with gas detection equipment and identified a trace of carbon monoxide. The Birsters, Marion Laughlin, and Annie Ryan, a mine foreman's widow, scattered, taking shelter with relatives and friends. Outside the Birsters' home the next morning, the inspector lit a safety lantern, the kind miners had used for generations to prowl for underground gases. Seconds later, inside the living room, the flame vanished.

As anyone who had slung a dinner pail over his shoulder and trudged into a gangway knew, the Birsters' half-double harbored a potentially lethal cocktail of insufficient oxygen and excess carbon dioxide. "Black damp," miners had long dubbed it, just as they nicknamed the colliery ambulance, with its mortally wounded cargo, the Black Maria. In naturally occurring proportions, the earth's atmosphere contains roughly 21 percent oxygen, 78 percent nitrogen, and .03 percent carbon dioxide. Around the high-intensity combustion of an anthracite mine fire, though, atmospheric conditions bear little resemblance to average ecosystems.

Like a car engine, burning coal devours fuel—oxygen—and spews emissions: carbon dioxide, carbon monoxide, and methane. Like a hurricane, a mine fire advances as a front, inhaling oxygen at its leading edge, where boreholes drilled into the surface register a downdraft. Near its core, where the blaze expels superheated waste gases, boreholes register an updraft, temperatures range between 600 and 1,500 degrees, oxygen plummets, and carbon dioxide soars.

In canaries, long carried into mines to warn of dangerous gases, even low-level doses prove fatal. In humans, black damp spawns a range of symptoms that vary with the oxygen deprivation's severity, beginning with headaches, dizziness, and shortness of breath. On the spectrum's opposite end, where carbon dioxide robs the lungs and induces suffocation, lie convulsions, coma, and death. When a safety lantern went out, mining officials had long known, carbon dioxide hovered at 10 percent, more than three hundred times higher than normal and twenty times higher than permitted under federal workplace safety guidelines. If the Birsters had slept in their home, the official said, they would have died.

For Mary Lou, the wife, daughter, and granddaughter of miners, word of her next-door neighbors' fate sent an unmistakable signal: The mine fire is right here.

MARY LOU, the eldest of five children, had grown up about a mile south of Centralia in Byrnesville, a forty-five-family patch that sprang into existence before the Civil War to house Locust Run Colliery's miners and laborers. Only outsiders called the hamlet, actually twin settlements, by its formal name. To natives such as Mary Lou, it was the Shanties, with lace-curtain Irish occupying the high ground in the Upper Shanties and the rest, such as Mary Lou's family, consigned to the Lower Shanties, about halfway down Locust Mountain from Centralia.

Even by coal region standards, Mary Lou had endured a childhood fraught with peril. When the stock market crashed in October 1929, she had just turned two. Her family rented a company-owned home with an outhouse in back. All five children were crammed into one bedroom, with two double beds and a crib. Her uncle, an alcoholic who once imbibed witch hazel out of desperation, and her grandfather, a potato famine migrant from County Mayo who helped build St. Ignatius, lived with them as permanent boarders. Mary Lou and her siblings each had one set of clothes and little in the way of toys: no bicycles, sleds, or ice skates. The hardship that loomed largest in her mind, however, was the shortage of food.

For years, soup and scavenged berries formed the backbone of Mary Lou's diet, a regime of cornmeal mush, baked beans, and huckleberry bread. Slight variations gave rise to celebration, including scraps foraged from her father's lunch bucket: a half-eaten apple, sandwich, or Tastykake, still bearing the musty aroma of the mines. When her dad hawked a load of bootleg coal, she walked with him to Ashland or Centralia, where they splurged on hamburger or minced ham and brought the meat home for supper.

As collieries lay idle throughout the 1930s, government giveaways crept into their home and onto their table. More than once, she and her brother pulled a red wagon up to the Mammoth Store to fetch a twenty-five-pound sack of cornmeal, a relief staple. The taint of charity lingered, even though, for many miners' families, the handouts warded off starvation. Eventually, Mary Lou rebelled. She and her brother slit the corner of the bag, hoping its contents would spill on the way home. When officials distributed girls' dresses crafted from feed bags, she ditched the garments in the woods so she wouldn't have to wear them to school. On Saturday nights, when her parents slipped out to the Moose and left her in charge, she pulled the sugar jar from the kitchen cupboard and mixed a batch of fudge, a project her mother had forbidden before heading out the door.

Only in the postwar years, when the coal region basked in relative prosperity, did Mary Lou achieve a semblance of stability. In 1948, while she was working in a garment factory and living at home, she married Tony Gaughan, a stripping-pit mechanic whose parents had been born and reared in Centralia. As newlyweds, they bunked with her family for three months, then moved in with his parents on Wood Street, next to the Laughlin row. From the outset, Mary Lou relished Tony's neighborhood, with its hilltop setting and wide-open sky, a kaleidoscope of weather patterns unveiled first atop Locust Mountain. After years of exile in Byrnesville, whose residents hiked into Centralia for Mass, mining supplies, and groceries, she had landed at the center of the local universe, two blocks from St. Ignatius School and four blocks from St. Ignatius Church. She even felt closer to God.

Up on the hill, dubbed Quality Hill by some of its long-term denizens, Mary Lou had landed among the Centralia equivalent of lace-curtain elites, a handful of barkeeps, bootleggers, and mining officials who climbed out of the mines: Jack McGinley, the bar owner, Jim Laughlin, whose wife owned a pub, and Ollie Ryan, a mine boss. Tony's clan, also well represented on the Hill, proved no exception, with his surname attached to a saloon, owned by his uncle Phil, and a justice of the peace, his cousin Joe. Tony's parents, meanwhile, had garnered distinction of their own. During Prohibition and the Depression, they peddled home-distilled whiskey, potato chips, chickens, and eggs. Long before many coal region families, and certainly well before Mary Lou's, they enjoyed indoor plumbing, a furnace, and a car. Their homestead, a detached two-story wood frame dwelling with a long wraparound porch, reflected their status and entrepreneurialism. From Locust Avenue, it looked like a regular row home, just wide enough for two windows on each floor. From Wood Street, though, where its long end paralleled the sidewalk, it graced the block like a residence befitting a doctor or lawyer.

Inside the Gaughans' home and out in the neighborhood, Mary Lou felt the embrace of welcome. On weekdays at five A.M., Tony's mother rapped a furnace pipe with a knife to rouse Mary Lou and Tony, plied them with toast and oatmeal, and packed them off to their shifts at the garment factory and the colliery, where Tony worked as a hoisting engineer, operating the lift that heaved coal cars in and out of the mine. After Mary Lou and Tony left, their neighbor Annie Ryan shuffled over for coffee in her housecoat and slippers. In the evenings, as the sun set behind St. Ignatius Cemetery, Mary Lou could hear whippoorwills and crickets, children roller-skating, riding bikes, and playing jacks, and the St. Ignatius bell, tolling at six P.M.

A few years later, when Mary Lou and Tony needed space to raise a family, they co-opted the bottling shed and chicken coop next door, where his parents had based their hooch and poultry enterprises. In a town with no shortage of handymen—miners mastered carpentry or risked perishing in a roof collapse—Tony hired neighbors and friends to handle the construction, from installing electrical wiring and hanging doors to plastering the walls. Under his supervision, they transformed the barnlike structure into an L-shaped three-bedroom house covered in maroon asbestos shingles, with a sloping gray roof and front and back porches.

Once installed in a home of his own, next door to his parents, Tony rarely contemplated straying. He had lived his entire life on Wood Street, even the war years, when his poor vision barred him from military service. When Mary Lou ventured out, she left him supper, and he ate at home, preferring her fare and his kitchen to anything he might experience elsewhere.

WITHIN A FEW DAYS of the demise of the Birsters' canary, panic seized Wood Street, home to about twenty families. Gas samples from the Laughlin row, analyzed by a federal lab in Pittsburgh, registered only

18 to 19 percent oxygen, 2 to 3 percent lower than normal. Outside the Laughlin and Birster homes, underground temperatures ranged between 65 and 120 degrees, 15 to 70 degrees higher than normal. Steam flowed from metal cylinders jammed into the government's boreholes like exhaust pipes and drifted into Mary Lou's yard.

Meanwhile, officials redoubled their efforts to pinpoint the fire, much farther north and west from the dump than they had anticipated. They cased Mary Lou's neighborhood with thermometers and gas detection devices, poking into boreholes and recording drafts, temperatures, and toxicity. About 150 feet southeast of the Laughlin row, near the Buck outcrop—and only about 400 feet from Locust Avenue—they logged temperatures of 760 and 900 degrees, within range of anthracite's 800-degree ignition point. The fire, they now estimated, loomed about 65 feet below the surface. It had charged along the fly-ash barrier's proposed southern border, near Wood Street and the Odd Fellows Cemetery, threatening to surmount the obstacle before workers erected it.

Four days after the Birsters' canary died, Mary Lou pressed her heels into the gravel outside Annie Ryan's home, with her arms clamped across her chest. Tony hovered nearby, with a handful of retired miners from the neighborhood, clad in shirtsleeves, windbreakers, and baseball caps. Helen Womer, who lived in Tony's childhood home, flanked her in a sleeveless white dress, interrogating a county commissioner who looked like a NASA engineer with his buzz cut, white shirt, and dark tie. One by one, the residents said they opposed the fly-ash curtain. They wanted a trench to safeguard their properties.

Mary Lou and the neighbors who clustered around her, especially Tony and the miners, knew that fly-ash flushing had smothered mine fires only in the bituminous fields, where the topography bore no relation to their own. They doubted that the technique—staging its hard-coal debut in their backyards—would work in Centralia, with its sharply pitched seams and unmapped bootleg workings. There were too many chutes and gangways, too many air passageways feeding oxygen to the fire. With time running out, they did not appreciate serving as lab rats. They needed a ditch now, to quarantine their blocks from the mine fire. Even if workers had to ram through the Laughlin row, a furrow would save the rest of Wood Street, one retired miner said.

Just a week ago, Mary Lou had ignored the mine fire. Now she stewed about gases leaking from the boreholes and into her home. Her head ached. A cave-in had ruptured the topsoil at the rear of the Womers' property, several feet from one of the boreholes, and they complained of headaches, too. As an envoy from the county, however—and an agricultural stronghold, at that—the commissioner lacked authority to alter a multimillion-dollar mining project underwritten by the federal and state governments. At best, he might raid the county's urban renewal coffers, reimbursing the Birsters, Marion Laughlin, and Annie Ryan for temporary housing.

The next day, federal officials announced they would proceed ahead of schedule with fly-ash flushing to the borough's east, from the landfill north toward Wood Street. The Laughlin-Birster-Ryan contingent vowed not to return, saying it wouldn't work. Mary Lou and Tony pledged to keep fighting, but with smoke and steam cascading from the ground less than a hundred feet away, where the Laughlin row stood vacant, she questioned how long they could stay. "How do they expect anybody to sleep peacefully around here with all that gas coming out of the ground?" she asked a reporter, one of several who materialized on her block. "It's like living on a powder keg."

Three days later, on May 26, eighteen-wheel tanker trucks rumbled up the street outside Annie Ryan's porch and Mary Lou's bedroom, kicking up dust. Inside their shiny metal cylinders they hauled noncombustible fly ash, supplied at no cost by Metropolitan Edison Company in Reading. Crews bulldozed the woods, opening roads and parking spaces for the rigs. Rotary drills dotted the landscape, grinding through rock, coal, and shale until they pierced the mine workings, fifty feet or more underground. From a distance, with their latticed three-story booms, the drills looked like oil wells.

Behind the Laughlin row, just east of Mary Lou's backyard, workers in leather boots and work gloves dragged four-inch hoses from the tankers and clamped them onto boreholes. Day after day, truckload after truckload, they flushed fly ash underground like pneumatic turkey basters. One ton every minute, the powder spilled through four-inch chutes and piled into mine voids, like sand into a beaker, layering atop tunnels, passageways, and bootleg holes. Under the Laughlin homestead alone, they pumped more than fifteen hundred tons.

In the pit near the Odd Fellows Cemetery, behind Mary Lou's house, crews delved into the fire once again. At night they beamed a spotlight on the work site to guide the shovel operator. From her bedroom, Mary Lou could hear the chains, with links the size of forearms, clanking against the blade. Workers sank six more vents in her backyard and Helen's. Hot fumes laden with carbon monoxide gushed from the voids.

Later that week, a bulldozer smashed into the fire about twenty feet below the surface and just a hundred feet from the Laughlin homestead. *Apollo 10* astronauts had just splashed down in the South Pacific after an eight-day mission, orbiting the moon thirty-one times and photographing potential landing sites. Federal and state mining engineers, however, could not muster the know-how to vanquish a mine fire in Centralia. A Harrisburg reporter who trawled the block, interviewing residents, filled a notebook with their spleen.

A few days later, Mary Lou's next-door neighbor, Helen Womer, wrote their congressman, Daniel J. Flood, and asked for a meeting. She and Mary Lou needed the intercession of a higher authority, one with the clout to steer pet projects to completion. Like legions of voters from Wilkes-Barre to Centralia, they knew one politician who fit that description, a member of the House Ways and Means Committee who siphoned federal pork into the coal region, a wealth of spending initiatives ranging from interstate highways to post offices: Dan Flood.

INSIDE A TRAILER between St. Ignatius ballfield and Mary Lou's backyard, Roland Harper, a surveying agent for the federal Bureau of Mines, fished out three house keys. As the morning sun beat down on

Wood Street, he and a colleague, Bob Bentz, ambled toward the Laughlin row to troll for black damp—which, at almost twice the weight of air, hunkered in low places. Over the past three weeks, their reconnaissance had evolved by rote. In the kitchen, where they knew they had plenty of oxygen, they lit a gray steel safety lantern the size of a tennis ball can, with a glass shield surrounding the flame. Each time, the lamp choked in the basement, near the furnace.

This time, though, on June 11, the lantern sputtered halfway down Marion Laughlin's cellar steps, about five feet from the landing. Harper, a surveyor, not a mine inspector, thought his equipment had malfunctioned. Huddled in the beam of Bentz's flashlight, he twisted a dime-sized metal loop at the lamp's base, striving to generate a spark, like a cigarette lighter. Nothing happened, even after six attempts, until he realized he couldn't breathe, as if he were trapped inside a paper bag and had sucked out all the oxygen. His face felt warm. Bentz radiated pink, as if he had a fever.

Harper and Bentz bolted up the stairs, through the kitchen, and into the backyard, panting for air. Back in the trailer a few minutes later, their cheeks still ruddy, Harper updated Danny Lewis, a federal technician: The light snuffed out before they landed in the cellar. The Laughlin homestead, where Michael and Anna Fowler Laughlin had landed after fleeing Lower Manhattan in the 1860s, had emerged as the mine fire's ground zero.

CHAPTER TWO

Where The Dog Star Never Glows

My great-great-grandfather fled Ireland in a hurry. At least that's what I heard, about 150 years later, when details about his 1837 departure remained scarce. According to the lore, Patrick Quigley staged a protest against the Crown, then embodied in King William IV, whose eighteen-year-old niece, Victoria, had not yet ascended to the throne. Patrick's offspring, to the extent they spoke of it, knew this as "the Londonderry incident." With the benefit of hindsight, I assume he was provoked.

Throughout Ireland in 1837, tenant farmers scraped to rent quarter-acre plots, stave off eviction, and, when the crops did not fail, survive on potatoes. That spring, the season when British landowners expanded their pastureland by ejecting Irish renters—and, in some cases, dispatching them to the United States—five children named Quigly landed in New York. The ship's manifest, which might have misspelled their last name, provides no clues about whether they hailed from my great-great-grandfather's clan, but Quigley was not a common name, 1837 predated the potato famine by several years, and something spurred him to radicalism. From his Galway home on Ireland's western coast he ventured to a Londonderry county fair, where he and two other men staged their demonstration. British officials chased him to

Westport, where he boarded a ship bound for the United States, abandoning, by some accounts, a wife and child.

New York Harbor's guardians notched Patrick's arrival on July 14, 1837, a twenty-four-year-old Irishman who signed his name with an *X*. Cursed by misfortune on both sides of the Atlantic, he disembarked amid an economic depression, the aftermath of a bank panic still reverberating across the city. Fifty thousand unemployed laborers and recent immigrants roamed the streets, trolling for work. Thousands more, including women and children, begged for charity. That winter, relief committees exhausted food stockpiles and shuttered their doors. Patrick Quigley appeared before a Manhattan court clerk the following spring. And in his naturalization petition, the first step toward easing from banishment to citizenship, he declared himself, of all things, an English national.

From there, his trail disappears for a few years. According to oral history, he bolted to northeastern Pennsylvania and found work in Towanda, digging a canal along the Susquehanna River. Given his ultimate destination, this makes sense. Forty miles southeast of Towanda lay a swath of woodland and mountain ridges, dubbed St. Anthony's Wilderness. In 1749, white settlers had procured the region from the Lenape Indians for five hundred dollars. The tribe, no strangers to victimization, had already sold Manhattan to the Dutch, and the Pennsylvania deal proved no less a swindle. Underneath blue-green hills, dotted with mountain laurel and pine, lay three-quarters of the world's anthracite deposits: bands of slate and shale and dozens of side-by-side coal seams, varying in thickness from a few inches to forty feet.

For decades, Pennsylvania's anthracite lay buried and landlocked, miles from navigable water. Even scientists remained baffled by its properties. The so-called stone coal, comprised of 85 to 95 percent carbon, burned with a nearly colorless flame. It yielded the same heat as charcoal at about half the cost, retained its shape, and produced little smoke, only a dusting of white or yellowish ash. Many locals assumed its energy could not be harnessed.

During the War of 1812, however, when hostilities blocked the influx of bituminous coal from Virginia and England, two Philadelphia iron manufacturers, Josiah White and Erskine Hazard, tinkered with anthracite combustion in their nail and wire works, developing a furnace fired by hard coal. By the mid-1820s, metalworkers and mill operators leaped to convert to the fuel. Entrepreneurs and investors scrambled to feed their demand, canvassing the anthracite coalfields, snaring mineral-rich property, and charting canals to reach it: the Schuylkill Canal, which opened in 1825, and the Lehigh Canal and the Delaware and Hudson Canal, both of which opened in 1829. A secondary canal network finalized the distribution web during the 1830s, connecting the region to mid-Atlantic ports.

Anthracite usage soared. By 1839, hard coal cornered 76 percent of the market, a 73 percent spike in less than twenty years. Still, canals froze during the winter, impeding further progress until the next transportation revolution, when anthracite realized its potential as fuel and investment. In January 1842, the Philadelphia and Reading Railroad Company laid the last segment of track on a ninety-eight-mile stretch linking the southern coalfields, near Pottsville, to Philadelphia. Pottsville's civic leaders, mainly Philadelphia coal magnates and their attorneys, heralded the coup with an eleven-hour, forty-three-car train ride between the destinations, accompanied by three militia companies, four bands, and twelve hundred local residents.

My great-great-grandfather, who must have arrived in Pottsville just after the Reading, ended his ditch-digging career, embraced the nascent boom, and severed his remaining Galway ties. In April 1842, he filed in to St. Patrick's Church, an Irish Catholic stronghold atop a Mahantongo Street hillside. There, next door to the Yuengling brewery, he wedded Bridget Carey, a twenty-six-year-old Irish immigrant. The church's marriage log identified him as Luck Nolan, a name likely to foil relatives or in-laws in Ireland—if he still had any—who might disfavor a second run at the sacrament, even after the coercion of his flight. The following August, he strode into Schuylkill County courthouse, registered his intent to become a U.S. citizen, and renounced all loyalty to Queen Victoria.

ANTHRACITE PROSPECTORS fanned out ahead of the railroad lines, into the Western Middle Field. Alexander W. Rea, an agent for the newly organized Locust Mountain Coal and Iron Company, reached Centralia, then known as Centerville, in February 1853. Centerville, situated just up the mountain from the Centre Turnpike, an early-nineteenth-century toll road between Reading and Fort Augusta, offered little more than sanctuary to stagecoach travelers, who paused overnight at the Bull's Head Tavern. When Rea arrived, a twenty-eight-year-old Flemington, New Jersey, native and Lafayette College graduate, the hostelry remained the lone structure, a squatter's log frame home surrounded by forests and swamps.

Centerville, however, straddled a morass of anthracite, and Rea's employer, Locust Mountain Coal, had amassed acreage encircling the outpost in every direction. From a basin measuring two miles long and one mile wide, the coal seams spiked upward, tilting at 33- to 45-degree angles, unimpeded by geographic faults. One vein, the Mammoth, measured thirty to forty feet wide. And thanks to a recently inked railroad deal, the valley lay poised for development.

Rea, a civil and mining engineer, surveyed a grid with streets and lots spilling down the mountainsides and across the valley. He named the main north-south artery Locust Avenue and designated the east-west thoroughfare, which sliced through the basin, Center Street. For the next few years, railroad tracks encroached from the south and mines sprouted in their wake: Big Mine Run and Bast collieries in 1855, Locust Run in 1856, and Hazel Dell in 1860. Seven years after Rea arrived, Centerville boasted about four hundred residents, most of whom had settled near the mines.

ACROSS BROAD MOUNTAIN, a 1,700-foot peak that separated the Southern and Western Middle fields, Patrick and Bridget Quigley ensconced themselves in Crow Hollow, a mining patch about five miles northeast of Pottsville. Crow Hollow sprang into being to harvest and ship anthracite from Pine Forest Colliery, a three-hundred-foot vertical shaft into the Mammoth vein owned by the heirs of Samuel Wetherill, a Philadelphia lead and paint mogul. From the colliery, a squat shed near the mine's entrance, the processed coal shuttled along the Schuylkill Valley Railroad, a Reading affiliate, to Port Carbon, about a two-mile trip, and then by rail to Philadelphia and New York.

By 1860, Patrick and Bridget had seven children. To swill a beer at a tavern, mail a letter, or seek God's forgiveness during Sunday Mass, they trudged to St. Clair, one mile to the east, or Pottsville. Inside the colliery, an ethnic hierarchy prevailed. Contract miners, predominantly Welsh and English immigrants who had honed their skills in British mines, dislodged their quota and quit for the day. Laborers, mainly unskilled Irish immigrants, remained long after the miners retired, wading through passageways choked with dust, shattering anthracite with their picks, and shoveling coal chunks into wagons. For their efforts, they received one-third to two-thirds of a miner's wage.

The hazards of the mines did not discriminate, however, even if the pay scale did. Coal seams and deposits harbored pockets of highly flammable methane. Gushers burst forth without warning, like steam from a boiler. Explosions killed, burned, and maimed nearby workers. Falling rock and coal crushed laborers to death. Coal cars jumped the tracks and ran them over, severing arms and legs. Miners tumbled down slopes and shafts, falling hundreds of feet to their deaths. For each 35,164 tons of coal unearthed in Schuylkill County in 1870, one person died—almost three times the fatality rate in British mines.

For those who managed to survive, subsistence aboveground proved no less precarious. Accidents closed collieries, stranding families without income. Eruptions and fires set coal seams ablaze, forcing crews to flood the workings and pump out the water before resuming operations. Pine Forest, plagued by gases and poor ventilation, averaged 52,342 tons per year after 1866—about half its yield in the 1850s and far less than its estimated capacity of 150,000 tons per year.

After the Civil War, mine workers took a cue from Schuylkill

County's draft protesters, whose Irish conscripts saw no reason to perish in another country's internal strife. In 1868, about a dozen Schuylkill County miners formed the Workingmen's Benevolent Association, mobilizing to improve pay and conditions. At its peak, the union boasted twenty thousand members and pressured the state legislature to adopt mine safety legislation, the nation's first, including ventilation standards and misdemeanor criminal liability for violators. State-appointed inspectors circulated among the collieries to enforce the new requirements, taking notes, policing infractions, and writing annual reports to the governor.

Still, most Irish workers remained frozen at their entry point, including Patrick Quigley, who still toiled as a laborer in 1870, almost three decades after arriving in Schuylkill County. His two oldest sons, including my great-grandfather James, had snagged coveted mining slots. His two youngest sons hovered near the colliery hierarchy's bottom, poised to follow their brothers and father into the mines.

In 1865, Alexander Rea rechristened his town Centralia, meaning "center of commerce." Three new mines had opened during the Civil War, including Centralia Colliery, near the town's center. By 1866, the population had swelled to more than a thousand residents, most of whom cleaved to the religious and national identities they brought with them. Mining officials, predominantly English and Welsh bosses, organized Protestant congregations, chartered their own benevolent associations, and barred Catholics from joining: the Independent Order of Odd Fellows, a secret society with initiation rites and community improvement projects, which dated back to eighteenth-century England, and the Patriotic Order Sons of America, dedicated to flag and country.

The borough's Irish Catholic mine workers hiked down Locust Mountain and into Mass at St. Joseph's Church in Ashland, about a four-mile round-trip. For recreation, they slaked their thirst at one of Centralia's twelve saloons, including the Bucket of Blood, a bar and billiard hall at the corner of Locust Avenue and West Main Street. And without a union to channel their grievances, they targeted Alexander Rea, who emerged as the industry's local face, darting through the borough in a horse-drawn carriage, managing seven collieries, and generating profits for his Philadelphia-based officers and directors.

On October 17, 1868, at about eight A.M. on a Saturday, a band of six men clad in black coats and hats ambushed Rea in the woods about two miles west of Centralia, where he had paused to let his horse drink from a stream fed by an underground spring. The bandits, thinking he was carrying an eighteen-thousand-dollar cash payroll, surrounded him and demanded his money. Rea, who had paid his miners the day before, surrendered his gold watch and wallet, containing just sixty dollars in cash—far less than the plunder they had envisioned. Unwilling to leave a witness to their botched heist, they started shooting. Rea fled along an old logging road and the thieves chased him, firing as they ran. About forty yards later, he sank to the ground, riddled with gunshot wounds. The assailants approached, pumped a bullet into the base of his skull, and scattered across the mountain. The next morning, a search party found Rea's blood-splattered glove, and ten yards away, his body, with bullets lodged in his brain, liver, and spinal column.

For years, mining officials blamed Rea's death on the Molly Maguires, a band of labor activists to their adherents, with roots in eighteenth- and nineteenth-century Ireland. Their detractors, including the coal industry and the Catholic Church—which excommunicated Mollys from the fold—denounced them as terrorists, bent on violence and mayhem. Although the source of the Mollys' name remains a matter of dispute, shrouded in legend and myth, they originated as an agrarian protest movement, with men dressing in women's clothing to symbolize starving mothers begging for bread. In Ireland, the Mollys retaliated against landlords for tenant evictions, ripping down fences and reclaiming pastures for farmland. In the Western Middle Field, where Molly activity spiked in the 1860s and 1870s, they punished transgressions by external authorities: collieries, railroads, and Protestant mine bosses.

One month after Rea's murder, officials rousted four reputed Mollys—none of whom hailed from Centralia—and charged them with the crime. Columbia County prosecutors tried them separately, beginning in February 1869, with the district attorney delivering the first opening statement. But the clandestine society, with its loyalty oaths, taboo against squealing, and enthusiasm for intimidating and bribing witnesses, stymied efforts to build a case. Each jury returned an acquittal. Prosecutors, stung by three straight losses, dropped the charges against the fourth defendant.

Meanwhile, Centralia's first Catholic pastor, the Reverend Daniel Ignatius McDermott, confronted a handful of the borough's reputed adherents at home. Not long after the pastor's arrival, a parishioner had approached him in tears, saying the Mollys had plied her son with poteen (home-distilled Irish whiskey) and initiated him as a member. McDermott, a twenty-five-year-old Londonderry, Ireland, native and a recent seminary graduate, peppered the boy with questions, eliciting the tormentors' identities. In a sermon the following Sunday, he lashed out against the secret society.

Centralia isn't big enough for both of us, said Father McDermott. Next Sunday I will identify these cowards by name. The following Sunday, after fielding death threats from Mollys seeking to derail him, Father McDermott appeared before his congregation, swathed in a black stole. He asked two men to stand. They rose, with the eyes of the parish boring into them. Three times, the priest asked if they belonged to the Mollys. Each time, they denied the allegation. Father McDermott snuffed the altar candles and, as women and men sobbed in their pews, leveled an oath against the pair. If you are innocent, as you swear you are, this curse will turn into a blessing, he said. But if you are guilty, may God have mercy on your souls. Within a decade, one of the men was crushed to death in the mines, and the other was sentenced to a prison term for murder.

One year later, an 1870 census taker roamed the mountain around St. Ignatius Church, a Romanesque fieldstone structure whose rectangular steeple rose about sixty feet over South Locust Avenue, dominat-

CECIL COUNTY
PUBLIC LIBRARY
301 Newark Ave.
Elkton, MD 21921

ing the borough's skyline. On Wood Street, about four blocks from the new parish, he found my great-grandparents Michael and Anna Fowler Laughlin, who had grown up together in eastern Galway, in thatched-roof cottages on adjacent farms in Bally Kiltormer, near Ballinasloe. As the potato famine subsided, Michael emigrated to New York; he sent for Anna two years later, and they married in 1863. Several years later, they ventured to Centralia and staked a claim to a corner lot near the top of Locust Mountain, with commanding views of the surrounding terrain.

BACK IN ST. CLAIR, my great-grandfather James Quigley filed in to St. Mary's and married Maggie McKeone, the Pennsylvania-born daughter of Irish immigrants. As newlyweds, they squatted in Crow Hollow with his family. But the St. Clair basin, once a haven for independent investors and operators, had emerged as the Reading Railroad's corporate fiefdom. By late 1871, after a four-year, $40 million to $45 million spending spree, the Reading had secured about 70,000 acres of coal lands: enough, the railroad crowed, to fill its freight cars for centuries. Four years later, when miners called a strike against a proposed pay cut, Reading Coal and Iron, the railroad's mining subsidiary, owned 60 to 80 percent of Schuylkill County's coal reserves and one-third of Pennsylvania's anthracite—one-quarter of the world's hard coal.

The Reading seized on the strike to crush the union, summoning the state militia to patrol the streets. Miners slunk back to work, and the Reading, bloated with debt, started shedding colliery jobs, dumping about five hundred workers, roughly half of St. Clair's mine labor pool, into unemployment. In the decade between 1870 and 1880, St. Clair's population plummeted by 27 percent as miners bolted for newly opened collieries in the Western Middle Field. At some point, my great-grandparents must have decided that they, too, had to leave. By November 1877, when their son Thomas was born, Jim and Maggie had hauled their family over Broad Mountain, a route that took them six miles up the face and six miles back down the other side. From Ashland, which spilled through the valley at Broad Mountain's base, they climbed Locust Mountain, about a two-mile ascent, into Centralia.

By the mid-1870s, however, Centralia reeled from many of the same forces that had shattered St. Clair. The Lehigh Valley Railroad, the Reading's chief competitor, owned more than a thousand miles of track, stretching from Wilkes-Barre to Perth Amboy, New Jersey, and the Great Lakes. Centralia and Mount Carmel sat at the western tip of its Western Middle Field holdings. By 1875, the Lehigh Valley Railroad had wrested control of the Centralia basin from Locust Mountain Coal and Iron, Alexander Rea's former employer, and flipped its real estate holdings to a wholly owned mining subsidiary, the Lehigh Valley Coal Company.

Meanwhile, in February 1877, the coal industry convened in Columbia County's brick neoclassical courthouse to avenge Rea's demise. The two-week trial riveted Bloomsburg, an iron ore and manufacturing hub severed from the coal region by mountains, farmland, and the Susquehanna River. Spectators crammed the courtroom for a glimpse of the star prosecution witness, a Molly henchman sprung from prison by gubernatorial pardon and shoehorned into the witness seat, where he fingered three accomplices: Patrick Hester, a tavernkeeper from Locust Gap Junction, Peter McHugh, a Molly chieftain in Northumberland County, and Patrick Tully, an Irish immigrant who joined the Mollys after settling in Centralia. Coal and Iron police dredged up witnesses, subpoenaed them, and shepherded them to Bloomsburg at no charge on specially commissioned Reading trains. One defense lawyer likened himself to the giant-taming Lilliputians in *Gulliver's Travels*.

The twelve-man jury, predominantly German American farmers from hamlets surrounding Bloomsburg, reached a verdict in two hours. Before a courtroom filled with onlookers, the jurors rose one by one from their Windsor-back chairs and pronounced each defendant, starting with Hester, guilty of first-degree murder. Hester's wife fainted. From Pottsville to Shamokin, the local press hailed the outcome. Newspapers, whose pages were larded with ads for Locust Mountain coal from Centralia collieries, assured readers that the Mollys' reign had ended.

Lawyers for Hester, Tully, and McHugh appealed to Pennsylvania's supreme court, saying anti-Molly hysteria had polluted the jury pool, making a fair trial impossible. The Reading president affixed his name to the prosecution's appellate brief. On January 7, 1878, the court upheld the convictions and death sentences, ensuring Columbia County's first public execution.

Two and a half months later, on March 25, 1878, about three thousand gawkers streamed into Bloomsburg for the hanging. The county sheriff, who printed tickets for the event, ushered about 200 local dignitaries into the prison yard, where the gallows rose from the center: a two-story assemblage of oak posts and crossbeams, on loan from Carbon County, where it had already hanged four Mollys. Several hundred men and boys perched on the rooftops of nearby buildings. Just after ten A.M., McHugh climbed the steps to the platform, followed by Hester, then by Tully, who had confessed his guilt—and implicated Hester—in a pre-execution statement to his attorney. Priests hovered nearby, mumbling prayers. Sheriff's deputies clamped steel manacles around the prisoners' hands, bound their legs with straps, slipped white hoods over their heads, and positioned their feet over the wooden trapdoors.

At 11:07 A.M., a lever sprang. The floors opened, yanking the condemned into the air. Hester, Tully, and McHugh dangled from their nooses for nine to twelve minutes, suffocating slowly as onlookers howled. Doctors monitored their pulse beats, waiting to log the times of their deaths. At 11:30 A.M., an undertaker cut the bodies down and dumped them into pine coffins. Spectators rushed in through a side door, pressing for a glimpse of the corpses and scrambling for a souvenir strand of hanging rope.

HUNDREDS OF FEET underground, very little had changed. By 1878, when Hester, Tully, and McHugh swung from the Bloomsburg gallows, the eight Centralia-area collieries swallowed more than eighteen hundred men and boys. My great-grandfather Jim Quigley landed work as a miner, toiling for absentee landlords: Lehigh Valley or Reading Coal and Iron, which together controlled Centralia's eight operations.

In Centralia, miners punctured the coal seams from an underground lair, like a subway tunnel riddled with chimneys. Teams of two to four miners toiled inside narrow chambers called breasts, latticed with timbers and dripping with water and mud. Inside the breast, they blasted uphill and over their heads, chasing and exhausting the vein, sometimes as far as a hundred yards. Between each breast they left blocks of coal, called pillars, measuring fifteen to forty feet wide. The pillars buttressed the roof, the remaining workings, and the surface aboveground, like anthracite retaining walls. To operators tempted by short-term profits, however, the pillars often proved irresistible, spawning one of the most lucrative and dangerous projects in the mines: removing them with dynamite, a practice known as pillar robbing.

In July 1883, my great-grandfather and three other miners were robbing pillars inside Continental Colliery, where the Mammoth vein measured twenty-five feet wide. With a new slope poised for production, the boss had decided to pillage the old one before abandoning it. Jim and his crew worked from back to front, inching closer to the mine entrance, blasting pillars with dynamite. As each pillar detonated, the tunnel became less stable. On July 28, Jim's partner, Peter Colihan, stood between the sixth and fifth breasts, lining the tunnel with extra timber. The overhead roof collapsed, burying him in a rush of coal. Colihan, a thirty-nine-year-old father of four, died fifteen hours later, one of fifteen workers killed in Centralia area mines that year.

One year later, in August 1884, Jim and Maggie bought a home at 120 East Center Street, two blocks east of Locust, on a double-width corner lot. Their wood frame house, twelve feet wide and two and a half stories high, perched at the eastern end of its block, buttressing a row of side-by-side homes. From east to west, each featured a front door and a window downstairs and two windows upstairs, capped by a triangular peak, like teeth in a jack-o'-lantern. From his front porch, Jim could chat face-to-face with his next-door neighbor without leaving his property.

Across East Center Street from Jim and Maggie's home, about five hundred yards northeast of their parlor, loomed Centralia Colliery's breaker, a wood frame tower dotted with windows. The breaker, equal parts factory and train depot, soared about a hundred feet over the mine entrance, spilling downhill from the summit at a 40-degree angle, like a covered bridge over a ski jump. Inside, iron tracks hoisted coal cars from the workings. A ribbon of Lehigh Valley Railroad tracks unspooled at the base, extending west to Mount Carmel and Pittsburgh and east toward Shenandoah.

Throughout Centralia and across the region, breakers and their effluvia dominated the landscape. Unmarketable waste lay heaped behind them on culm banks, towering black lava fields of rock, slate, shale, mud, and anthracite pebbles. Puffs of coal dust floated from the tipple, coating the miners' homes and seeping in through their windows.

Even worse than living with the breaker, though, was coping without it. Operators flooded the market in the mid-1870s, seeking to boost revenue and meet six-figure interest payments on their multimillion-dollar real estate loans. Excess supply clogged the ports, and profits sagged. As a hedge against volatility, operators hashed out secret agreements to slash production and inflate prices. If stockpiles grew and the market softened, especially during the spring and summer, they locked the collieries. In the fall and winter, when customers clamored for anthracite, they recalled the workers. In Centralia, Lehigh Valley and the Reading suspended mining for an average of 135 days in 1880 alone.

Jim and Maggie lurched between booms and busts, saddled with a six-hundred-dollar mortgage and struggling to support their family. Of twelve children born to them between 1874 and 1889, five died as newborns or infants, including their first son and a daughter whose twin sister, Nell, survived. After my grandfather, a boy and two girls died at birth.

Maggie, however, proved adept at massaging the cycles. When the mines lay dormant, she opened a bar in the parlor, catering to her neighbors in the Swamp—until patrons realized Jim siphoned her whiskey on the sly and refilled the bottles with water. When one of her sons ripped both knees of a new pair of pants playing leapfrog, she sent Nell to the Mammoth Store, a company-run enterprise on North Locust Avenue named for the coal seam it straddled. Nell, hewing to Maggie's script, demanded a refund. What kind of cheap merchandise are you selling us? she said. When my brother knelt down to pray in church, the trousers tore open.

During one work stoppage, Maggie pooled a collection of free railroad passes and hauled the family to Philadelphia. Her son James, at eight or nine, looked young enough to circumvent the fare, she thought. When the conductor asked for his ticket, she eyed the rest of her brood, all endowed with her dark hair, and said he, with his reddish locks, belonged to a neighbor. Throw him the hell off the train, she said. He's nothing to me. The conductor caved, and my grandfather, who had entertained visions of orphaned exile, rode out the journey with his siblings. In the city, Nell secured a job in a shoe factory, earning about two dollars per week. Maggie, impressed by their relative affluence, lobbied to stay. As soon as the mines reopened, however, Jim insisted on returning to Centralia.

Given the obstacles he encountered there, it's hard to say what drew him back. Maybe he took pride in his work, especially assignments fraught with peril, such as robbing pillars in a Mammoth gangway. Maybe, after starting over in Centralia, he grew determined to stay put. Or perhaps, as a first-generation Irish American, his immigrant father instilled in him a reverence for soil and the act of owning it. Whatever the explanation, Centralia and the mines prevailed over Maggie.

Back in Centralia, Jim ushered his wife and children into a photographer's studio, where they assembled in front of a Victorian cottage backdrop. Surrounded by his family, Jim projected an air of well-fed professionalism, like a Bloomsburg lawyer with a walrus mustache, attired for court in a three-piece suit and tie. Only the black crescents ringing his fingernails, coal dust embedded in his skin from years of blasting, betrayed his profession. His sons, the two oldest of whom had already endured several years in and around the mines, tucked white pocket squares into their suit jackets. One looped a watch chain across his vest, poking the fob through a buttonhole. Maggie, enrobed in a dark, high-necked dress, struck the lone note of dissidence, frowning into the camera, decrying the frivolity.

MAGGIE HAD REASON to scowl. In 1890, she and Jim took out a two-hundred-dollar second mortgage on their home, and my nine-year-old grandfather, who had finished third grade, entered the ranks of Centralia's breaker boys. Pennsylvania's mine safety laws prohibited employment of children younger than twelve, but many parents circumvented the restriction. In 1891 alone, the state mine inspector tallied 664 slate pickers in Centralia's eight breakers, 21 percent of the borough's mine labor force. Every paycheck mattered, with Centralia's collieries averaging 111 inactive days that year, even one earned by the smallest hands.

Early in the morning, often before sunrise, my grandfather left the East Center Street row home and walked to the breaker. Inside, high overhead, workers upended wagons into the hopper, where cast-iron rollers crushed coal chunks and forced them through chutes. Wooden troughs angled downhill from the chutes, funneling processed anthracite to the breaker boys. For ten or more hours, a stream of coal swept past my grandfather, glistening with water and sulfuric acid from the mine. He crouched over, grabbing pieces of slate, wood, and rock with his bare hands and flicking them into a waste chute. Shards of anthracite, like broken glass, tore into his fingers, slicing them raw: red tops, the boys called them. During the winter, when he filed to and from the colliery in darkness, he saw the sun only on Sundays.

By 1901, at age twenty, my grandfather had attained the rank of laborer, like his older brothers. Up on Wood Street, my great-grandparents Michael and Anna Fowler Laughlin had replicated their childhood farms in Galway, with chickens, indoor and outdoor cats, and a smokehouse for butchered pigs. My sixteen-year-old grandmother Helen lived with them, surrounded by three generations of her extended clan, who coexisted side by side in three adjacent homes, under Anna's watchful eye.

FAR FROM the Laughlins' Wood Street compound, two New York financiers dominated the principal anthracite railroads: the Vanderbilts and J. Pierpont Morgan. The Reading and its coal company slipped into receivership in 1893, just before a bank panic. Three years later, J. P. Morgan and Company snatched both concerns at foreclosure. With Morgan's backing, the Reading grabbed a $23 million, 53 percent stake in New Jersey Central, and with it the second-largest mineral reserves in the anthracite fields. The Reading and New Jersey Central also acquired a $12 million, 30 percent stake in the Lehigh Valley Railroad. The coal operators, buffered by overlapping ownership and shared directorates, anticipated an era of unprecedented harmony and prosperity.

For colliery workers, the outlook was far less promising. About four hundred miners died in the hard coalfields each year. In the 1890s, Pennsylvania's anthracite mining ranked as the world's eighth most hazardous profession, surpassed only by the likes of Gloucester fishermen and South African diamond miners. Wages, too, had stagnated. At Centralia Colliery in 1901, a miner's average daily earnings hovered at $2.48.

By 1902, more than seventy-eight thousand anthracite mine laborers had joined the United Mine Workers of America. On May 12, when operators rejected proposals for a 10 percent wage hike and a nine-hour day, the union's president, John Mitchell, called a strike. More than 140,000 anthracite workers laid down their drills and shovels. All 357 collieries ground to a halt.

Across the region, miners scrambled to feed their families. Women and children roamed the mountains with buckets and baskets, picking huckleberries and selling them for five cents a quart. Miners sneaked onto Lehigh Valley Coal's property outside Mount Carmel and looted seams near the surface; coal and iron police materialized to arrest them. On July 31, one day after the deputy sheriff's brother died in a riot at the Shenandoah train station, twelve hundred national guard troops massed, pitching their white canvas tents on a hill overlooking the town.

In St. Ignatius Church, the pastor stood before his congregation and told his parishioners to go back to work. The strike has "impoverished you and ruined our town," said the Reverend Thomas W. Hayes, a silver-haired Holy Cross College alumnus who entertained Reading officials in his residence and blocked the strikers from meeting in the parish hall. "The longer you delay, the greater the injury you inflict upon yourselves and your families." The day before Labor Day, with Mitchell slated to lead ten thousand marchers in Philadelphia's parade, Father Hayes again sided with the operators, saying the union had delivered nothing but broken promises. "You have been gulled long enough," he said.

By late summer and early fall, strikers were scaling the mountains that encircled Centralia and Mount Carmel, pillaging farms for corn, apples, chickens, and potatoes. Tempers flared across the region, with strikebreakers bearing the brunt of the ire. In Lansford, about a hundred women surrounded and beat another woman as she carried supper to her brother, a strikebreaker at a nearby colliery. A dynamite blast detonated under a nonunion boss's home in Gilberton, demolishing his front porch. Even teenagers entered the fray, surrounding a house in Forestville, banging tin buckets and washtubs, and taunting the colliery workers who lived there, deriding them as scabs.

In private, Mitchell, a thirty-two-year-old Illinois bituminous miner, despaired of crafting a peaceful resolution. The operators, who claimed the moral high ground, refused to negotiate. "The rights and interests of the laboring man will be protected and cared for, not by the labor agitators, but by the Christian men to whom God in His infinite wisdom has given the control of the property interests of the country," said George F. Baer, the Reading president, in a widely published letter. As winter approached, Mitchell pressured President Theodore Roosevelt to intervene.

In Centralia, just a few miles from the cavalry's Shenandoah base camp, the military occupation stiffened the union's resolve. On September 26, just before midnight, one hundred to two hundred union leaders and strikers converged on the Lehigh Valley Railroad depot and refused to scatter. When a train pulled in to the station, loaded with ten to twenty nonunion workers, strikers surrounded the coach. Two union leaders spoke to the passengers, urging them to respect the strike.

The next morning, strikers poured into Centralia's depot again, lobbying the scabs before their shift. This time, only three strikebreakers boarded the train. Columbia County's sheriff telegraphed the governor asking him to deploy troops to Centralia. Instead, with the military diverted to larger towns, six sheriff's deputies and the deputy sheriff wended through the borough the next day, serving warrants and arresting men and boys for unlawful assembly. At an emergency meeting, the strikers forged their response: Surrender peacefully, refuse to make bail, and insist on a hearing in Bloomsburg. All but seven—a total of 127—honored the pact. Law enforcement officials herded the suspects into the Odd Fellows Hall on East Center Street, a block uphill and across the street from Jim and Maggie's house, and detained them overnight.

The following day, as the sheriff loaded the Centralia prisoners into thirteen horse-drawn wagons, President Roosevelt broke his silence. At 1:29 P.M. on October 1, he zapped a telegram to Mitchell—and identically phrased invitations to the operators—bidding them to meet him in Washington, D.C., in two days. The summit's topic, he said, was "the failure of the coal supply, which has become a matter of vital concern to the whole nation."

Meanwhile, the Centralia procession lurched north toward Bloomsburg. The Patriotic Order Sons of America band, arrested for participating in the disturbance, headed the convoy, clutching their drums, tubas, and trombones. Union members with names such as McGinley,

Dempsey, Gaughan, and Cleary sat shoulder to shoulder with Centralia school directors, borough council members, and the chief burgess. Inching up North Locust Avenue, over the railroad tracks and past the fire department, they serenaded Lehigh Valley Coal's divisional headquarters, where corporate officials monitored collieries from a wing of the Mammoth Store.

After a five-hour trek across the mountains, the wagon train rolled into the county seat, where lawyers inhabited Georgian mansions and young women and men trained for teaching careers at Bloomsburg State Normal School, overlooking the Susquehanna River. Gliding down the broad expanse of Main Street, lined with brick commercial storefronts, the band played "Marching Through Georgia," a Civil War tune with lyrics about liberating the slaves. Onlookers knotted the sidewalks. Strikers bellowed cheers for Mitchell, the union, and Centralia. In front of the courthouse, a four-story redbrick and brownstone edifice whose clock tower lorded over the thoroughfare, they jumped out, fell into place behind the band, and marched several blocks to their lawyer's office.

That evening, Justice of the Peace Guy Jacoby, a member of the Patriotic Order Sons of America, convened a hearing inside his second-floor courtroom, where windows soared from the floor to the ceiling, as in a New England church. Strikers and band members crammed onto the wooden benches, facing the judge, and spilled into the jury box. Local spectators packed the center and side aisles. The prosecution, fronted by a Lehigh Valley Coal attorney, called its witnesses to the stand: the Centralia-based divisional superintendent, a Lehigh coal and iron policeman, and Centralia's deputy sheriff. When pressed, they said the strikers had not brandished weapons or resorted to violence.

The union's lawyer offered leaders Patrick Cain and John O'Donnell, who said the strikers had never used force. He also called my great-uncles Pat and Tom Quigley, who confirmed their account. At 11:30 P.M., Jacoby made his ruling: In a decision transcribed by hand into the court's docket book without explanation or rationale, he dropped the charges against thirty-one Centralians, including my great-uncle Pat. He scheduled the rest for a December trial, including my great-uncle Tom and my grandfather, and released them on their own recognizance.

The strikers, band members, and school directors arrived back home the next afternoon, after spending the night in the courthouse. News of President Roosevelt's planned meeting with Mitchell and the operators leaped from the Mount Carmel newspaper's front page, paired with a report on the Bloomsburg proceedings. "Things Seem Brighter than for Many Moons," said the headline.

WITHIN TWO WEEKS, Roosevelt appointed a seven-member strike arbitration commission to investigate conditions in the anthracite fields. Miners ended the walkout and returned to work. The depot disturbance vanished from the Bloomsburg court's docket. For the next four months, the strike commissioners toured the region's collieries, including Potts, and heard testimony from mine workers and breaker boys. Clarence Darrow, the Chicago-based trial attorney, represented the miners. "Trade unions are for today, for the present," he said in his closing argument. "They are the greatest agency that the wit of man has ever devised for uplifting the lowly and the weak, for defending the poor and the oppressed, for bringing about genuine democracy amongst men."

With the union, anthracite miners gained economic leverage that had eluded them for decades. By 1906, Centralia boasted nineteen general and grocery stores, five hotels, two jewelry stores, two theaters, and twenty-six saloons. Immigrants from southern and eastern Europe and Russia flooded the borough, adding two new churches with onion-shaped domes to the skyline: St. Mary's, a Greek Catholic church on the mountain overlooking town from the north, and Sts. Peter and Paul, a Russian Orthodox church.

Meanwhile, my grandfather married Helen Laughlin, whose relatives called her Ella, at St. Ignatius. Her father, Michael, my great-grandfather, had died six years earlier, one of Centralia's oldest and earliest settlers, according to his obituary. Eventually they settled in

Mount Carmel, where they bought a row home at 45 North Chestnut Street, next door to his brother Pat. Their upstairs bedroom, at the back of the house, faced east, toward Centralia.

By November 1915, when Maggie died of a stroke at the breakfast table, each of her three sons had climbed into colliery management. The *Mount Carmel Item* gave her a front-page obituary, calling her one of Centralia's best-known residents. Three years later, when Jim died at home of miner's asthma, the local term for black lung disease, his page one obituary hailed him as the father of mine bosses—and one of Centralia's most prominent citizens.

When the stock market tanked in October 1929, my grandfather's state salary as a mine inspector—not more than six thousand dollars, but enough to support a middle-class lifestyle—insulated his family. Beierschmitt's grocery made weekly deliveries to my grandmother's kitchen, just as it had before the crash, bearing cakes, jelly, cream, sugar, milk, and pretzels. Once a week, a cleaning lady scrubbed my grandmother's floors and a neighbor laundered the family's clothes.

For my grandfather, who spent evenings at his desk, filling the lined pages of leather-bound notebooks with handwritten investigation reports, the rhythm of work did not deviate. Day after day, he rotated through collieries, probing into accidents, screening for poor ventilation and hazardous gases and, if necessary, shutting down mines until foremen improved conditions. On December 15, 1931, after preparing a report about unemployment in his district, he toured Centralia Colliery, one of his territory's most productive mines. On this day, just before Christmas, he found water slowly filling the lower level.

For years, Lehigh Valley Coal had struggled to turn a profit from its mining operations, let alone honor interest payments on the multimillion-dollar mortgages securing its mineral lands. The company, which borrowed cash from its railroad patron to meet operating expenses, did not pay a dividend between 1874 and 1914. Across the region, operators faced similar straits: Railroads forgave their mining companies' debt and renegotiated their low-interest loans. The railroads, not the collieries, remained the revenue centers. In some years, more than 40 percent of the Lehigh Valley Railroad's revenue derived from anthracite cargo.

During the Depression, the mining operations proved expendable. Centralia, perched on the western frontier of Lehigh Valley's rail network, was especially vulnerable. After the 1929 crash, Lehigh Valley closed twenty-one mines, including its three in Centralia. About eight hundred mine workers, more than one-third of Centralia's workforce, tumbled into unemployment. Between late 1931, when my grandfather noticed water levels rising in Centralia Colliery, and 1932, when Lehigh Valley jettisoned Continental, the company abandoned Centralia altogether.

Reading's Centralia area collieries initially fared better, retaining about a thousand employees, until a mine fire shuttered Bast, tossing about six hundred more workers into joblessness. By 1936, Reading had scrapped thirty of its forty-two mines in Schuylkill and Northumberland counties, flooding the idle workings. Potts closed every other year, lurching between full and zero employment.

Sidelined miners fended for themselves, staking a claim to an outcrop—a spot, like the tips on a V, where the vein spiked to the surface. They labored in teams, often veteran miners and their extended family members, clearing rock, dirt, and debris with picks and shovels. If, after several weeks of digging, they tapped the coal seam, they sank a bootleg hole, propped it with timber, blasted into the vein with dynamite, and opened a tunnel anywhere from twenty to a hundred feet deep.

During the summer, women and children again scoured the mountains for huckleberries, as they had during the 1902 strike. Boys toiled with their fathers, cracking, cleaning, and sorting anthracite for sale to independent truckers, the outlet to customers from Baltimore to Connecticut. After expenses, a bootlegger pocketed about twenty dollars per week. Law enforcement officials and parish priests acquiesced, knowing the practice warded off starvation.

Up on the Hill near St. Ignatius, the Laughlins, Ryans, and Donahues—the multigenerational Wood Street offspring of Michael and

Anna—operated a bootleg hole about a hundred feet south of their front steps, on the Buck vein's outcrop. Inside their operation, and hundreds just like it, miners served as their own safety police, relying on judgment and experience to keep them alive, but often skimping on timber and ventilation that could have bolstered their chances. By 1937, cave-ins and toxic gases had claimed about a hundred bootleggers, two to three times the fatality rate in officially sanctioned mines. My dad's cousin John Donahue, who had already lost a leg in a mining accident, perished inside the brood's enterprise.

ONLY WITH THE OUTBREAK of World War II did Centralia's collieries spring back to life. In 1942, the first full year of combat for American troops, Continental, Midvalley, and Potts engaged about thirteen hundred mine workers, almost doubling the borough's 1936 deep-mine workforce. Across the region, posters urged employees to churn out more anthracite: "Every Minute Counts," they read. "It's Up to Us. Work Will Win." Meanwhile, more than 220 St. Ignatius parishioners joined the armed services, including another of my dad's cousins, Jackie Ryan, who perished in the Battle of the Bulge.

After the war, as Americans decamped for the suburbs and launched the baby boom, Centralia enjoyed a construction renaissance. The Lynch-Gugie Post No. 608 of the American Legion, named for the first Centralia soldiers killed during World Wars I and II, erected a pink cinder-block hall on West Park Street after a fire destroyed its previous lodge, Alexander Rea's former home. St. Ignatius razed its parochial school on South Locust Avenue, a three-story wood frame structure across from the church dating back to Father Hayes's tenure, and dedicated a one-story brick building, with four classrooms and a social hall, on the same site.

Still, anthracite teetered on the brink of obsolescence. The operators blamed the United Mine Workers and its president, John L. Lewis, for alienating customers with strikes during the winter, when their bargaining power peaked. Even before the Depression, however, consumers had begun gravitating toward heating oil. Regional anthracite production peaked in 1917. During the postwar housing boom, the slide accelerated as homeowners swapped coal storage bins for automatic furnaces, freeing their basements for rec rooms. Demand for hard coal, long confined to the home heating market, plummeted and did not rebound. Even the industry's once-fabled mineral reserves commanded only pennies on the dollar.

Congress, long silent about the operators' environmental abuses, took its first step toward compelling the industry to underwrite the toll of its demise: mine fires. Between 1949 and 1952, the federal Bureau of Mines spent $1.3 million dousing infernos in abandoned mines and stripping pits in five states, including $570,000, almost half its national budget, on five anthracite mine fires. In 1954, blazes consumed seventy-five inactive coal deposits in Pennsylvania, 48 percent of the nation's total. That summer, Congress proposed shifting the federal government's tab to the coal companies, requiring them, as owners of the affected mineral lands, to finance 50 percent of the fire containment costs.

In Centralia, the industry parried with a dodge: If it didn't own the mineral rights, it didn't have to foot the firefighting tab. In mid-August, with the federal bill slated for passage, Coates Coal Company, Centralia Colliery's successor, unloaded its underground mineral rights—the once-vaunted claim to anthracite still wedged underneath the Centralia basin—on the borough for one dollar. Two weeks later, on August 31, 1954, the legislation cleared Congress, saddling the town—now the owner of the borough's subterranean mineral largesse—with liability for half the cost of any future mine fires in its midst.

Within a year, the industry and Centralia's economy cratered. Continental closed in 1955, followed by Germantown in 1960, together jilting about five hundred workers. Between 1950 and 1960, the town's mine workforce shrank by 93 percent. Many residents fled to northern New Jersey and southeastern Pennsylvania, where they joined other ex-miners on assembly lines in steel, automotive, and plastics factories. Those who stayed behind commuted to work outside the region or cobbled together income from odd jobs and construction, tending bar and digging graves. Women filed into garment factories and emerged as the family's primary wage earner, just as their mothers and grandmothers had anchored family finances through strikes and wars.

By 1960, the borough's population had slid to about fourteen hundred residents, including a handful of my aging relatives. Annie Quigley remained at home in the Swamp, alone and unmarried, with doilies coating overstuffed furniture and pictures of Saint Theresa and the Sacred Heart lining the walls. Up on the Hill, Jim Laughlin, my grandmother's older brother, lived in his parents' Wood Street homestead. During baseball season, he lounged on a round bench encircling a weeping willow tree near his tribe's old bootleg hole. From that vantage point, on a slight mound overlooking St. Ignatius School's baseball field, he and a posse of neighborhood men disputed the calls, arguing the balls and strikes.

About five hundred feet to their east, across from the Odd Fellows Cemetery, pickup trucks and sedans bounced along a dirt and gravel road to the dump, an abandoned stripping pit perched atop the Buck vein.

WHAT FIRE?

PART TWO

CHAPTER THREE

Trench Warfare

MARY LOU GAUGHAN couldn't help staring. Across Helen Womer's parlor, on a maroon velour sofa, sat Congressman Flood. He had swept onto Wood Street only minutes earlier, bedecked in a white Panama suit, white shoes, and a white cape, disrupting the Friday supper hour. Ordinarily, she would be dishing out bean soup right now, or hot dogs, hamburgers, and fried potatoes. Instead, she found herself a few feet from Dapper Dan, as his constituents had dubbed him, with his handlebar mustache tapered into points like waxed apostrophes. Whatever happened as a result of this meeting, she viewed one outcome as a certainty: federal funding. If a congressman comes to your house, you're going to get money.

Flood, a Wilkes-Barre lawyer and twenty-year veteran of Capitol Hill, knew better than to show up unprepared. Earlier in the day, he had clamored for a Centralia update, tracking down a Washington-based Bureau of Mines official at home and pressing him for details. And as the congressman had learned, the news was grave.

In fact, in the private confines of interoffice memos, far from Wood Street's ears and eyes, federal officials had labeled the situation an emergency. The mine fire had surged through a labyrinth of Depression-era bootleg holes along the Buck outcrop, including the old Laughlin-Donahue-Ryan enterprise. Now, just behind Mary Lou's and Helen's backyards, both the coal bed and the surface above it smoldered. Earlier that day, federal mining engineers had recommended a hundred-thousand-dollar ditch, tunneling more than half the length and width of a football field and five stories deep, from the outcrop to the Laughlin row: another effort to root out the fire and stop it from spreading farther west, down Wood Street and into the borough.

Flood, a former Shakespearean actor who had paraded through Centralia's centennial in the back of a pickup truck, attired in a top hat, tails, and white gloves, hewed to an upbeat script. In deference to Mary Lou, Tony, and Helen, he expressed concern. With federal engineers from Schuylkill Haven and Wilkes-Barre in the room, nursing wounded egos, he explained the procedure for modifying the federal fly-ash contract. The trench proposal, he said, had received special treatment and could win approval as soon as Monday, June 16, just three days away.

Even as Flood delivered what sounded like good news, though, Mary Lou had trouble concentrating. Why, she wondered, had he come all the way to Centralia? Who had ever heard of a congressman coming to someone's home? It must have been the notoriety, the press coverage. The pressure brought him to town.

Mary Lou hovered near Helen's parlor door, with her back to the front porch and Wood Street. To her right, facing the congressman, sat Helen in a wine-colored armchair, part of a living room set just like the one Mary Lou had acquired after marrying Tony. As Flood spoke, Helen filled the pages of a yellow pad, line after line, with her elegant script. None of this surprised Mary Lou, whose friendship with Helen dated back to St. Ignatius School, when they were Mary Lou Donahue and Helen Bergan. For several years, Mary Lou knew, Helen had monitored mine fire projects from her kitchen and dining room windows, logging her observations on legal pads. Now, as Mary Lou stood in her mother-in-law's former living room, too charged with nerves and adrenaline to sit down, she watched Helen take charge of the meeting.

HELEN, LIKE MARY LOU, had grown up, the oldest of five girls, in a mining family gripped by the Western Middle Field's depression. But from an early age, Helen's academic aptitude set her apart. At St. Ignatius School, when the Reverend Patrick J. Phelan barged into the classroom and sat at the nun's desk with a pile of report cards arranged in alphabetical order, he lingered over Helen's marks and pronounced them excellent. Two consonants later, when he reached Mary Lou, he said: You have to try harder.

Nine months after the Japanese bombed Pearl Harbor, Helen and Mary Lou enrolled at Conyingham Township's public high school in Aristes, Con-Cen High. Helen should have matriculated at Hubert Eicher, the borough's high school, near the American Legion on West Park Street. After eighth grade, though, without explaining why, she left her parents and younger sisters and settled with her aunt Kathryn Bergan, an unmarried teacher, in the Swamp, where high schoolers enrolled at Con-Cen.

Helen's decision hinged less on school zoning than family dynamics. Her father, Bill Bergan, a St. Ignatius parishioner, grew up on East Wood Street a block from the Quigleys, the son of a union official. Her mother, Josephine Bergan, also grew up in Centralia, a seamstress from a clan of Eastern European immigrants who worshipped at St. Mary's. Inside Helen's childhood home, Bill held sway with rage and alcohol, a combination not unheard of in neighborhoods throughout the coal region. As a young teenager, Helen bolted, seeking refuge with her aunt Kathryn, who nurtured her intellect and encouraged her to read. For Helen, who also absorbed her aunt's demeanor, the arrangement reaped dividends. On the school bus, riding up the mountain to Aristes, Mary Lou overheard other students marveling at Helen's grades, her 95's and 98's in civics and typing.

For Mary Lou, who lost her front teeth to decay after eighth grade because her parents could not afford a dentist, high school proved torture, with its whirl of dances and skating parties. Students poked fun, stretching their top lips over their gums and imitating how she spoke. Halfway through sophomore year, just before Christmas, she decided to drop out. Her mother, whose maiden name was Mary Magdalene Dougherty, discouraged her, saying she'd have to find a job. Mary Lou, a fifteen-year-old who didn't know how to sew, walked to Centralia, rode a bus to Mount Carmel, and landed a slot as a collar setter in a children's clothing factory.

Helen, meanwhile, with her fair skin and shoulder-length curls, thrived at Con-Cen, where classmates signed up for the Red Cross and sold war bonds. She joined the glee and press clubs and penned the junior class history for *The Iris,* the school's yearbook. Senior year, she served as class secretary and edited the yearbook, with its can-do postwar tributes to peace, prosperity, and success. In a two-page prophecy charting careers for each graduating senior, from mechanic to movie star, Helen's classmates predicted she would enjoy a corporate bookkeeping career in New York. After graduation, she pulled the Centralia equivalent: a secretarial job at the Mammoth Store, and from there a lengthy tenure as a Centralia Bank teller.

Over the years, while she lived in a Locust Avenue apartment, Helen developed a fondness for the Gaughans' Wood Street homestead, with its parklike setting and Quality Hill address, its spacious backyard and freedom, unlike most row homes, from walls shared with neighbors. On Friday afternoons, when the borough's Catholic faithful eschewed meat and Tony's mother filled the void, selling dozens of cheese and potato pierogies, Helen sat on the front porch, waiting for her order while fawning over the view. Once, Mary Lou even heard Helen ask Mrs. Gaughan to offer her the house first if she ever parted with it. When Mrs. Gaughan decided to cast about for a buyer, Mary Lou reminded her mother-in-law about Helen, who bought the home and moved in with her husband and children.

NOW, A DECADE LATER, Congressman Flood presided over Helen's living room, with its three-directional view of Locust Avenue, Wood

Street, and the mine fire. Steam and fumes trailed from vent pipes behind her house. Flood, ever the showman, assured his constituents they remained in capable hands. The federal mining engineers were the most dedicated mine fire experts in the world, he said. Still, even he could not resist a note of caution. Up in Bloomsburg, Columbia County officials were deliberating about the Birsters, Annie Ryan, and Marion Laughlin, mulling whether to underwrite relocating them to homes elsewhere in Centralia. Tony, Helen, and Mary Lou should meet with their county commissioners, Flood said, just in case.

After the meeting, Mary Lou, Tony, Helen, and the congressman traipsed across the muddy field behind Wood Street. Up near the Odd Fellows Cemetery, they showed Flood where the fire had started and where workers, with their bulldozers and dragline shovels, had tried to extinguish it. Helen narrated the tour, reading from her notepad. From the aborted 1962 excavation to the more recent fly-ash flushing, she knew each project's cost. She knew where and when the digging had stopped, where the boreholes, even the ones without exhaust pipes, were located, and how the fire had spread. Like a lawyer marshaling evidence for trial, she had saved newspaper articles and prepared a scrapbook, and now she argued her case. Afterward, when the officials scattered, Mary Lou knew Flood would deliver.

Three days later, the Bureau of Mines authorized the emergency trench. Flood dispatched a telegram to the Bloomsburg *Morning Press* that afternoon, trumpeting his efforts. Helen, meanwhile, engaged in some freelance media relations of her own. That day, she dashed off a letter to the editor of the *Pottsville Republican*, where recent coverage had focused on distant phenomena, from racial unrest in Newark, New Jersey, and Indianapolis to long-haired student antiwar protesters clashing with college-town police. In five column inches, she set the record straight. "Upon our request, Congressman Daniel Flood from the 11th Congressional District of Penna. met in my home, with federal mine officials and engineers along with area residents, to discuss the matter at length," she said. For her kicker, she embellished the text with initial capitals, a headline-style flourish: "Result—We Have Been Successful in Obtaining the Unobtainable."

FOR THE REST of the summer, when the *Apollo 11* moon landing riveted Americans to their television sets and music pilgrims converged on a farm near Woodstock, New York, Mary Lou and Helen thought they had saved Centralia. By day, federal contractors bored into the Buck outcrop, scooping out smoldering chunks of sandstone and siltstone, blasting and drilling open a carrot-shaped wedge extending east from Mary Lou's backyard to the Odd Fellows Cemetery. Inch by inch, cubic yard by cubic yard, they closed in on the Laughlin row, hovering within twenty-five feet of a garage behind Mary Lou's house. In the evenings, neighbors stood at the rim of the crevasse like mountain climbers: Mary Lou in floral print A-line shifts, with mud spattering her ankles, and Helen belted inside a raincoat and slacks. Beneath their feet, curtains of steam rippled from the rock walls like fog washing ashore at dusk.

As summer faded into fall, workers drew close to the fire's core. Behind the Laughlin row, they grubbed out the surface blaze and kept digging away from the borough, following the outcrop. About two hundred feet east of the Laughlin homestead, they exposed a burning coal pillar, glowing red under a white ash veil, like molten lava. Seven years after the dump flared, workers had the conflagration within their grasp. But in October, with the fire still scorching along the north dip, contractors exhausted the last of Dan Flood's hundred-thousand-dollar appropriation. Federal officials ordered them to fill in the trench and proceed with the fly-ash barrier. A battalion of dump trucks plugged the cavern with clay and rocks as Mary Lou and Tony watched from St. Ignatius baseball field.

That's the end of Centralia, said Tony.

Mary Lou, who still had faith the government would devise another containment plan, snapped Polaroids of the excavation before it disappeared: four shots of orange and gray striated rock walls, shimmering like the base of a charcoal grill, with her maroon house and garage in the background. Later, she added them to her mine fire scrapbook, now spanning several pages of press clippings and color photographs. At the bottom of the page, in red Magic Marker, she wrote, "Covering Over the Fire."

When officials congregated for a photo op the following August, pledging to conquer the blaze by other means, a local reporter suggested that Centralians no longer had anything to fear. Helen clipped the story and fired off a letter to her sister in Alaska. "The enclosed article is a joke, and needless to say, I was spitting mad when I read it," she wrote. "I told one of the Federal Inspectors if all the Government Departments were run like the Department of Mines, our country is sure in a sorry state of affairs."

Three years and $2.8 million later, in late 1973, workers completed the fly-ash barrier: actually two underground blockades, one on the west, coursing north-south from Mary Lou's backyard to Center Street, and one to the east, a semicircular barricade beyond the Odd Fellows Cemetery. During the initiative's seven-year life span, contractors had sunk 1,635 boreholes, sprayed 123,000 tons of fly ash into mine workings, and excavated about 60,000 cubic yards of burning rock and coal. In February, Congressman Flood inspected the site and pronounced the project a success, hailing it as a landmark achievement for environmental protection.

Within months, however, trouble signs emerged. About 350 feet northeast of the Odd Fellows Cemetery, just beyond the aborted 1969 trench, inspectors spotted a hole at the surface, measuring about five feet in diameter, spewing smoke and steam. Federal and state engineers who scrutinized the cave-in, exchanging interoffice memos about their surveillance, recognized the opening as a cropfall, technical parlance for a cave-in over an old mine chute. From the physical clues, they knew the blaze had seared along the Buck outcrop from the filled-in trench.

A few months later, in the fall of 1975, federal officials pried the metal cap off a borehole diagonally across Wood Street from Mary

Lou's house, about fifty feet northeast of her bedroom window. Inside a mine cavity about seventy feet underground, they discerned a trace of carbon monoxide. Federal engineers knew then that their fly-ash experiment had failed: Any carbon monoxide in the monitoring holes they had punched along the barricade's western flank, the so-called cold side, proved they had not thwarted the fire or its signature emissions. Instead of suppressing the blaze, they had buried it alive.

TONY, WHO SPENT his mornings in the kitchen with a cup of coffee and a pair of binoculars spying on federal contractors and technicians, knew almost as soon as the government did that the fly-ash barrier had flopped. After supper most evenings, he and Mary Lou crept around their neighborhood with a colorimetric tester—a handheld gas detector the size of a garage door opener—and a twelve-inch steel thermometer looped onto a blasting wire. Tony encased his hands in leather work gloves, unbolted the borehole covers with a wrench, and brandished his gadgets at the opening, dropping them, like an angler on a frozen lake, to depths of one hundred to two hundred feet. Mary Lou tabulated his gas and temperature readings on a notepad, taking comfort in their resourcefulness. Still, with potentially lethal mine fire gases lodged seventy to ninety feet under their foundation, she worried about their safety inside their home, especially at night, when a sudden gas surge might asphyxiate them in their sleep.

Had she known as much as the government, though, she would have spun into hysteria. In June 1976, state officials probed a borehole thirty-seven feet from Mary Lou's bedroom window, roughly where Annie Ryan's front porch once stood. Sixty-five feet belowground, they found 1 percent carbon monoxide, or 10,000 parts per million, more than eight times the concentration the government deemed life-threatening. One of the officials drew a map for his boss and his boss's boss depicting Mary Lou's home and the adjacent boreholes, with arrows reflecting the distances among the points. He did not, however, share his findings with Mary Lou or with Tony, who had, over the years, earned a reputation as a hothead, with access to a shotgun. For all Mary Lou knew, the government's highest reading, and one its technicians had obtained repeatedly, was 0.1 percent carbon monoxide, or 1,000 parts per million, 83 percent of a life-threatening dose.

Within days of the 1 percent reading, though, state and federal officials met in Schuylkill Haven to discuss the fly-ash barrier, which they had jointly funded under then prevailing federal mine reclamation law. Federal engineers, who had footed 75 percent of the bill, remained unconvinced of a breach. The state detailed a mine inspector to sweep through Mary Lou's home every week, prowling for carbon monoxide, methane, and black damp. Each time, as he recounted in memos to his boss, the tests proved negative. His results provided little assurance to Tony and Mary Lou, however, especially since they had no basement. If a life-threatening dose of carbon monoxide, 1,200 parts per million, burst through an underground fissure, the fumes would surge into their living space, and with only a thirty-minute margin for survival, they might not realize their peril in time to escape.

Mary Lou and Tony, who had seen the bureaucracy buckle under Dan Flood's touch, labored to rouse interest in their plight. Throughout the summer of 1976, they placed phone calls to public officials and swamped them with letters, highlighting the potentially fatal carbon monoxide swirling beneath their pavement. When that didn't work, and with their own data depicting a spike in underground temperatures, they spoke to the media, from local reporters to *The Wall Street Journal* and CBS News.

"We're trying to get something started to save our home," said Mary Lou.

Tony, in a forecast that ricocheted across the AP wire, was even more blunt. "What I'm trying to do is get this fire put out and get the gas stopped," he said. "It's going to wipe the whole town out."

Federal officials, however, remained unmoved. Over and over, they insisted everything was fine. In statements to the media, Congressman

Flood, state officials, and Centralia residents, they said the fly-ash firebreak had worked as planned, the town faced no danger, and the mine fire gases posed no harm to residents. Most people in Centralia, including some of its elected officials, just wanted Tony and Mary Lou to keep quiet, even after Tony warned borough council that the fire would reach Coddington's gas station within a year. They didn't want the rest of the world to hear about the mine fire.

Meanwhile, the Gaughans' health deteriorated. Tony, who was already disabled by heart disease and miner's asthma, lost sixty pounds and had trouble sleeping. In June 1977, three months after *The Wall Street Journal* chronicled Wood Street's predicament on the front page, Mary Lou was diagnosed with breast cancer. Practically overnight, she shelved her mine fire obsession. After her mastectomy, when flowers lined her hospital room and more than two hundred get-well cards poured into the house, she had no energy to cultivate reporters or combat the government. Instead, she lit candles and prayed at St. Ignatius. Every six weeks, she yielded to her mother-in-law, who moved in and ran the household while Mary Lou underwent chemotherapy. One week later, after bouts of nausea and vomiting so intense she could swallow only a few teaspoons of Gatorade, Mary Lou returned to the factory.

Once, at Tony's insistence, Mary Lou posed with officials for a publicity shot near the Odd Fellows Cemetery. The photo landed on the Shenandoah *Evening Herald*'s front page, featuring Tony locked in a handshake with the federal government's chief mining engineer and a semicircle of his technical staff. Mary Lou, racked by chemotherapy, swam inside her sleeveless polka-dot blouse, with cheekbones jutting out beneath her Lucille Ball curls and eyes sunken behind her cat's-eye glasses. The caption read: "Mine officials assure Centralia residents Tony and Mary Lou Gaughan they have nothing to worry about."

For the most part, though, Mary Lou was bargaining with God, not ruminating on mine fire gases or whether they had caused her illness. She had cancer; this was what happened in life and she had to deal with it. By August 1978, four months shy of finishing her eighteen-month treatment regimen, her two oldest children, Patricia and Tony, had reached adulthood. She wondered if she would live to see her son Joe—her baby, now thirteen—earn his driver's license.

MARY LOU dragged herself out the front door. At the curb in front of her house, a cluster of neighbors and borough officials had gathered around Mayor Joe McGinley's 1970 Chrysler Newport: Tony, Fran Jurgill, and Sam Devine, from borough council. McGinley, a truck driver and union steward who had just driven back from a Wilkes-Barre meeting with federal and state officials, unfolded a color-coded map of Centralia across the hood of his car.

What the hell are they going to do now? said Tony.

This is what they've proposed, said Joe, whose great-grandfather Patrick McGinley, a County Mayo immigrant and the patriarch of an extended Centralia clan, had perished in the mines 101 years earlier.

Mary Lou studied the map while Tony sputtered and cussed. A light green wedge lay superimposed across the borough's southeastern quadrant, a coffin-shaped parallelogram extending north from the stripping pit to East Park Street, over the vacant lots where the Laughlin row once stood. A red border surrounded the green core for two hundred feet in every direction, like a picture frame. Federal engineers, with their colored pencils and perfectly formed capital letters, had labeled the outer region a safety zone: a rose-colored sea blanketing Wood Street, stretching from St. Ignatius ballfield to the Swamp.

Tony, Fran, and Joe ticked off the monuments inside the red boundaries. The Russian Orthodox church on East Park Street (still known as the Onion Church more than two decades after a hurricane demolished its bulbous gray domes)? Gone. Mary Lou and Tony's house? Gone. Helen Womer's house? Also gone. As far as Mary Lou could tell, they were taking more than half the town.

On Wood Street, of course, frustration over the mine fire had brewed for several years, and not just in Mary Lou's house. Bob Domboski, the father of then eight-year-old Todd, had distilled the prevailing cynicism about a year earlier, telling a reporter, "I guess some kid will have to get killed by the gas or by falling in one of these steamy holes before anyone will call it an emergency."

Now, in October 1978, Wood Street faced a new kind of peril: its own obsolescence. Two months earlier, at a hastily convened caucus in Bloomsburg's courthouse, the federal government conceded what it had been denying for three years: The fire had penetrated the fly-ash barrier. As an emergency measure, federal officials proposed a $464,000 trench that would obliterate East Wood and Park streets, uprooting the families who ate, slept, and hung their laundry out to dry in its path, including Mary Lou's and Helen's. The excavation, measuring 410 feet long, 140 feet deep, and 30 feet wide, required the demolition of twenty-six homes and a church. Still, it remained an emergency measure, designed to reduce gas emissions. At some future date, if they could obtain the funding, officials hinted they would oversee an even larger excavation, estimated to cost as much as $9 million, to control the fire.

Most of the proposals, however, including the emergency trench, had little chance of progressing beyond the concept stage. Under a law signed by President Jimmy Carter, federal officials could, for the first time in anthracite mining's 150-year history, compel the industry to pay its environmental cleanup costs. On its face, the 1977 Surface Mining Control and Reclamation Act seemed tailor-made for Centralia. Unlike previous legislation, which drew on federal appropriations, this statute taxed coal producers: thirty-five cents for each ton they gouged from strip mines and fifteen cents for each ton hauled from underground. Penny by penny, the tariff's proceeds—$157 million in 1978 alone—spilled into a trust, the Abandoned Mine Reclamation Fund, to help mining states and federal officials remedy past abuses by the operators, including abandoned-mine fires.

At the very moment when the federal government and Pennsylvania could have joined regulatory coffers and whipped the Centralia blaze once and for all, they did the opposite. The legislation, instead of fostering cooperation, exacerbated rifts between the mining agencies, like relatives squabbling over an estate. Pennsylvania officials announced their position in Bloomsburg and did not yield: The federal government had dictated Centralia strategy for more than a decade and should finance any projects after the $464,000 emergency trench from its share of the new fund, including the $9 million excavation.

Down in Washington, federal officials hoarded their principal like penny-pinching heirs to the family fortune. From the outset, they questioned the logic of investing $9 million in Centralia when the borough's combined real estate portfolio—five hundred homes, four churches, a state-of-the-art municipal building, and a decommissioned high school, now housing a furniture outlet—carried an assessed value of only about half a million dollars. Even with a former peanut farmer in the White House promoting solar power, Centralia wasn't worth saving.

This time, Dan Flood could not intervene to convince officials otherwise. Weeks earlier, he had commandeered an Air Force spy plane to swoop over Centralia and snare infrared photographs of the mine fire. In the interim, however, a federal grand jury in Los Angeles had indicted him on three counts of perjury stemming from allegations that he swapped votes for cash. The congressman, whose Wilkes-Barre supporters were staging fund-raisers for his legal defense, had diverted his energies to proclaiming his innocence and salvaging his reputation and career.

Still, when Mary Lou heard that officials had condemned her home, she knew her media campaign had backfired. Within days, she and Tony reentered the fray, granting interviews to local reporters. Tony insisted, on the record and for publication, that he would never leave. He and Mary Lou, whose minimum-wage checks supported the family, lacked the resilience to withstand the stress of moving. Even if they wanted to uproot themselves—and they did not—they could never afford a comparable residence somewhere else, on a hillside four blocks from the church where they were baptized and the school they and their children attended.

As far as Mary Lou knew, only one event would pry her husband loose from his homestead: his burial, across the street in St. Ignatius Cemetery.

CHAPTER FOUR

Bureaucratic Shuffle

Up at the top of Locust Avenue, in a row home next door to St. Ignatius Convent, Catharene Jurgill needed a spatula. Fifteen hours earlier, she and Leon Jurgill, Jr., the borough maintenance worker's son, had stood together on an Indian summer evening, exchanging vows at the altar of her hometown parish in Ringtown. Before an audience of siblings, parents, aunts, uncles, and grandparents, she had finessed the traditional covenant, pledging to love and cherish, but not to obey. Now, on October 21, 1978, their first day as a married couple, she wanted to prepare her husband's favorite breakfast, eggs over easy.

In the weeks leading up to their marriage, Catharene and Peacho—Leon's childhood nickname, adopted by residents across the borough—had outfitted their home with hand-me-downs and new acquisitions, befitting their budget and thrift. At K-9 Furniture World in the old high school building, they splurged on a queen-size cherry four-poster canopy bed with a matching Queen Anne highboy. In the living room, overlooking Locust Avenue, they installed Peacho's yellow and brown plaid bachelor sofa set. In the kitchen at the back of the house, where Catharene now stood, they placed his grandmother's 1950s stainless steel table with its red Formica top and surrounded it with mismatched wooden chairs. Yet somehow, in their quest to furnish the living spaces and inventory the shower gifts, from hand-crocheted hanger covers to brown earthenware dishes, they had neglected the one cutlery drawer staple she needed to flip an egg.

Peacho, a twenty-two-year-old lathe operator with the six-foot-two-inch frame and chiseled form of an athlete, headed to the rotary phone in the dining room and dialed his mother. Elaine Jurgill, a coal region native with seven children who had long ago adapted to feeding a crowd, invited them over. But Catharene, who had sprinted through high school and graduated a year ahead of schedule, rebuffed the overture. She and Peacho faced a lifetime of Sunday dinners at her mother-in-law's, assembled around the kitchen table for stuffed cabbage or turkey with dressing and cranberry sauce. On their first morning together as husband and wife, she, not Elaine, would assemble the morning repast. Peacho slid into his vintage Pontiac Catalina and drove across town to North Paxton Street, where his parents lived, and borrowed a spatula from them.

As AUTUMN DESCENDED on the coal region, Polish Americans from Shamokin to Shenandoah heralded Pope John Paul II's elevation from Cracow archbishop, the first non-Italian pontiff in more than four centuries. Catharene settled into a routine, acclimating to life as a newlywed. While Peacho manned his shift at Goyne Pump in Ashland, she scrubbed her floors and rode her stationary bike, entertained friends and hiked across town to drop by her in-laws'. Up and down Locust Avenue, as she fetched her mail at the Kennedy-era post office and made her rounds, she overheard retired miners holding forth about the planned excavation.

Three days before her wedding, Centralia borough council voted to approve the emergency trench. One of the councilmen, Bob Lazarski, injected a series of stipulations into the resolution, including weekly progress reports by federal engineers. In the end, though, the elected representatives felt they had little choice. Officials had rejected their plea to shift the ditch a hundred feet to the east, an effort to spare

Helen's and Mary Lou's homes. The excavation, an imperfect solution at best, offered their only hope for salvaging the rest of the town.

Unbeknownst to Centralia's councilmen, however, federal officials had already consigned their gesture—an act of courage, given the stakes—to oblivion. In Washington, a federal mining official deflected a demolition contractor, saying the agency had no immediate plans to raze any of the town. In Schuylkill Haven, the Bureau of Mines arranged to order ten carbon monoxide monitors, at eighteen hundred dollars each, for homes near the mine fire. Meanwhile, Centralians girded for blasting, dust, and an onslaught of trucks rumbling over the borough's streets.

The trench piqued Catharene's curiosity. Her father-in-law, a former bulldozer operator and Korean War veteran who grew up in Centralia, trusted the government and its engineers. But he lived on the northern periphery, near St. Mary's Church, far from the fire's trajectory. Before long, she found herself wondering why Centralia residents seemed to hope, at best, for containing the blaze with the emergency excavation, not extinguishing it with a more ambitious undertaking. As the daughter of a small-businessman who majored in economics, their resignation to the short-term trade-off didn't make sense.

Still, her interest remained academic, an outside investor's conundrum. Like her father, who owned rental properties, she viewed a home as a long-term bet. Before the wedding, with Peacho scouting real estate near St. Ignatius Church, she pressed him for assurances the property would appreciate, especially before he sank five thousand dollars in savings into a row home at 34 South Locust Avenue, across the street from St. Ignatius School. She knew a few families had relocated from the borough after their houses became unsafe. And as she and Peacho pooled their finances and mapped their future, she grew concerned that the mine fire might zap their equity, saddling them with an unmarketable asset.

Peacho, who had lived in Centralia his whole life, persuaded her not to worry. He knew their row, like the church itself, straddled a rock deposit near Locust Mountain's crest, about four hundred feet from the Buck outcrop. Catharene trusted his judgment. He worked hard, saved money, shunned alcohol, and nurtured ambitions of rising into management at the plant. With a baby due in April, she focused on more immediate concerns: buying groceries, cultivating a garden, and preparing the nursery.

CATHARENE LOVED BABIES. Growing up in Ringtown, in a white clapboard nineteenth-century farmhouse just north of Centralia, she had tended to her younger sisters and brother, feeding them in their high chairs and pushing them in their strollers. Her mother, a teacher who bore six children in nine years, returned to the classroom full-time when Catharene was eight. As the oldest, she felt like a second mom.

Responsibility, especially at a tender age, sprang from the territory, like tractors and pickup trucks, dairy barns and covered bridges. Ringtown sprawled across a valley just a few miles from the Western Middle Field, humming with the agrarian pulse of the Susquehanna River plain. After school, Catharene donned overalls and pedaled her bike to a commercial chicken farm, where she draped netting over her face to ward off chicken lice, collected eggs, and stacked them in a refrigerator, pocketing twenty dollars a week. She and her friends, even those whose parents owned coal companies, toiled in the fields when the crops ripened, picking potatoes and tomatoes for twenty-five cents a bushel alongside Mexican migrant workers.

Still, Catharene did not hail from a farming family; her paternal ancestors, who emigrated from County Mayo in the 1860s, had long eschewed the mines for the law. Joseph Burke, her grandfather, owned a hundred-acre tract of Ringtown woodlands, belonged to a local country club in Fountain Springs, and practiced in a third-generation Shenandoah firm, Burke and Burke, founded by his grandfather. Her parents, who raised their children and pursued their own careers, attended St. Francis College in Altoona, where they met.

At home, the Burkes maintained a zero tolerance policy for laziness and boredom. Catharene's father, a Republican, learned speed-reading as a Vietnam-era Navy pilot and devoured *The Wall Street Journal* every day. He taught his children the Evelyn Wood technique so they could plow through periodicals and newspapers delivered to their Main Street address, from the *Pottsville Republican* and the Shenandoah *Evening Herald* to *National Geographic* and *Reader's Digest*. Her mother, a Democrat, once dreamed of moving to New York to pursue a career as a model and dancer. She subscribed to French *Vogue,* paced her children through yoga stretches before bedtime, and helped organize a public library because she couldn't imagine living in a town without one.

When Catharene landed in ninth grade, her upbringing, with its Montessori-influenced premium on inquiry and engagement, collided with the county's bent for warehousing teenagers. Every day, hundreds of students spilled from school buses into North Schuylkill High, a mid-seventies brick facility with windows shaped like locker doors and the low-rise profile of a prison complex. Administrators and teachers struggled, with a thousand adolescents under their command, to preserve law and order, from maintaining discipline to busting alcohol and marijuana infractions. Across the grades and pay scales, pedestrian traffic consumed the institution's psyche. Officials color-coded lockers and hallways so their charges would not stray off course between classes. Yearbook scribes riffed on the chaos up front, in the introduction, even before tributes to football, homecoming, and wrestling.

Catharene, whose parents pronounced the school a failure at the design phase, when blueprints revealed its shortcomings, viewed her schedule like a puzzle. She strategized to avoid study hall in the cafeteria, where students in cowl necks and bell-bottoms sat confined to every other seat, dozing, passing notes, and plotting breakouts. To stave off boredom, she doubled up on English and science, her favorite courses, and enrolled in physical education four days a week instead of two. She plowed through her homework on the bus, bagged A's and B's (at least in nonmath subjects), and still squeezed in glee club, mixed choir, and a role as Alice in *Bye Bye Birdie*. No one questioned her industriousness, and even if she had wanted guidance, she wouldn't have known where to turn. If students avoided addiction, violence, and wholesale academic failure, they were invisible.

Outside school, though, Catharene joined the festivities, partying with coal region kids and friends from school and speeding home in time for curfew. On weekends, keg bashes sprang up around old stripping pits, where boys guzzled Yuengling, the local favorite, and Rolling Rock. Girls sipped Blue Nun, Malt Duck, and Boone's Farm Strawberry Hill wine—from the bottle, with a straw. In the spring and summer, partygoers plunged off the cliffs into swimming holes fed by underground springs. Before long, boys began to hover. Peacho, then twenty, spotted Catharene in a Centralia soda shop when she was fifteen, with fair skin, shoulder-length brown hair, and a size 6 figure, dating a boy from town. Peacho asked around, found a mutual friend, and engineered a Saturday night fix-up.

But Peacho arrived late for the date. Catharene thought he had stood her up and filed off to Mass at St. Mary's. When she came home, she found him chatting with her parents, reviving his prospects. Later, they drove around in silence, nestled inside his muscle car with tail fins and a dashboard turn signal shaped like an Indian headdress. She knew he was a catch: gainfully employed, living at home to save money. He could bench-press three hundred pounds. And her parents loved him.

For the next two years, they saw each other only on weekends. On date nights, they climbed into Peacho's car and cruised through nearby towns, from Shenandoah and Frackville to Mount Carmel and Shamokin. Along the way, with Yes, Foghat, the Steve Miller Band, and Electric Light Orchestra blaring from the eight-track cartridge player, they stopped at ice cream shops and high school football and basketball games, staples on the coal region weekend calendar.

Eventually, though, Catharene's antiboredom crusade at school backfired. At the beginning of her junior year, she alerted administrators that she had compiled enough credits to graduate. Only then, as seniors mocked and sniped, saying she'd never belong to their class, did she realize what she had done. Briefly, she entertained notions of flunking all her courses so she could graduate with her friends. Just before Christmas, she confided in her mom and dad. They scrambled to dispatch her to Marywood, a women's Catholic college in Scranton with an enrollment no larger than that of her high school and a service mission shaped by the Sisters of the Immaculate Heart of Mary. Catharene, who overheard her mother making arrangements on the telephone, flipped through the course catalogue, hoping in vain that some sliver of the curriculum, with its bias toward home economics, would spark her interest.

From the outset, Catharene knew she would never matriculate at Marywood, even if her parents packed her bags, drove her there, and deposited her on campus. She might have relented for a college near a beach, with the promise of sand, surf, and lifeguards—but she had never pined for four years of single-sex exile in the northeastern coal region. Her father, a small-businessman, had defied family tradition. He enlisted in the Navy, even though his father, a World War II veteran, said war was no place for a gentleman. He ducked law school and a fourth-generation berth in the family firm to open a tool and die shop, pursuing his passion and aptitude for mechanics. Catharene's mother, meanwhile, though happily married, had once entertained a vision of Manhattan stardom. Her father, a Brooklyn refugee, and her mother, a Pottsville native, had disapproved and funneled her instead to college.

Catharene was confident that her parents, who had allowed her to switch to public school when her parochial school's dress code barred her from strapping on her favorite red shoes every morning, would not thwart her. They had five other children to raise and their own careers and a business to manage. She and Peacho announced their engagement.

A BLOCK DOWNHILL from Catharene's house, Dave Lamb spotted a cave-in in his backyard. The fissure, measuring about ten inches wide, sat about ten feet from Coddington's gas station. A ribbon of steam puffed from its interior. Oddities had plagued the Lambs' house for several months, almost since they moved in, phenomena he couldn't explain or dismiss, such as his daughter's worsening health. But for Dave, a five-foot-seven-inch ex-Marine with shoulder-length brown hair, a pencil-thin mustache, and oversized aviator glasses, this eclipsed them all.

Federal technicians mounted a daily watch, equipped with thermometers and carbon monoxide detectors. Within five days, the temperature at the opening doubled, to 126 degrees. Within two weeks, a state fire marshal ordered Coddington to drain his underground storage tanks, closing the station. A state inspector had sunk a probe into the basement's dirt floor, about twelve feet from the four-thousand-gallon canisters, and notched a temperature of 136 degrees, 60 degrees shy of gasoline's boiling point. Inside one tank, the fuel had heated to 64 degrees, 14 degrees higher than normal.

For Dave, the evidence pointed in one direction: It's here. The fire was right next door.

Dave knew about the mine fire, of course, before he bought the house. He and his wife, Eileen, both grew up in Centralia, junior high school sweethearts who stole kisses in a garage behind his parents' West Park Street house. The dump ignited during his sophomore year in high school, when he sported a ducktail and thick black glasses, like James Dean with a science bent. Even into the 1970s, when he and his family lived on the borough's western end, the blaze seemed far away.

In March 1979, when they moved to the top of South Locust Avenue, Dave thought he'd spend the rest of his life up there. Their new home, a former mine clerk's abode with a wraparound front porch and a white picket fence, presided over the heart of uptown: a block downhill from St. Ignatius Church and next door to Coddington's station. For his young children, Rachel and David, the neighborhood abounded with babysitting potential. Their grandmother Mary Kane lived diagonally across the street, in a corner house adjacent to Wood Street, where she had reared fifteen children, including two future nuns.

The Lambs' home, however, also sat eight hundred feet west of the dump. For the rest of the winter, a season whose chill could extend into early June, the furnace conked out several times a week, usually late at night. At first, Dave tinkered with it himself, creeping down into the basement in bedroom slippers and a jacket, pressing the reset button and replacing parts. As a mechanic who owned the Speed Spot, the motorcycle shop at Center and Locust, he understood how the oil burner's combustion chamber functioned. He knew the electrodes, which fired sparks off the ignition coil, could not light fuel without oxygen. Still, he never fingered oxygen deficiency as the culprit. It seemed too far-fetched, even after he unearthed hand-cranked mining drills and drill bits in the basement, caked with rust and silt.

A few months later, he hired two furnace repairmen, who scrambled upstairs from his cellar, pale and rattled, saying he had black damp. Dave, a child of the coal region bust in the 1950s and early 1960s, had never heard the term. All he knew was that after fifteen minutes in the basement, he felt dizzy and his head ached. Two days later, when state and federal mine inspectors braved his cellar, their safety lantern extinguished.

Meanwhile, Rachel's health deteriorated. In their old house, a doctor's regimen of immunization therapy had controlled her dust allergies and the asthma they triggered, restricting her to one or two episodes a year. On Locust Avenue, though, Rachel's attacks spiked, coming as often as once a month. A few times, her breathing grew so labored that Dave drove her over to Ashland Hospital in the middle of the night, hoping an epinephrine shot would ease her suffering.

The day after officials closed the gas station, a *Philadelphia Inquirer* reporter surfaced, scouting for reactions from Coddington's neighbors. Dave unleashed. He felt trapped, he said, in a home he had inhabited for less than a year, with little faith in the government leaping to his rescue. "They're going to wait till somebody's dead before they do anything about it," he said.

A few weeks later, Dave's foot sank into his basement floor where a twenty-foot concrete slab merged into an expanse of coal dust littered with cobwebs and anthracite chunks. At the back of the house, about ten feet from the furnace, he had exposed a bootleg-mine entrance. The previous owner, Frank Brennan, had tapped into the Buck outcrop—lodged just a few feet beneath the cellar—and tunneled into an east-west gangway adjacent to Coddington's station. For Brennan, who shared his booty with neighbors, the enterprise yielded a free source of domestic heat. For Dave, it functioned like an exhaust fan, sucking mine fire gases into his home. Inside the slope, a mine inspector recorded 10 percent oxygen, 4 percent carbon dioxide, and a temperature of 120 degrees.

In mid-January 1980, a federal technician unplugged a carbon monoxide monitor from Nance Maloney's house and deposited it in Dave's cellar, where it began notching traces of carbon monoxide, from 2 to 7 parts per million. The machine, called an Ecolyzer, functioned like a ten-pound electronic sentry, with dials like a transistor radio and a needle like a grocer's scale. If the needle swung to the dial's midpoint of 50 parts per million, the maximum allowable exposure under federal workplace safety guidelines, the monitor wailed. Still, one official said the gases in Dave's home emanated from sewer vents, not the mine fire.

Throughout the winter, Dave and Eileen hosted a few meetings in their living room, where neighborhood parents exchanged morsels of intelligence: what they knew and what they had heard. For Dave, though, the sessions enhanced his sense of isolation. Many of his neighbors yearned to protect their families, but no one agreed on whom to blame, from borough council to federal figureheads. No one, at least in this cross section of Centralians, sanctioned confronting officials and demanding better treatment, not with the government's authority to audit income taxes and ax state employees. No one else stood ready to shoulder the risks, real or imagined, of engagement.

THROUGH THE PANES of glass just above the windowsill, where potted Easter lilies basked in the morning sun, St. Ignatius ballfield loomed in the distance. In the coming months, players from Centralia would don jerseys and shag fly balls, the crack of each bat a ritual dating to the era of Mary Lou's grandfather, when breaker boys and miners whiled away summer work stoppages. On this mid-April Sunday in 1980, however, the view from her kitchen window, for all its familiarity, offered little solace. In fact, the outlook had never seemed so bleak.

Two weeks earlier, officials had cased Wood Street for gases and shuttled samples to West Virginia for analysis. Mary Lou had procured a copy of the lab results. The data, spread across the second typewritten page, heralded her neighborhood's straits: 20.6 percent oxygen in Helen Womer's coal bin; 13.6 percent oxygen at John Coddington's washing machine. At borehole X-33, outside Mary Lou's bedroom window, the government had measured 11.6 percent oxygen and 9.6 percent carbon dioxide, more than twice the amount the federal government deemed immediately dangerous to life or health.

Mary Lou and Tony had written dozens of letters over the years, to politicians and bureaucrats and officials: all of them, as far as she could tell, useless. They had even appealed to the president of the United Mine Workers, hoping he, with his Washington savvy and Irish surname, could help save their home. But he, like almost everyone else, parroted generalities: a one-paragraph exegesis on the history of anthracite mine fires and the difficulties of containing them.

Still, Mary Lou clung to hope. A newcomer had installed himself at the Office of Surface Mining, the latest figurehead atop the federal government's mining bureaucracy. She pulled out a legal-sized pad of lined paper and a black Bic pen from her stash, stockpiled in one-dollar ten-packs from the A&P. In the hush of her oak-paneled kitchen, without telling Tony, she drafted a letter to Wesley R. Booker, OSM's Washington-based chief of federal mine reclamation programs. Maybe he, unlike all his predecessors, would tell her what she wanted to hear.

"Dear Mr. Booker," Mary Lou wrote, "My name is Mrs. Anthony Gaughan." In her Catholic-school cursive, she inked her East Wood Street address and phone number, slipping them into the text of her missive. Mining engineers had made her feel stupid for years, like an immigrant who hadn't mastered English, so she wasted little time with pleasantries.

"Mr. Booker, if you don't help us on the Centralia mine fire, we will have to look for help somewhere else," she wrote. This represented, of course, an empty threat. She had nowhere else to turn, so she continued pleading her case, hoping to sway him with specifics. Her husband had heart trouble and diabetes and she herself had cancer, she went on. "We have been fighting this mine fire since 1962 and if these *'Smart'* men knew what they were doing, we would never have this condition in 1980."

In other words, if these federal engineers, with their college degrees, had listened to Tony years ago, families across Locust Avenue would not have mine fire gases in their basements. And they did—the lab report said so. Carbon monoxide had infiltrated three locations in the Oakums' home, next door to the Lambs', including the basement and first floor, where the children played. As a mom who had wondered for years whether gases might fell her own family, Mary Lou simmered with indignation.

"There is no way under God's Creation we are going to leave our home," she said. Still, the lies, betrayals, and broken promises had wounded her, battering her psyche. "This mine fire is nothing more than a 'Bureaucratic Shuffle,'" she said. "We took as much as we can take. We can't take any more."

FIVE DAYS LATER, on April 18, an assistant interior secretary in Washington authorized the Office of Surface Mining to buy eight East Park Street homes, a block from Mary Lou's. In an interoffice memo, the official fretted about the $225,000 venture, the agency's inaugural foray into relocating homeowners away from a mine fire, and the message it might send. "In particular," she said, "the Centralia Project should not be perceived as a precedent for rewarding people who have been imprudent in purchasing or building houses in known unsafe locations, insurance companies seeking to avoid paying valid claims, or other persons or companies not willing to accept responsibility for their acts."

DAVE LAMB cradled his push-button phone. Scattered before him on the dining room table, an oval mahogany piece he had inherited from his aunt, lay handwritten notes from telephone conversations. Phone messages, recorded in triplicate on white and yellow six-by-nine-inch pads, sat in piles. Over and over, he had pressed his cause, hopscotching among agencies, lingering on hold, and badgering secretaries who covered for their bosses, telling him to call back in fifteen minutes.

Dave woke up that morning wanting to punish someone. Over the past week, mine fire gases inside his home had soared. In the basement, federal technicians logged oxygen as low as 9 percent and carbon dioxide as high as 8 percent, almost three hundred times higher than normal. Upstairs, they found 18.5 percent oxygen and 1 percent carbon dioxide in the kitchen and 20 percent oxygen and 0.4 percent carbon dioxide in the dining room. Rachel wound up in the hospital with pneumonia.

For thirty-three years, the world had pummeled Dave. His biological mother had abandoned him as a child after her husband went to jail for bank robbery, fobbing him off on relatives who made him eat alone in the pantry. The relatives in turn dumped him in an orphanage, where nuns smacked him on the knuckles with a paddle. His older brothers ran away and severed contact with him. In Centralia, where he settled after his biological aunt adopted him, kids taunted him, calling him jailbird and Black Protestant, because his adoptive family descended from a line of Welsh mine bosses and worshipped at the Methodist church. Even the coal industry landed a jab. His adoptive father, ditched in midcareer when the collieries closed, spiraled downward from middle-class coal assayer, analyzing seams and charting future operations, to part-time janitor, living above an Elks Club in Rahway, New Jersey, and numbing the pain with alcohol.

Now Rachel couldn't even come home from the hospital. Her doctor had ordered her not to return until the gases stabilized. Today, April 29, 1980, Dave's customers would have to wait. Even if he had to drive to Washington, he would make the government fix the situation in his basement. He'd call the president if he had to.

Dave pulled out the phone book and a list of numbers. Each time, he explained his predicament: He had spoken to the Department of Health and the mine inspectors who trawled his home for gas samples and shipped them off to a federal mine safety lab in West Virginia, often without sharing the results. He had gotten nowhere. Now he needed to talk to the person in charge of the Centralia mine fire. Eventually, after bouncing from office to office, he broke through to Earl Cunningham, the Office of Surface Mining's assistant regional director for abandoned mine-land reclamation in Charleston, West Virginia.

I have a serious problem in my basement, Dave said. I have a small child with asthma and she's having attacks. She's been in and out of the hospital and I think the mine fire gases are causing her problems.

We've done all we can for you, said Cunningham.

Dave bristled, thinking Cunningham was trying to placate him. He didn't want excuses. His daughter lingered in a hospital bed, fighting to breathe, and the government wouldn't even confirm that mine fire emissions had infiltrated his basement, let alone triggered her asthma. Rachel was his eldest, his firstborn, and he had tried, where his biological mother and father had failed, to forge a parental bond: He had bathed her, walked her, cradled her in his arms, listened to congestion in her chest. When he thought of what she had endured, he wanted to kill someone.

Finally, Dave tracked down Cunningham's boss in Washington, Dr. Charles A. Beasley, OSM's assistant director for abandoned mine lands.

If something's not done by tomorrow morning, Dave said, you're going to see me in front of your desk with a shotgun in my hand. Stashed in his gun cabinet, he had the means: a Remington 870, a hunting rifle. If he had to, he knew how to use it.

I don't think you need to get that drastic, said Beasley. Someone will be there tomorrow morning.

Dave hung up the phone, knowing he had to calm down. All he could do was wait.

The next morning, around eight A.M., mining officials and federal contractors descended on Dave's property. The Office of Surface Mining had dipped into its own till, proclaiming a state of emergency. As a precaution, the agency extended the order to Dave's next-door neighbors, John Coddington, who lived above his former gas station, and the Oakums. On site, officials held a prebid conference, the first step in an estimated thirty-thousand-dollar effort to mitigate mine fire gases by pumping sand and water into boreholes around the three structures.

Dave eyed the tumult in his yard, a three-lot expanse where Katie Brennan, the previous owner's sister, had planted fourteen trees, representing the stations of the cross. Even he, who had browbeaten officials into responsiveness, reeled from the pace of their mobilization. He couldn't wait to tell Rachel.

Still, as he ricocheted between the shop and the house for the next few days, monitoring progress, this convergence of federal prowess rankled him. Why did it have to take so long? he wondered. Why did he have to get on the phone and threaten a guy? He had served his country during the Vietnam War. He paid taxes. This was how the government, his government, *should* treat him—and everyone else in Centralia.

FIVE MONTHS LATER, Catharene pointed her Buick Century downhill. A clutch of elderly neighbors roosted atop her vinyl passenger seats, speculating about what they might hear. In the two years since she married Peacho, Catharene had forged a bond with the neighborhood's widows, including Tony Gaughan's aunt, Mary Tyson, and Clara Gallagher, who lived next door. Now that Catharene had a car—after Katrina was born, she had insisted on it—she ferried Clara to the grocery store, doctors' appointments, and family dinners in Ringtown. When Catharene entertained friends, Clara sent over sherbet or Jell-O.

Four blocks from home, Catharene glided into the Center Street intersection, where the borough exhibited a manger scene every Christmas, with plastic wise men and a blond baby Jesus. On her left, in a former building supply store, Dave Lamb's shop towered over the corner, a three-story outpost and ground-floor showroom stocked with motorcycles from Japan, Germany, and Czechoslovakia. Ahead on the right, as Locust Avenue arched uphill toward Aristes, Centralia's new municipal building hummed with industry, like a chocolate-colored concrete beehive, with solar heat, energy-efficient needle-shaped windows, and truck bays for the fire engine and ambulance.

Inside borough hall, several hundred copies of a report known as the Red Book, encased in a scarlet cover, lay stacked in piles. At the far end of the meeting room, across an expanse of polished gray linoleum, county, state, and federal officials were arrayed at the borough's folding banquet tables. In the woods behind them, beyond the cinder-block walls at their back, lay the remains of Centralia Colliery, a tangle of spill banks and crumbling brick buildings. Residents idled side by side in rows of metal folding chairs under the glare of overhead fluorescent lighting. Catharene and her neighbors wended their way up the aisle toward the front, where they scored chairs on the right side, overlooking the Swamp and facing the government's emissaries.

Even in high school, where close-in seating bore the taint of the nerd, Catharene preferred to camp near the teacher. In borough hall, she knew, if she ensconced herself up front, she could focus on the government's presentations and comments from the audience. With the first row jammed ten to fifteen minutes before the proceedings began, she contented herself with her perch, a few rows back, and chatted with her neighbors. She didn't need to pore over the Red Book, with its hundred-plus pages of data and single-spaced narrative. She knew from perusing the tome before the meeting that it failed to recommend a course of action.

Still, she brimmed with expectations. For months now, she had seen officials rolling through town in government vans and trucks, poking into boreholes near St. Ignatius School and scrawling their measurements in logbooks. Tonight, she thought, engineers would unveil their design and disclose their intentions, their blueprint for trouncing the mine fire.

Throughout the Red Book's text, amid three-dimensional temperature studies and computer-generated thermal contour maps, the Bureau of Mines had evaluated eleven options for subduing the blaze, without settling on one as its preference. From excavation to flooding, flushing, and controlled burnout, the prescriptions represented the bureau's engineering judgment—one year in the making—on the hazards and costs of containment. The option laundry list, with price tags ranging from $20 million for an experimental underground water curtain to $84 million for total excavation, had rattled residents across the borough, stoking hostility (now almost a generation old) over bureaucratic ineptitude and generating anxiety about what would happen next.

By September 29, 1980, of course, uncertainty hardly ranked as news in Centralia. More than two years had elapsed since officials first proposed the emergency trench and still no agency, state or federal, had initiated any project to tackle the blaze. Mine fire angst was, however, a novelty to Catharene, who had strolled into a meeting in Dave Lamb's living room and learned he couldn't keep his pilot light lit. If the Lambs' house lacked enough oxygen to sustain a furnace, she realized, it wasn't safe for children. If gases could surge into Dave's home, just a block away, they could seep into her house, too, where her infant daughter, Katrina, slept in a second-floor nursery, overlooking St. Ignatius Cemetery.

Peacho did not share her apprehensions, but his clan greeted John Coddington's shutdown with relief: Their family-affiliated enterprise, a gas station run by Fran Jurgill's son, would thrive from the lack of competition. From what Catharene had gleaned, leafing through neighbors' mine fire scrapbooks and researching the issue on her own, vapors could burst through cracks in the rock strata under her cellar and penetrate her home. On this point, she decided, she and Peacho would have to disagree.

Not long after the get-together at the Lambs', she drove to a pet store and bought two parakeets. Back at home, she enclosed them in a cage in the dining room, where they inhaled seeds, spat shells, and shed feathers. Still, she knew from neighbors, who said miners had relied on canaries underground, that they would protect Katrina.

By seven P.M., between three hundred and five hundred spectators had packed into the municipal building, one-third to one-half of Centralia's population. Peacho had remained at home with Katrina, but Catharene derived more than a little satisfaction from the standing-room-only crowd. For several weeks, she had conducted a door-to-door campaign, like trick-or-treating for UNICEF. During afternoon walks with Katrina, she parked the stroller and paused to chat with neighbors. On their front porches and in their kitchens, while widows cooed over her baby and young mothers tended to their own, she prodded them to attend the meeting. Now she hoped the evening's turnout sent a message: Centralians cared about their fate.

Catharene listened as the federal government staged its presentation, with a slide show depicting how mine fires spread and an overview of the Red Book's proposed fire control modes, including how many structures and buildings would perish under each. Even Catharene, who had grown up schooled in the etiquette of not interrupting, inscribing her questions on a child-sized notepad until her parents finished their dinner-table discussions, wearied of the abstractions. She had more immediate concerns: emissions trickling from vent pipes and boreholes around her neighborhood; the health of her seventeen-month-old daughter, who breathed the fumes; and the long-term effects these gases might have on her family's health. The pediatrician had already drawn Katrina's blood to scan for carbon monoxide. None of this corresponded to any vision she had entertained of motherhood.

Since she and Peacho settled on Locust Avenue, Catharene had noticed another phenomenon, one she had not encountered in Ringtown, where her father had served on the zoning board and her mother circulated door-to-door, touting library events. In Centralia, many of the women she met hesitated to express opinions about the mine fire, especially in public. From what she deduced over Diet Pepsi and iced tea in their kitchens, they even feared interrogating public officials. Many had grown up in Centralia, steeped in its folkways and taboos. In their minds, making an inquiry was tantamount to taking a stand, a gesture fraught with the risk of shredding the borough's social fabric: alienating someone next door, down the block, or across town, from former classmates to fellow parishioners and extended kin.

Catharene, however, had no reluctance to speak out. She had inherited this community by marriage, not birth, and its code of silence did not bind her. Over and over, she heard neighbors complain about the government's mendacity, from declarations about extinguishing the blaze to insistence that the fire had not breached the fly-ash barrier. Someone had to challenge officials to address public health issues, even if only to make them squirm. If she could invoke her daughter and her family to jump-start the process, all the better.

When the discussion veered into health and safety territory, Catharene was ready. The state's public health official, Dr. Donald Reid, elaborated on how mine inspectors would track gases while federal decision makers pondered their alternatives. She rose from her beige folding chair and faced him.

When should we call for an inspection? she asked, projecting from the diaphragm so even the retired miners standing near the smoked-glass doors in the back of the room could hear her. And will we receive carbon monoxide monitors in our homes? I am worried, she said, about the safety of my daughter, Katrina.

Dr. Reid tried to reassure her. Side effects from exposure to low-level oxygen develop slowly, he said. There would be enough time to react.

Catharene had researched this issue. After consulting Katrina's pediatrician, she knew otherwise—and she knew a bullshit answer when she heard one. How could people react when they were asleep? If they lost oxygen, they didn't wake up.

A handful of women leaped in where Catharene left off, outraged by the government's failure to level with them about mine fire gases. One of them was Joan Girolami, a Mount Carmel native and East Park

Street resident who had backed the ill-fated emergency trench in 1978, mounting a letter-writing and media offensive to revive it. Everyone should have access to facts gathered by state and federal inspectors, she said. Another was Nance Maloney, a retired schoolteacher from the McGinley tribe who flouted the Wood Street consensus—and jeopardized her friendship with Helen Womer—by favoring the trench. Anyone who lived near someone with low-level oxygen and other hazardous emissions had a right to know about her neighbor's fate, she said.

For audience members skilled in reading subtext—and in a hamlet such as Centralia, many possessed the talent—these remarks crackled with heresy. Joan Girolami and Nance Maloney had not mentioned anyone by name, but as virtually anyone who paid attention knew, they wanted access to the readings in Helen Womer's basement. Therein lay their deviance.

For two years, Helen had contrived to block inspectors from sharing her emission-test scores, even penning "Do not reveal" across the bottom of one of her daily reports. Now, with the Red Book pitching four separate trenches, any one of which spelled catastrophe for her home, she had even more of an incentive to resist disclosure. Just that morning, a state inspector had registered 10 percent oxygen and 6 percent carbon dioxide in her cellar, a scenario that could have dimmed the flame on a safety lantern—and one she had to conceal if she intended to remain in her home.

Mary Lou, of course, knew that mine fire emissions had surged in Helen's basement, with or without the official tabulations. Over the summer, she had seen a report chronicling 11 percent oxygen and 9 percent carbon dioxide in Helen's basement. She knew Helen propped her cellar door open with a brick to boost ventilation. When Mary Lou and Tony asked Helen about gases in her house, however, she chided them for their curiosity, saying the information was private.

Catharene remained unaware of Helen's predilections. Still, as she piloted her car up Locust Avenue after the meeting, she felt overwhelmed. Her head swam with statistics and a litany of engineering options, in no apparent order of feasibility. The federal government had not committed to a course of action. It had unfurled its charts, clicked through its slides, and punted.

WITHIN WEEKS, the Red Book receded from view. Even before the Centralia meeting, federal officials had commissioned another study, dubbed the socioeconomic impact analysis, to evaluate two prospects the Red Book did not explore: letting the fire rage to its natural barriers until it exhausted the basin's anthracite reserves, and relocating the entire community. In the interim, Washington's power grid tilted, like a chessboard upended in midgame.

Five weeks after the Red Book meeting, President Carter lost his reelection bid in a landslide defeat to Ronald Reagan, a former actor and California governor who pulled many working-class Democrats into the Republican fold. In Centralia, where the Legion rocked to the beat of the 1950s on Saturday nights, voters bucked the national trend, backing Carter two to one. In Washington, where Republicans had recaptured control of the U.S. Senate for the first time in a generation and GOP donors and operatives jockeyed for their first White House and cabinet posts since Gerald Ford's administration, the 1980s had dawned. Populism and polyester were out. Pinstripes and cowboys were in.

Two weeks before Reagan's inaugural, the Office of Surface Mining released the socioeconomic impact analysis, a 187-page treatise accented with bullet points and bar graphs. The agency's consultants, who had spent six weeks in Centralia interviewing more than four hundred residents, unmasked widespread confusion about the Red Book's options. About half the population accepted excavation as an alternative; the other half opposed it as too disruptive. Slightly less than half the populace stood ready to relocate away from the mine fire. The remainder, about 60 percent, deemed quitting the borough unacceptable. Amid the static, one observation emerged: Centralia was a town divided.

DIVIDED WE STAND STILL

PART THREE

CHAPTER FIVE

Squaring Off

IN THE HOURS and days after Todd Domboski plummeted into the earth about seventy-five feet from Helen Womer's fence, print and broadcast reporters descended on Centralia, jockeying for firsthand accounts, hounding him on his way to school, and combing Carrie Wolfgang's yard for footage of the cave-in. Flo, still rattled from almost losing her only son, fielded interview requests from news organizations scattered across the country and around the globe, from Australia to New York to Sweden. By granting them, she defied Helen's admonition, engineering a miasma of publicity. Each press cycle, from the afternoon dailies to the evening news, confirmed the worst for Helen Womer: Events had spiraled out of control.

Overnight, the media transformed Todd into a celebrity, the boy in Nikes and corduroy pants who had survived a plunge into the mine fire—so close he could hear it breathing, he said. For photographer after photographer, he bundled into his parka and a knitted ski cap, plodded over to Apple Alley, and stared down into the chasm, with its snow-fence perimeter and plume of white steam. Editors splashed his image on front pages across the region, from Pottsville to Hazelton to Reading. The Shenandoah *Evening Herald,* whose reporter Terri Coleman had arrived on the scene moments after Todd's rescue, featured her close-up photo of the opening that swallowed him, with a tree root spanning the hole like a suspension bridge.

The local media also redoubled its mine fire coverage, delving into the what-ifs and might-have-beens. A Mount Carmel obstetrician said expectant mothers should avoid mine fire fumes to prevent harming their unborn babies. Another report said several residents had heard thuds in their basements, suggesting the fire had ripped through the mine workings, causing them to collapse and destabilize the neighborhood above them.

Politicians, in turn, scrambled to project their command and control. Governor Richard J. Thornburgh, a Yale-educated Republican and former federal prosecutor from western Pennsylvania, dispatched a deputy to Centralia to inspect the cave-in at Carrie Wolfgang's and report back about short- and long-term solutions. Congressman James Nelligan, who touted relocation within days of Todd's rescue, called for a referendum so residents could decide the town's fate. Borough council, reluctant to shoulder responsibility for ejecting families from their homes, endorsed the idea. For the first time, many residents awoke to the prospect of a future without Centralia, an outcome now looming as a distinct possibility, not mere jawboning in a federally funded report.

Todd's experience emboldened Helen, who had long ago resolved not to abandon Wood Street, pushing her to retool her strategy and tactics. She could no longer settle for prodding officials from her kitchen, scribbling on reports, and pressing for meetings. She had to expand her audience, appealing to residents who hadn't focused on the mine fire until now. She had to educate them, in a way no interloper with a notepad could, about what was really happening.

As the press converged on Flo's home across the street, Helen circulated an alternate rendition of events: Todd had stumbled into a hollow from a long-abandoned outhouse, not a chute from an abandoned mining operation. He had sunk no deeper than his ankles or knees. Contrary to what they might have read or heard, his life had never been in danger.

For some residents, especially those who lived on the safe side of town, Helen's explanation resonated on several levels. Privies once dotted the coal region landscape, like steeples, spill banks, and railroad tracks. Even now, with indoor plumbing the norm, the psychic footprint of privation lingered. For many Centralians, the media served as a convenient foil, just one more in a string of intruders intent on plundering their town, from Alexander Rea to Bloomsburg politicos, who seemed to surface only before elections. Helen, a teller at the borough's only bank and one of its few business establishments, held a position of prominence in the community. Many residents, from workers with paychecks to retirees and widows surviving on Social Security benefits, passed through her North Locust Avenue workplace, with its art deco façade, at least once a month. Few felt disposed to incur her wrath by questioning her reliability as an eyewitness, especially if they hadn't seen for themselves what happened.

Still, even in Centralia, where parents often learned of their children's hijinks before the transgressors woke for breakfast, the grapevine had its limits. With an NBC camera crew filming a report for the evening news, Helen launched a counteroffensive. And in post-Todd Centralia, where mine fire scrapbooking had witnessed a resurgence as residents clipped articles and pasted them into notebooks and binders, a natural platform beckoned.

In late February, Helen penned a letter to the editor of one of the local newspapers, the Shamokin *News-Item*. As a former cub reporter for Con-Cen High, she led with her strength, a point few could dispute even nineteen years after the dump ignited: No one, not even the government, knew the fire's location. Before voting on the community's fate in a referendum, she said, residents should demand that the government pinpoint the blaze. Any effort to chart the fire's progress, of course, would take months or even years. Delay and indecision numbered among her allies, allowing her to float an alternate explanation, one even Mary Lou and Tony could not countenance: The fire is not located under the borough of Centralia, she said. As proof, she cited "documented factual information," government borehole measurements allegedly showing no temperatures higher than 168 degrees near the borough's limits.

For Helen, the solution remained simple: Centralia had to be safeguarded in perpetuity, mine fire or not. She envisioned herself, whether by draft or by fiat, as the guardian of its long-term conservation. "As long as there is a shred of hope left in me, and I have the support of my family and friends, I will work tirelessly against monumental odds toward keeping as much of Centralia intact as is safely possible," she said.

IN WASHINGTON, meanwhile, Interior Department staffers scrambled to retrofit Centralia to the Reagan Revolution. President Reagan had, within moments of raising his right hand and reciting the oath of office, launched an assault on the federal government, reversing a social compact dating back to the New Deal. In his inaugural address, delivered against the backdrop of double-digit inflation and high unemployment that had helped derail his predecessor, he pledged an "era of national renewal," a burst of productivity and entrepreneurialism from slashing federal spending, downsizing the federal bureaucracy, and reengineering the relationship between the federal and state governments: a resurgence of states' rights, without the civil rights–era racism. "In this present crisis, government is not the solution to our problem; government is the problem," he said.

From the opening minutes of his presidency, Reagan kept his word. As his first official act, even before signing his cabinet secretary nominations, he imposed a hiring freeze on federal workers, hailing it as a symbolic first step toward taming the budget deficit. In the days and weeks that followed, as Americans celebrated the release of fifty-two hostages held for 444 days in the U.S. embassy in Tehran, the crackdown continued. Reagan ordered federal agencies to pare travel expenses, trim payments to outside consultants, and suspend furniture purchases. He directed his cabinet members not to redecorate their offices. In a speech before a joint session of Congress outlining his economic recovery package, he vowed to provide relief from federal regulation, just as he promised to slice income taxes by 30 percent over three years and boost military spending.

Reagan did not just target the rank and file, however; he remolded the bureaucracy from the top. As a ranch owner and former California governor, Reagan identified with the Sagebrush Rebellion, a coalition of western states and business interests seeking to dismantle the conservation movement, from the Clean Air and Clean Water acts to the Surface Mining Control and Reclamation Act. At the same time, they hoped to increase access to minerals, timber, grasslands, and other resources on hundreds of millions of acres of federally owned western land. As president-elect, Reagan revealed his allegiance to the sagebrush cause, tapping states' rights westerners for cabinet level and leadership posts at the Interior Department and the Environmental Protection Agency—many of whom had labored in the industries they now stood to regulate.

From the outset, the nominations aroused protests from environmentalists and Capitol Hill Democrats, who bemoaned the politicization of the EPA and the conservation movement, previously wellsprings of bipartisanship. Editorial and opinion page writers blamed brewery magnate Joseph Coors, a Reagan supporter, for plucking the nominees from obscurity, just as he had launched the Heritage Foundation as a conservative think tank and policy incubator. Still, no choice stirred as much alarm as Reagan's pick for interior secretary, another Coors protégé: James G. Watt, a six-foot-two-inch Wyoming native and evangelical Christian who ranked *The Waltons* as his favorite television show.

Watt had spent two decades in and out of the capital, burnishing his Republican credentials. In the early 1960s, he parlayed his University of Wyoming law degree into a staff counsel slot for U.S. senator Milward L. Simpson, a Harvard-educated lawyer, former Wyoming governor, and father of a future senator, Alan K. Simpson, then serving in Wyoming's house of representatives. When the elder Simpson opted not to run for reelection in 1966, Watt pounded the corridors of civilian and official Washington, from the Chamber of Commerce to the Interior Department and the Federal Power Commission.

In August 1977, when President Carter signed the surface mining act, Watt decamped to the Colorado headquarters of the Mountain States Legal Foundation, a public interest law firm founded and subsidized by Joseph Coors, with a mission carved from conservative bedrock: defending individual liberty, private property, and free enterprise. As the foundation's president, Watt litigated on behalf of the mining, timber, oil, and ranching interests who endowed the foundation, advancing their agenda through federal court dockets, including a constitutional challenge to the surface mining act. When the U.S. Supreme Court agreed to hear the case, Watt filed a friend-of-the-court brief, saying the law usurped state government functions and threatened to destroy the federal structure of government in America.

Back in the early 1970s, western bituminous mining, especially in Wyoming, was a nascent enterprise. The congressmen who crafted the surface mining law—and persevered through two Republican vetoes until President Carter affixed his signature—viewed it as a necessary evil, essential to address the nation's energy crisis and ease dependence on foreign oil. Still, given the environmental legacy of Appalachia, where cave-ins, acid mine drainage, and underground mine fires menaced the landscape, they sought to police the western coal trade up front, before it disappeared. The act, with a nod to the industry's past performance, imposed national standards on coal mining operations across the country, to safeguard the environment during extraction and compel reclamation—rehabilitating the site to its original contours—afterward.

From the outset, operators bristled. But the statutory scheme, spelled out page by page and paragraph by paragraph, from permits and performance bonds to inspections and fines, explained only a fraction of their antipathy. Across the West, with its wealth of publicly owned lands, the strip mine legislation cordoned off swaths of coal deposits—in national parks and forests, wildlife refuges, and wilderness and recreation areas—and placed them off limits. Reclamation dollars, meanwhile, threatened to pour into the anthracite region, where the devastation predated the western bituminous industry by decades. Out in Wyoming, operators saw no reason why they should forfeit their revenue, ranging from fifteen to thirty-five cents per ton, to rehabilitate northeastern Pennsylvania.

Watt, who inherited the act's Abandoned Mine Lands fund fresh from his tour at the operators' end of the spectrum, shared their predilections. Even before winning Senate confirmation, he pledged to restore balance to domestic energy development. In his first action as secretary, he proposed reversing a Carter-era ban on oil and gas drilling off the California coast, opening 1.3 million acres in the outer continental shelf to domestic production. One week later, he called for terminating a $105 million land acquisition program to expand the national parks.

In public statements, Watt professed himself the steward of the nation's natural resources. Still, with his assertions and policies, he invited criticism, including suggestions that his fervor stemmed, at least in part, from Scripture, which instructed mankind to occupy the land until Jesus returned. "I do not know how many future generations we can count on before the Lord returns," Watt said before a House Interior committee. "Whatever it is, we have to manage with a skill to leave the resources for future generations." However listeners construed this remark—and interpretations varied—environmentalists deciphered it as code for slash-and-burn exploitation: There's no need to preserve mineral wealth and scenic beauty, they saw him as reasoning, if Jesus is coming back soon.

Watt, a visionary in size 12D cowboy boots, did little to allay their concerns—though he did deny the allegation. By his own admission, he intended to rewrite the country's land management policies and alter the shape of government for generations to come. When Todd Domboski catapulted Centralia onto the front pages and network news, Watt seized the opportunity to place his imprimatur on the AML fund and the politics of its distribution.

MARY LOU HAD to admit, Helen did look pretty. She had outfitted herself in a ruffled white blouse and one of her business suits, the kind she bought in department stores at the mall in Frackville, not the pants and T-shirts Mary Lou snagged at discount merchants such as Kmart. She had visited the beauty parlor, too, where a stylist had coiffed her hair into a gray and white cap. And as she rose from her chair at the speakers' table and approached the microphone, a striated metal cylinder perched atop a floor stand, she clutched a wooden pointer.

A half-dozen witnesses had preceded Helen, including John Coddington, who stood before the microphone in a three-piece suit and tie, and Chrissie Oakum, who gripped a piece of white paper as she spoke. Their anecdotes about coexisting with mine fire gases had riveted the panel, a committee of lawmakers from across the state. "If any of you have trouble sleeping or have to take sleeping pills, come up to my apartment and you'll be asleep," said Coddington.

For almost two decades, Helen had nurtured her career and family while Tony monitored the blaze, feeding her regular updates. Now, when legislators convened in borough hall for a mine fire hearing, they slighted Tony, whose reputation for profanity and bluster preceded him, and summoned Helen. All of a sudden, on March 12, 1981, she ranked as an expert.

Even to Mary Lou, who knew Helen better than many Centralia residents did, Helen remained an enigma, a lifelong friend who placed her trust in very few. For years, she insisted—even to Mary Lou and Tony—that she never spoke about the mine fire at home. In private, with her intellect and facility for barbs, she occasionally hurt Mary Lou's feelings. Mary Lou forgave and forgot, making allowances because they had known each other so long. Still, Helen's inclusion in these proceedings grated on Mary Lou almost as much as Tony's exclusion.

Up at the microphone, Helen opened with a point on which most of her neighbors, including Mary Lou, could agree: perfidy and treachery among the coal barons. Across Centralia, many residents believed the borough's unmined anthracite remained a potential windfall, even with the industry shattered. To these Centralians, including many who grew up tasting their first Sunday roast only when World War II reopened the collieries, government officials had permitted the mine fire to burn at the coal barons' behest. The operators, the theory went, had plotted to regain control of the borough's still sizable coal deposits—an estimated 24 million tons. First, though, they had to wipe out the town, the only municipality in the anthracite region holding the title to its underground resources—thanks to the one-dollar transfer back in August 1954. That's why, conspiracy theorists held, the government successfully dug a massive trench to squelch a mine fire in Mount Carmel, which did not own its mineral rights, and bungled the job in Centralia, which did.

Helen, who maintained a multivolume scrapbook of mine fire articles, knew the conspiracy theory resonated with her neighbors: great-grandchildren of the Molly Maguires, children of the 1902 strikers and jilted ex-miners, hoping the industry would bounce back. Bob Burge, the council president, had caused an uproar several years earlier just by commissioning a confidential report, a feasibility study, to explore whether the borough could auction the mineral rights and channel the proceeds into relocating the town away from the mine fire. Burge, a high school valedictorian and World War II veteran whose uncle served as the Democratic Party's Centralia kingpin, doling out patronage jobs, survived the fracas. But ill will and sensitivity lingered. Two decades after the industry cratered, dispatching a generation of middle-aged miners into retirement without health benefits or pensions, the mineral rights remained a hedge against despair and capitulation, like an attic full of baby bottles, baseball cards, and old magazines waiting to acquire the cachet of antiques. In fact, in the eyes of conspiracy theorists, the town was worth more dead than alive.

"I would like to take you back to 1969, and trace for you what I feel is a conspiracy here in Centralia," said Helen. As she spoke, she faced the lawmakers, who were arrayed before her at banquet tables like a panel of appellate judges, with notes and papers spread before them and overcoats piled in the corner at their backs. A borough map rested on an easel beside her. From the audience, which saw the back of her head, a rumble of whispers, shuffling, and coughs ricocheted across the room, from the men and women spilled across rows of folding chairs and standing around the edges, leaning against the cinder-block walls. Only when she referred to the government's order to backfill the 1969 trench, calling it the first in a long line of conspiracies, did the chamber grow silent.

As Helen continued, her testimony confirmed that she bore many of the attributes of a leader. She could communicate with power brokers outside the borough and compel them to listen. She had a facility, from her makeup and clothing to her carriage and demeanor, for transcending her roots and high school education, for conveying a sense of respectability and rationality. Even her diction bore few traces of the coal region brogue. To visiting officials, she loomed like an apparition from Philadelphia's Main Line.

However, with about one-third of the borough watching, Helen had a built-in credibility gap, enhanced by her recent letter to the editor. Many residents knew the fire had seared along the outcrop from the dump to Wood Street, with gases and elevated temperatures plaguing her house and Mary Lou's. Vapors from the fire had licked Helen's back fence for years. Steam seeped through Carl's vegetable garden, on the fence alongside Apple Alley, where Todd had fallen. In the winter, snow melted in her backyard. For her to say otherwise, as she had on the *News-Item*'s op-ed page, tested the bounds of credulity.

"Very, very interesting," Mary Lou had written, in her red Magic Marker, when she taped Helen's missive into her scrapbook. Others in town, albeit in numbers that eluded quantification, were less charitable. They didn't like Helen and they didn't trust her.

Helen, meanwhile, peppered her statement with details that sounded incriminating, tapping her pointer against the map for effect. Workers reinforced the fly-ash barrier at five pounds of pressure, not thirty, she said. They backfilled a stripping pit behind her home and drilled six vent pipes into a field near the Odd Fellows Cemetery, instead of eight. Still, she failed to clarify how or why these events, if true, might prove relevant. Even Mary Lou lost interest and tuned her out.

Toward the end of her statement, Helen said the gases were spreading north and south, not east and west through her neighborhood. Several men coughed. A few spoke over her in hushed tones, prompting her to sigh. One voice pierced the din.

"How come I'm getting gases, then?" asked Terry Burge, one of the witnesses who had testified earlier. He remained seated at the speakers' table, just a few feet away from her.

"Pardon?" said Helen, rattled by the interruption.

"How come I'm getting gases, then, if they're going north and south?"

Burge, as most of the residents in the room knew, lived in a trailer behind Coddington's station, about five hundred feet west of Helen's backyard. His home straddled the same gangway that belched gases up and down Wood Street, from Mary Lou's house to Locust Avenue and beyond. State health officials had recently declared his house unsafe for habitation, along with the Coddington and Andrade residences.

Borough hall again fell silent.

"That I can't answer," she said.

Burge, the former borough council president's brother, barely reacted.

"Oh, okay," he said, his voice devoid of emotion or histrionics. He had accomplished enough just by asking.

"That I can't answer, Terry," she said again, talking over a hum of voices.

Helen thrust ahead with her text, ending with five suggestions that would have eased the mine fire gases in her home, including reinforcing the fly-ash barrier. As she read through each, hurtling toward her conclusion, her voice tightened. "I *strongly* recommend an *investigation* at the federal and state level toward an *indictment* of the individual or individuals who ordered the backfilling of the '69 trench, while the fire was still visible, in conjunction with an *investigation* of all questionable incidents that have taken place since then," she said.

When she finished, the audience responded with six seconds of polite applause.

After the hearing, Helen thought people had loved her speech. Mary Lou knew better. She heard the comments and queries, the befuddlement among her neighbors, colleagues, and parishioners. What was Helen talking about? they wondered. Helen, with her penchant for obfuscation, had squandered her opportunity. Rather than fill the borough's leadership vacuum, she had exposed it.

WITHIN A MONTH of Todd's rescue, an alliance of residents and parents materialized, forged in meetings in one another's living rooms and around one another's kitchen tables. For the most part, they hailed from East Park Street and the upper reaches of South Locust Avenue, near St. Ignatius, where a few had endured elevated temperatures, mine fire gases, and carbon monoxide monitors for more than a year. As a federation, they had no name, no officers, and no budget. They were wage laborers, housewives, and small-business owners, like Catharene Jurgill and Dave Lamb. They were moms and dads, aunts and uncles, churchgoers, and in some cases lifelong Centralians. Together, at an almost visceral level, they shared a common reaction to Todd's near fatality: The time for complacency had ended.

For their debut initiative, they seized on a petition, a technique so enshrined in democratic protest that the First Amendment mentions it by name, alongside freedom of speech. For their target, they aimed at the state capital, about sixty miles to the southwest. No Pennsylvania governor, including Thornburgh, had ever ventured from his Harrisburg office to witness the blaze. Since Valentine's Day, the *News-Item*'s opinion page had chided Thornburgh for not inspecting the mine fire himself rather than delegating the task, as he had, to subordinates. Photocopies of the most recent editorial, lobbying for a state-of-emergency declaration, had started trickling into the governor's office, snipped from the newspaper and photocopied, with passages underlined for emphasis. "Is a half-hour visit to Centralia, followed perhaps by a personal phone call to President Reagan, too much to ask?" it said. "We think not. And once again, Governor Thornburgh, we're asking you to do it."

Meanwhile, a cave-in ruptured the topsoil in Nance Maloney's backyard, about seventy-five yards from where Todd fell. The mayor pleaded with residents of the mine fire area to stay out of their backyards. Now more than ever, this smattering of parents and residents thought the commonwealth's chief executive should focus on their plight. In mid-March, they typed their missive onto onionskin paper, like pieces of tissue paper. "Dear Governor Thornburgh," they wrote. "Because of the danger to human life due to deadly mine gases emanating from the Centralia Mine Fire, we the undersigned urge you, the Governor of this Commonwealth, to visit this Borough of Centralia to determine first hand the gravity of the situation and learn that as stated in the March 16, 1981, Shamokin News Dispatch [*sic*] Editorial that '. . . a declaration of a state of emergency is still in order.' "

The national news media, too, had latched on to the mine fire story, ratcheting up the pressure on state and federal officials. In late February, *NBC Nightly News* featured a Centralia piece, with footage of the vent pipes spewing steam across Quality Hill and an interview with Todd Domboski in his mother's living room saying he was afraid to walk to school and play outside. Three weeks later, the *Los Angeles Times,* the president's hometown daily, splashed Centralia across its Sunday front page, with one photo of Todd beside the snow fence, another of steam curling from a vent pipe on South Locust Avenue, and a history of the government's containment efforts in all their appropriation-stretching failure.

As interior secretary, James Watt presided over a $40 million abandoned-mine reclamation budget, 20 percent of the AML fund's 1981 haul. It was enough, by one estimate, to relocate Centralia's entire population—with $25 million to spare. He also wielded broad discretion to tap the fund's federal allotment for contingencies, provided he craft two findings: an emergency existed, constituting a danger to the public health, safety, or general welfare, and no one else, no other agency or person, would hasten to fix it. In either case, the secretary's emergency response power seemed tailor-made for the mine fire. Cave-ins and potentially fatal gases menaced the upper reaches of South Locust Avenue, as well as Mary Lou and Helen and their Wood Street neighbors. No other governmental body, from the borough to the county to the state, boasted the multimillion-dollar resources to arrest its spread.

Pennsylvania officials, by contrast, languished on the fund's margins. Almost four years after the Rose Garden bill signing ceremony, when President Carter had praised the strip-mining legislation but lamented its failure to establish stricter standards, the commonwealth still had not received its slice, an estimated thirty million dollars. With Pennsylvania's proposed statewide reclamation plan mired in litigation, commonwealth officials held little hope of a windfall anytime soon. In public and on the record, they continued to assume, as they had since the ill-fated 1978 trench, that the federal government would bankroll any Centralia relief efforts, just as it had underwritten the relocation of about a thousand families from Love Canal, New York, a working-class Niagara Falls neighborhood built atop a nineteenth-century canal laden with toxic industrial chemicals.

Watt, however, did not share their faith in federal intervention. One day after the *Los Angeles Times* story, on March 16, he floated his mine fire solution within the privacy of his agency's upper ranks: Remove families from the immediate emergency area, buy and demolish their homes, and transfer the acquired property, along with all future liability for Centralia, to the state. In one stroke, his proposal realigned more than three decades of federal-state relations in the anthracite region and reversed the surface mining act's legislative intent, unloading the burden onto the commonwealth. To flush out his approach in writing, he conscripted two of his top lieutenants: Perry Pendley, the deputy assistant secretary for energy and minerals, who shaped policy facilitating private development of public lands, and Andrew Bailey, the Office of Surface Mining's acting director.

By delegating this task to Pendley and Bailey, Watt handed Centralia, the poster child of unpoliced strip mining, to foot soldiers of the anticonservation movement. Pendley, an ex-Marine and Wyoming law alumnus, had begun his Washington career as an attorney for then U.S. senator Clifford P. Hansen, a Republican rancher and former Wyoming governor who sat on the Mountain States Legal Foundation's board. Bailey, a veteran of the Interior Department's Geological Survey, once signed a memo saying staff should not inject environmental statements with "inflammatory words such as disturbed, devastated, defiled, ravaged, gouged, scarred and destroyed. . . . These are words used by the Sierra Club, Friends of the Earth, environmentalists, homosexuals, ecologists, and other ideological eunuchs opposed to developing mining resources."

ON SAINT PATRICK'S DAY, Tom Larkin set out on foot, bundled into a winter coat and boots. From his apartment near the intersection of Center and Locust, a spot known locally as the Four Corners, he trudged past Popson's grocery store, the post office, and the municipal building to the borough's northern reaches. Up near St. Mary's, with its panoramic view, Centralia tumbled across the valley: a patchwork of streets and alleys lined with side-by-side row houses, just as Alexander Rea had envisioned. At the hub, where Centralia Colliery once dominated the low-lying terrain between St. Mary's and St. Ignatius, snow coated the spill banks and rock piles like a white lace shawl draped over a black dress.

But Tom, a miner's son and ex-seminarian, had not hiked uptown to admire the scenery. He had helped craft the Thornburgh petition, a six-line synopsis of his frustration with the government. Now, undeterred by falling snow, he had devoted his day off to canvassing for signatures. Indeed, Tom's mother's cousin and her husband, Mr. and Mrs. Clayton J. Chappell, had landed the leadoff spot as supporters, inscribing their names just under the kicker, the request for a state-of-emergency declaration. Each gesture, in its own way, reflected Tom's stake and conviction: Officials had to do something before someone died.

By early evening, when darkness fell, Tom had crisscrossed Aristes Mountain from North Locust Avenue to North Paxton Street, knocking on doors, explaining the petition, and asking residents to sign. Many refused, as if he were a scab crashing a picket line. Why are you doing this? some asked. A few even slammed the door, stranding him on their front steps. Tom, who did not share their reverence for orthodoxy, forged on. One by one, he culled a handful of endorsements, names inked in cursive across a sheet of white paper.

Tom grew up during the postwar boom and bust, related by blood or marriage to many of the town's residents, from Pop Beaver, the school bus driver, to John Coddington. As the third of five children, born nine months and a day after his parents' wedding anniversary, his world revolved around his family and the Catholic Church, from the Immaculate Heart of Mary nuns at St. Ignatius School to the parish bell that rang at six A.M., noon, and six P.M., summoning the faithful to prayer. From the age of five, as soon as he was old enough to attend Mass and fall under the spell of ecclesiastical Latin, he knew he wanted to enter the priesthood.

For training ground, Tom landed in fertile terrain. At an early age, as a soloist in the annual Saint Patrick's Day minstrel show, he earned the regard of Father Phelan, the Irish immigrant who reigned over St. Ignatius for more than two decades, terrorizing Mary Lou on report card day, pounding his cane on the floor during funeral dinners to demand his repast, and driving his car down the center of the borough's streets. When the pastor needed to delegate a chore, he phoned the Larkin house looking for Tom, an altar boy who struggled with his weight throughout childhood. Is the fat boy there? the priest would ask.

For all Tom's budding spirituality, however, he hailed from a clan of independent thinkers, firebrands who toiled in the mines beneath Centralia and pitched in to erect St. Ignatius but did not bow to the borough's overlords: the anthracite magnates and the parish priest. When a coal company sought to relocate Tom's ancestors' homestead, uprooting it from a subsidence-prone block and dragging it to safer ground in the Swamp, his great-grandmother Sarah Reilly Maloney balked. You took my home from me in Ireland and you'll not take it from me here, she said. Company officials dislodged the structure from its foundation and hauled it away while she squatted on the front porch, glued to her rocker.

As a young boy, Tom also saw his family bristle under the yoke of parochial oppression. His grandfather John William Larkin, a miner with a glass eye and shoulder-length white hair, once lashed out at Father Phelan, who was hounding his unpaid staff on a parish improvement project. Goddammit, Pat, do *you* want to do it? he said, throwing down his tool. Tom listened in awe, mortified that his grandfather, whose sister Mame was a nun, had sworn in church and addressed the priest by his first name.

Nor did Tom's mother, a five-foot-two-inch plus-size convert to Catholicism, shrink from challenging the nuns. Once, Tom slunk home from detention with strands of his hair stashed in a book. When his mother saw the evidence, she marched him to the convent and confronted the sister who had grabbed his locks, threatening to knock off her headpiece and yank out her own tresses if she ever touched any of her children again.

Still, even in a family of iconoclasts, the matriarch held sway. When Tom was eleven, he moved in with his sixty-seven-year-old grandmother, Margaret Veronica Larkin, and began caring for her. Maggie, as he called her (but usually not to her face), was the youngest of fourteen children, an Irish Catholic born in the 1880s who did not accept Tom's German American mother, even after she abandoned Protestantism. When Maggie phoned, she expected Tom's father, her oldest, to leap into action and rush to her aid in the Swamp. After her husband died, Maggie feigned illness, exaggerating the gravity of a heart condition, and co-opted a series of grandchildren to board with her and minister to her needs: cooking her meals, fixing her tea, changing her clothes, and looking the other way when she nipped her brandy bottle at night from her stash in the bedroom closet.

Only Tom lasted more than a month. He survived by striking a balance between accommodation and rebellion, honoring Maggie's commands and escaping her regime. On Wednesday nights, he donned a pair of jeans or chinos, anchored his jet-black pompadour with Brylcreem, and lost himself at the American Legion, where the jukebox hummed with the sounds of Tony Bennett, Rosemary Clooney, and Patti Page, and the girls sported poodle skirts and see-through blouses. On Saturday afternoons or evenings, he fled to one of Mount Carmel's three movie theaters for a Western, musical, or drama, from *The Outcasts of Poker Flat* to *How Green Was My Valley* to *Gone with the Wind*. Ten minutes after the bus pulled into Centralia, he had to report back to Maggie.

After eighth grade, when the nuns packed their charges off to high school, Father Phelan urged Tom's parents to dispatch him to seminary. He even offered to pay the tuition. Tom's father, who started in the mines at fourteen and weathered the industry's demise as a part-time electrician, plumber, and bartender, refused, insisting his son finish twelfth grade. In 1957, after Tom stood in the honor guard at Father Phelan's funeral and graduated from Con-Cen High, he enrolled in a seminary in Ontario, Canada.

Tom, who had ceded much of his childhood and adolescence to Maggie, relished the seminarian's daily routine: the regimented layering of prayer and meals and classes, the silent meditation, Gregorian chants, and solitude. After four years, though, halfway through the program, he changed his mind about his vocation and deliberately flunked out. Academic insufficiency was easier to explain to his parents than the truth: He didn't know what he intended to do with his life, but he knew he didn't want to be a priest. With his staged failure weighing on him, he opted not to return to Centralia, where locals tallied the borough's native-born priests and nuns like Yankees fans notching division titles. Instead, he bounced around the mid-Atlantic in search of a toehold, from a stint as a Navy chaplain's assistant in Norfolk, Virginia, to a series of service industry jobs including bartender, hotel reservations manager, and restaurant manager.

In 1965, Tom was tending bar in Pottstown, an industrial hub twenty-six miles east of Reading. He was there when a waitress learned that her son, a high school graduate who had enlisted in the Army, had died in Vietnam. For Tom, who watched his friend grapple with her loss, the event jolted him into awareness. These high school kids were dying—and for what, he wondered. Under the tutelage of the activist who employed him, Tom gravitated toward the antiwar movement. He grew his hair long, bought a Nehru jacket, donned leather sandals and a peace sign pendant, and started frequenting meetings of the local peace committee. By 1969, after Senator Robert F. Kennedy's assassination, Tom was attending candlelight vigils and marching on the Washington mall, singing "Blowin' in the Wind" and listening to speeches and Peter, Paul and Mary.

On Sundays, Tom drove home to Centralia, outfitted in his hippie regalia, for dinner at noon, polishing off his mother's pot roast or chicken or ham with mashed potatoes, stuffing, and canned corn with milk. His dad, who had left Centralia only once—to work at a Camden, New Jersey, Campbell's Soup factory during the Depression—nagged him to chop his shoulder-length tresses, held in place Jimi Hendrix–style with a suede strap around his forehead. Tom demurred for years, only to relent in 1978, before visiting his father on his hospital deathbed, where he lay incapacitated by lung cancer and miner's asthma.

A year after his dad died, Tom moved to Girardville, a few miles from Centralia. He wanted to be near his mom, now a sixty-four-year-old grandmother who smoked Pall Malls, crocheted afghans, and structured her day around housework, phone calls, soap operas, and crossword puzzles. On September 12, 1980, a month after suffering a brain aneurysm, Gladys died of a pulmonary embolism. Tom, who sobbed at her wake, moved in to her two-story, two-bedroom apartment at 514 Locust Avenue, just north of Center Street. For several days, he couldn't leave, not even for work in a Pottsville restaurant.

Tom had revered his mother as the embodiment of Christian love, a woman whose lemon meringue pies and chicken-soup-and-waffle Christmas Eve dinners had earned her fans across the borough. Her funeral attracted the second- or third-largest crowd he had ever seen at St. Ignatius. He had planned to dote on her into her old age, chauffeuring her to the grocery store and doctor's appointments. Instead, as a forty-year-old bachelor whose siblings had scattered and acquired families of their own, he contemplated a future alone.

Still, Tom had landed back in Centralia, and a network of his mother's friends and relatives looked out for him. Ellie Chappell, his mother's cousin, offered him a job as a short-order cook at Snyder's, her Ashland restaurant, where homemade ice cream and soups vied for menu space with hamburgers, hot dogs, and cheesesteaks. Just after Christmas, his mother's friend and across-the-street neighbor, Eva Moran, invited him over to chat about the mine fire, hoping to pull him into a loose coalition of the dissatisfied. Tom knew nothing about the blaze, but he agreed to peruse the Red Book, to enlighten himself about what he had missed during his twenty-three-year hiatus. He read the report twice.

AT THE INTERIOR DEPARTMENT in Washington, meanwhile, Bailey sent Pendley an eight-page single-spaced briefing paper about Watt's Centralia proposal, analyzing its legal and political considerations. Under the secretary's emergency powers, he said, the agency could buy the twenty-eight or so homes in the mine fire area for an estimated one million dollars, or fifteen thousand per house plus fifteen thousand in relocation expenses per family—roughly three times the borough's median income. This remedy, he said, boasted several advantages: It would minimize federal involvement, demonstrate federal concern, and return reclamation responsibility to the state.

Bailey knew the federal government's action would spark controversy, however, with previous estimates for extinguishing the fire ranging as high as a hundred million dollars. To offset criticism, Bailey said the agency should hire outside experts to validate the one-million-dollar approach, orchestrate a public relations campaign, and relocate residents as quickly as possible. He devised selling points for wooing the state, saying recent media coverage might have exaggerated the mine fire's magnitude and the cost of its abatement. Finally, he noted, Pennsylvania had one of the country's oldest and best reclamation programs.

In outposts beyond the beltway, though, midtier management failed to decode the signals from headquarters. On March 19, a federal mining official in West Virginia convened an advisory group of local, county, and state officials to finalize its nonbinding recommendation: The Office of Surface Mining should undertake an $84 million excavation, the Red Book's long-neglected Plan A, to extinguish the mine fire once and for all. The group's advice, as dated as a mirror ball, proved moot before it hit the morning papers.

Later that evening, John Coddington passed out in his bedroom and landed in the hospital, felled by oxygen deficiency. The next day, Congressman Nelligan held a press conference at the Wilkes-Barre airport. With the television cameras rolling, he said the Interior Department had authorized a one-million-dollar buyout of fifteen to twenty-five homes in the mine fire area. State and borough officials, many of whom learned of the plan from the evening news, expressed surprise. Still, they exerted little influence over the Office of Surface Mining's Washington staff, which seized control of press relations and policymaking from the West Virginia upstarts, leaving the Watt team in command.

On March 30, the day John W. Hinckley, Jr., shot President Reagan outside the Washington Hilton, Watt and Governor Thornburgh entered into a one-page memorandum of understanding. In five terse paragraphs, it contained a blueprint for containing the Centralia crisis. The federal government agreed to purchase homes and relocate residents from the neighborhoods most endangered by fumes and cave-ins. The buyout region, dubbed "the 16-acre area," encompassed the upper expanses of South Locust Avenue and East Wood Street. Beyond that, the document fell silent. "As soon as practicable thereafter," it said, "the entire site will be conveyed to the Commonwealth of Pennsylvania, which will undertake any further activities which it deems appropriate." The Interior Department had lobbed the mine fire onto Pennsylvania's doorstep, like a states' rights hand grenade.

THE NEXT MORNING, Tom Larkin stepped into the sunbathed warmth of early spring. Overhead, a sign hanging from his threshold read *Pax intrantribus,* Latin for "Peace to all who enter here." Outside, on this late March Tuesday, serenity eluded him: Centralia crackled with news. Two blocks west of K-9 Furniture World, a state police helicopter had touched down on a baseball field and disgorged Governor Thornburgh, with his wingtips and horn-rim glasses, clutching a sheaf of papers. Traffic streamed past the Four Corners. Pedestrians filed toward the municipal building. A gaggle of reporters, representing media outlets from Harrisburg to Wilkes-Barre-Scranton, had entrenched themselves outside borough hall.

Tom crossed Locust Avenue and veered toward the municipal building, with its mustard-yellow trim, a block and a half away. Beyond the bank, where he deposited his paycheck, and Popson's grocery, where he bought his eggs, the regulars huddled outside the post office. Next door, at borough hall, journalists trailed TV cameras and microphones, clamoring for comments from residents. The first-ever visit by a sitting governor towered over the borough's history, eclipsing Dan Flood's cameo during the 1966 centennial, and Tom brimmed with curiosity. Some confluence of factors had driven the governor here to address a crowd at borough hall, and he wondered what he planned to say.

Meanwhile, up at Dee Fashions, where she and dozens of other women stitched spaghetti straps and wire corsets into satin and taffeta prom gowns, Mary Lou hunched over her sewing machine. Ordinarily, when a dignitary alighted in Centralia, she would plant herself on the sidewalk for a glimpse and snap a photograph for her scrapbook. Not today. Not with Thornburgh poised to announce, according to a local paper, whether he would accept a federal offer to relocate thirty families affected by the mine fire. Even if she hadn't had to work, she would have snubbed his appearance.

From the outset, Mary Lou had opposed the notion of hounding Thornburgh to visit. A gubernatorial look-see now, after everything that had unfolded in Todd Domboski's aftermath, would only intensify pressure for relocation, and Mary Lou did not want *anyone* to leave. Still, she knew his press conference did not bode well. Her house would likely qualify for the buyout no matter how officials drew the boundaries, and she and Tony would have to leave, the result they had resisted for more than a decade.

Outside borough hall, a television reporter collared Tom for a man-on-the-street reaction. Tom, who had emerged at the core of the nascent opposition, with its petition drive and dozen or so adherents, did not leap at the opportunity. His compatriots increasingly looked to him as their leader and spokesman, but they had not yet elected officers. As a group, they still didn't have a name. So, not wishing to presume that he spoke for anyone other than himself, he answered a few questions and slipped inside.

In the borough hall meeting room, row after row of Centralia residents sat facing a lectern flanked by a bank of television cameras. The overflow crowd, men in truckers' caps and windbreakers and late-arriving women in raincoats and blazers, stood against the wall at the back of the room, facing the crowd and the speaker's rostrum. Not long after Tom arrived, the governor strode in, a white handkerchief tucked into his suit jacket. The audience burst into applause. Thornburgh, whose ancestors traced their roots back to colonial America, including a maternal forebear who arrived on the *Mayflower,* wended his way up the aisle, smiling and shaking hands.

Up at the lectern, a pair of egg-shaped microphones jutting toward his sternum, Governor Thornburgh made his announcement. The federal government had agreed to buy twenty-five to thirty homes in the mine fire area and provide financial assistance to help the families move. In a concession to the community's polarization, though, he went one step farther, offering residents such as Mary Lou an option she had not anticipated: The relocation would remain voluntary. "No one, whether for financial or personal reasons, will be forced to sell their properties and move out of their homes," he said. "Those who feel threatened by the fire will be able to relocate, while others may stay. This is a sensitive and humane approach to a difficult issue."

After his remarks, the governor fielded questions and retreated back down the center aisle. In his wake, he trailed a band of local and elected officials, borough council members, and aides. Tom elbowed his way over to the aisle, shook Thornburgh's hand, and thanked him for coming. The encounter—indeed, the entire event—left Tom filled with hope: Something positive had happened. Something would be done.

FIVE BLOCKS uphill from borough hall, Dave Lamb hovered on his front porch, scanning the horizon. From his post, he commanded a view of Locust Avenue, looking toward downtown. In his front yard, along Locust, red satin ribbons encircled his tree trunks, rustling in the afternoon breeze. Up and down the block, crimson strands dangled from tree limbs and fluttered from wrought-iron porch railings, like presents wrapped for Christmas.

Volunteers from Dave and Tom's coalition had swept through the neighborhood before the governor's arrival, looping streamers around stationary objects from construction sawhorses to utility poles, anchoring them with bunny-ear bows. The crimson bands, inspired by the yellow ribbons that had proliferated across the country during the Iran hostage crisis, had deepened divisions in town. For proponents, the strands symbolized the fire and bureaucratic red tape. Helen Womer snipped the filaments from the poles near her house, triggering a shouting match between her husband and one of the borough's two part-time police officers. For Thornburgh's visit, she reciprocated with a message of her own. At her request, Harry Darrah hung a hand-lettered sign from his front porch, up near St. Ignatius. "When the church goes, we go," it said.

For Dave, who had battled inertia for more than a year, the red ribbons lodged more than a symbolic protest. Within the past week, after Coddington collapsed and public health officials ordered a battery of medical tests for Dave and his family, the state had offered to install the Lambs in emergency housing: a trailer home four blocks away, on a western Centralia baseball field. Dave viewed the gesture with wariness, not relief. If he accepted, he feared officials might abandon him. Worse still, they might bar him from participating in a relocation program, if they authorized one. Either way, he was trapped.

Downhill, about half a block away, Dave spotted the governor on the Andrades' front porch, at the corner of Wood and Locust. Thornburgh had just sipped coffee in their kitchen and crouched down in their living room, under a shelf lined with their son's athletic trophies, to inspect the carbon monoxide monitor. He had also dropped in on John Coddington next door, where he ribbed the ex-mayor, saying his recent hospital visit was "a heck of a way of getting attention." Outside the gas station, Thornburgh knelt on the pavement and held his hand over a vent hole. "We'd better get you away from there, Governor," said Coddington. "We don't want you to die."

Now Thornburgh strode toward Dave's house, a few paces ahead of his retinue. Dave tracked the governor's approach up Locust, where a vent pipe trailed steam across the street from his mother-in-law's. As Thornburgh drew closer, past Coddington's station and just beyond the white picket fence that surrounded the Lambs' front yard, Dave climbed down the steps from his porch and walked out to the sidewalk, where he shook the governor's hand and thanked him for coming. Inside, away from reporters and photographers, Thornburgh asked about Rachel, who lay upstairs in her room recovering from an asthma attack. He said he'd like to see her.

Dave ushered the governor upstairs. They walked up the steps and down the hallway, past David's room and the bathroom. Near the end of the hall, next to Dave and Eileen's room, they turned left. Rachel's room, about thirteen feet square, with white walls and hardwood floors, was unadorned by carpeting, to minimize dust. Her twin bed with its colonial-style headboard faced Locust Avenue, to the right as they entered. A pair of windows overlooked Coddington's station.

Rachel was sitting up in bed in her pajamas, her brown hair spilling around her shoulders and glasses framing her face. A clear plastic tube snaked across her chest, with one end clamped to a green canister the size of a scuba tank and the other threaded into her nostrils. Under doctor's orders, she now breathed with supplemental oxygen inside the house. The governor and Dave stood at the foot of her bed, side by side, surrounded by her drawings and Madame Alexander dolls, some still sheathed in boxes.

Thornburgh shook Rachel's hand. She handed him a letter she had written, and he thanked her. He was there to see if he could help, he said. He'd do his best, but it would take time, more than a day or two.

Dave presented the governor with his group's petition, now an eighty-five-page document, strewn with coffee-cup stains and hand-lettered pleas to "Save Centralia." Volunteers had garnered more than sixteen hundred signatures, including many from out-of-towners. Dave had displayed a copy at his store, on the counter just inside the Center Street door. Many customers—about 90 percent of his patrons hailed from outside Centralia—added their names. Still, within the borough, the petition had exacerbated tensions, like the red ribbons.

Within the span of a few minutes, however, Dave's encounter with Thornburgh—and Thornburgh's conversation with Rachel—had transcended the realm of protest, of neighbors unleashing frustrations in each other's living rooms and canvassing door-to-door. The governor, a father of four, had followed him up here alone, unencumbered by handlers and staff. When he talked to Rachel, cofined to bed at age nine, his eyes welled with tears. Now, as Dave elaborated on Rachel's illnesses, her doctors' visits and difficulty breathing, her asthma attacks and hospitalizations, he realized Thornburgh, whose first wife was killed in a car accident that severely injured one of their sons, was someone he could talk to, not just a figurehead hewing to a script. He was a man and a dad, just like him, and that insight heralded another for Dave, about his own family's ordeal: Officials would probably buy his property. If so, he and his wife and children could leave and buy a home somewhere else.

Dave had not felt welcome on Quality Hill, where even some of his wife's relatives viewed her as a rebel, a black sheep who worshipped at the Methodist church after marrying him. Up near St. Ignatius, Dave remained the Protestant on Catholic turf, the long-haired dirt biker and amateur drag racer in a town that revered traditions dating back to the Civil War, from Memorial Day to July Fourth bonfires. Still, he had negotiated a psychic truce about the mine fire, convincing himself, as he had to, that his family was safe enough. If Locust Avenue were to collapse in front of his house, he reasoned, he would detect signs in advance, such as cracks in the pavement. If another cave-in opened in his yard, where the coal seam almost hugged the surface, the mine workings under his grass wouldn't be very deep and his children wouldn't tumble very far.

All the while, of course, evidence of his family's distress mounted. He knew his property abutted the same gangway as Helen Womer's; he could see her back lawn from his front porch. Snow dissolved in about 40 percent of his yard each winter, as it did in hers, exposing a green patch that crept from his porch toward Coddington's station and the cemetery. Each year, the snowmelt expanded, like a retreating glacier, and he knew the mine fire gases aggravated Rachel's asthma, even if state health officials had long insisted otherwise: Her doctor had counseled him to move. He was nurturing a business, however, living day to day, and couldn't afford to buy a new house, especially after borrowing money from an elderly aunt and sinking his savings into this one. He relied, as he had to, on luck and technology to fend off disaster: the carbon monoxide monitor, Rachel's oxygen tank, and their proximity to the Ashland hospital.

Now that officials might help him relocate, though, Dave yearned to stay. Even in middle age, the former orphan's dread of dispossession haunted him, as did a twinge of guilt. He had not intended to cause a commotion. He just wanted to relieve Rachel's suffering.

A few minutes later, Thornburgh went back downstairs and out of the Lambs' house, where a reporter tarried with questions. Dave doubled back upstairs to check on Rachel, still dazed from the governor's visit.

Do you think he'll do anything, Daddy? she asked.

CHAPTER SIX

Outside the Norm

Catharene scrambled to get ready. Inside her living room, a newly installed carbon monoxide monitor ticked like a clock. Outside her front door, with its trio of graduated windowpanes, gray clouds hung over the borough. Along Locust Avenue, trees sported a veil of kelly-green leaves. In less than three weeks, veterans from the American Legion would dust off World War I–era rifles for their annual parade among the borough's cemeteries, stepping in time to a snare drum. Today, however, the wind gusting from the north across Aristes Mountain evoked Ash Wednesday more than Memorial Day, and Catharene pulled on a windbreaker. The jacket, more tailored to Peacho's frame than hers, ballooned over her maternity pants. She bundled Katrina into a sky-blue princess coat, plopped her into the stroller, and grabbed a stack of poster-board signs. With that, they bounded out the door, down their three front steps, and into the early evening.

By the time winter loosened its grasp on Centralia, when snow dissolved even up near St. Mary's and crocuses and daffodils were coaxed into bloom in the basin, few mourned its passage. This year, when Todd Domboski dominated the news between Valentine's Day and

April Fool's Day, Catharene greeted spring with relief. She and her family could finally return home.

After the Christmas holidays, Catharene, Peacho, and Katrina had decamped to the opposite end of town, to bunk with his parents and siblings. For Catharene, then a nineteen-year-old mother in her second trimester of pregnancy with their second child, the temporary quarters provided a much-needed haven. She had tuned in to this baby from the outset, even predicting conception, on her second wedding anniversary, weeks before any test confirmed her suspicion. With tenacity born of instinct, she insisted: Either we move together, away from the gases, or I'm renting an apartment for the duration of my term. They ruled out settling with her parents in Ringtown, where Peacho would have added eight miles to his two-mile commute. As a compromise, they installed themselves with Leon and Elaine.

Now, though, with temperatures nudging into the mid-double digits, Peacho and Catharene had heaved open their windows and migrated back up Locust Avenue, where she dived back into her routine, relishing her privacy and independence. Once again, she stayed awake long after Peacho retired, tuning in to the news and *Nightline,* lounging on the living room sofa, and lugging the phone in from the dining room so she could dial her mother. From Centralia, Ringtown was a long-distance call, and Catharene waited to chat with her mom until after eleven P.M., when the rates dropped.

Soon, she knew, after the rhododendrons, lilacs, and mountain laurels flowered, she and Peacho would gravitate to the backyard, a strip of grass measuring about fifteen feet wide and a hundred feet long, dotted with blue hydrangeas. In the evenings, just a few feet from Clara Gallagher's back door, they would sink into lawn chairs, grill dinner on the hibachi, and swap highlights of the day. Invariably, their discussion hinged on Katrina, a two-year-old with porcelain skin, shoulder-length blond ringlets, a teddy bear named Nose, and an imaginary friend named Bobby Blue. So much about her intrigued them, from her fondness for peanut butter and jelly to her devotion to Richard

Scarry books and the Cookie Monster. With another child due in July, their sense of wonder only stood to multiply.

Still, Catharene's winter with her in-laws, living under their regime, had exposed strains in her relationship with Peacho. Almost from the outset of her marriage, she had absorbed pressure from his family to conform. Leon and Elaine, who numbered among Helen Womer's closest friends, disapproved of Catharene's research and curiosity, her questions at public meetings, and her association with David Lamb and Tom Larkin. They were, in Elaine and Leon's parlance, stirring things up. Not long after Catharene and Peacho moved in, Elaine said she would not babysit Katrina if Catharene planned to attend a meeting. Catharene, who knew her mother-in-law would supervise Katrina if she ventured to the grocery store, chafed at the edict. But Peacho, who was reared to revere and obey his parents, encouraged her to respect their preferences. For the sake of harmony, within the clan and her marriage, she shelved her mine fire interest, at least while cohabitating with his mother and father.

On the one hand, Catharene understood the Jurgills' misgivings. They viewed her as one of their own, an emissary of the tribe, and they wanted her to embody their beliefs, not fraternize with troublemakers. Peacho shared their uneasiness and sense of loyalty, fretting that Centralians would form an inaccurate impression of his wife. He urged her not to disagree with his parents in public and to keep her name out of the papers.

On the other hand, Catharene's mother-in-law braved the fray without incident, siding with Helen Womer. Elaine had submitted a letter to the editor, which the *News-Item* published, saying she did not believe the mine fire lurked under the borough—only gases. Indirectly, she took a swipe at her daughter-in-law. "If council and other groups would spend more time urging the government to solve the gas problem rather than to buy the homes [and/or] sell the coal then many of our elderly residents would not be so frightened and upset," she said.

Somewhere beneath the veneer of kinship and fidelity, though, Catharene thought she detected a deeper issue. For two decades or more, ever since the collieries slammed shut, women such as Mary Lou had supported their families with garment factory wages. Yet, as Catharene grew to realize, her in-laws expected her to stay at home with their son and grandchildren. Catharene, whose mother had taught school and contributed to the community while raising her children, had long expected to achieve the same balance for herself, juggling motherhood, marriage, work, and civic engagement.

On top of that, Elaine and Helen Womer had entreated her to cease her activities as a matter of piety. Catharene failed to see how pestering officials for information had corrupted her soul, consigning her to purgatory or worse. She was raised in a Catholic family, no stranger to the faith, with an aunt in the convent and a mother who played the organ in church. She attended Sunday Mass, prayed for devotions before her first Communion, said the Rosary, and taught CCD, the hierarchy's nomenclature for Sunday morning religion classes. As she analyzed her conduct, filtering it through her knowledge of doctrine, she did not perceive any lapse. Jesus was a political radical, she thought, who questioned the status quo. She had not sinned by failing to keep her mouth shut.

In fact, Catharene could not fathom why St. Ignatius's longtime pastor, the Reverend John Suknaic, had retreated to the sidelines. She knew he had long battled ill health and, most recently, surgery to remove a blood clot in his brain. He served as the borough's spiritual leader, so beloved that his parishioners called him Father John, and his parish and parochial school sat within a few hundred feet of the blaze's trajectory. In a rare interview—with a Catholic newspaper—he declined to press for greater accountability, deferring to the government to resolve the borough's predicament.

Catharene, by contrast, sprang from a tradition valuing independence and investigation, in which farmers bristled at federal oversight and lawyers marshaled evidence to cement their claims. Ask questions and speak out, her parents had taught her, as long as you buttress your stance with facts, not emotion. Haul out a copy of the Constitution. Form an opinion and articulate it. Doing so stamps you as an enlightened citizen, not a bad person.

Besides, if compliance were Catharene's forte, she would have enrolled at Marywood. She had not heeded what people thought about her before, an outgrowth of springing from a large family, and had little inclination to adapt now. She and Peacho loved each other, with reservoirs of passion. Even with their differences, the intensity of their attraction had not diminished. They looked, with their dark-haired athleticism, like a couple ripped from the pages of *Seventeen*'s back-to-school issue, as if the football captain had betrothed the head cheerleader. Back in her own home and bedroom, Catharene tuned her in-laws out, just as she had her parents, and mapped her own trail.

ON THE SIDEWALK alongside Locust Avenue, outside St. Ignatius Cemetery, a batch of Catharene's neighbors and friends had gathered, swaddled in winter coats. The petition drive coalition had just emerged as an official entity, the Concerned Citizens Action Group Against the Centralia Mine Fire, a nonprofit corporation with a charter and bylaws. Its mission, according to its incorporation documents, was to provide remedies for the mine fire. About three dozen families and individuals had joined, paying five dollars in annual dues: the Locust Avenue and East Park Street residents who flocked to each other after Todd Domboski's incident, including Dave Lamb and Catharene. At their first meeting, they elected Tom Larkin president.

For Tom, the intervening weeks had flown, a blur of phone calls, get-togethers, and inquiries from far-flung locations. A Brazilian camera crew filmed one of the first meetings he chaired, in the borough hall meeting room. Ralph Nader's Washington-based organization, the Public Interest Research Group, dispatched several representatives, including an environmental scientist, to caucus with Concerned Citizens about health issues and tour the mine fire area. Tom fished out his Underwood and typed a letter to the editor of several local papers, railing against the Interior Department, sending copies to President Reagan and James Watt.

Still, one event, more than all the others, had consumed the confederation. With the borough slated to vote in a mid-May referendum, the group brainstormed about boosting its membership rolls, galvanizing support across the community. At their debut meeting in late April, they seized on organizing a protest march, right down Locust Avenue. In a burst of enthusiasm, born of novelty and fed by solidarity, they believed visibility would trump indifference, converting skeptics into comrades.

The local press, whose reporters had slogged through mine fire meetings at borough hall and teased news from government reports and contracts, featured articles about the alliance and its planned demonstration. One report said marchers would carry signs and wear red armbands. Another said they might don surgical masks to dramatize the danger of toxic emissions. The *Evening Herald* and the *News-Item* ran the same advertisement—free of charge, as a public service—urging neighbors to band together and join the "march for survival." "If we don't care, why should the government?" it read. "We need your help now!"

Tom, who ranked Scarlett O'Hara among his favorite screen heroines, endorsed the demonstration from the outset, embracing its theatricality. From his stint in the antiwar movement, he knew marches enticed the media, with their stew of rebellion, slogans, and (at least in the sixties) costumed participants. He also knew a procession down the borough's main artery—even an orderly one, without tie-dye and peace signs—threatened to rile the opposition, a risk he shouldered without hesitation. As a concession to community sensibilities, though, he and his cohorts jettisoned the gas masks.

Tom had already antagonized Helen Womer, and the prospect of provoking her further did not figure into his calculus, except perhaps as an inducement. Not long after the Todd Domboski incident, she confronted him from her window at the bank, asking if he had allied with Joan Girolami, the East Park Street housewife who now served as

Concerned Citizens' vice president. When Tom said yes, Helen narrowed her eyes and glared at him—a reaction that surprised him. In his mind, he was still Gladys Larkin's boy, the tenor soloist with a flair for baking.

Still, Tom knew Helen counted Joan as an enemy for agitating to revive the 1978 trench and lobbying for disclosure of gas test data. Now, he realized, Helen had etched his name on her list. Helen, with her absence of nuance, reminded him of Maggie, who had denounced everyone from Methodists and Black Protestants to St. Ignatius parishioners who stinted on the collection plate. In the end, he didn't care what Helen thought. The real obstacle, he believed, was the government.

Recent events only confirmed his thesis. A few weeks after Governor Thornburgh's Centralia press conference, federal officials had disclosed their strategy, the one they presaged with the memorandum of understanding. Interior would pay one million dollars to relocate families from the mine fire area, but not a penny more. Any future efforts to contain the fire or remove residents devolved to the state, a department spokesman said. Homeowners who qualified for the buyout, such as the Lambs, the Coddingtons, and the Andrades, felt the squeeze of Reagan-era austerity. Under Andrew Bailey's guidance, the Office of Surface Mining said it would discount appraisals as much as 50 percent to reflect the mine fire's effect on real estate values, and participants would have only ten days to accept or reject their offers.

For Tom, who initially cheered Thornburgh's announcement, the relocation package smacked of betrayal: by the governor, for acquiescing to the memorandum of understanding, and by federal officials, for their million-dollar bait-and-switch. Before the demonstration, he vented his frustration with red paint and four-inch stenciled letters, stacked in rows across a slab of white poster board. "Ask not what your government can do for you," he spelled out, riffing on President Kennedy's inaugural address. "It doesn't give a damn."

By 6:30 P.M. on May 12, 1981, the announced kickoff time, about three dozen members and supporters of Concerned Citizens had materialized. In pairs and clumps, they advanced down Locust Avenue, past

Coddington's station with its red, white, and blue Amoco sign. Into the wind and toward borough hall they proceeded en masse, a column of children and adults wearing sneakers and blue jeans, nylon jackets and baseball caps, with red satin ribbons circling their biceps. In their hands and around their necks they clasped cardboard placards, like a cordon of striking airline pilots. Volunteers such as Catharene had made the signs by hand in the weeks leading up to the march, adorning them with a host of messages. Letter by letter, in tempera paint and Magic Marker, they scripted their pleas, like mine fire haiku, from "Stop Talking, Start Digging!" to "Centralia Held Hostage 6,940 Days by Mine Fire."

Just below Coddington's station, as Locust Avenue straightened and dipped downhill, the convoy streamed along the center of the street, with a canyon of row homes soaring overhead. Catharene found herself near the head of the line, surrounded by children: a mom and mom-to-be with a model's sculpted cheekbones, a red satin armband clinching her right bicep, and a sign hanging around her neck from a grosgrain ribbon. As she marched, with her hands guiding the stroller, her placard batted against her pregnancy bulge. "Save Our Lives," it read. Trish Burke, Catharene's eleven-year-old sister, bounded alongside, smiling and pushing Katrina. "Please Help Us," said the placard around Trish's neck, in white letters stenciled on a blue background. Katrina, nestled in her perch between her mother and her aunt, sat upright like a china doll in white tights and Mary Janes, red satin streamers fluttering from her left wrist and arm.

In front of Catharene, two small boys marched in parkas, with hoods drawn around their faces, gripping a sheet of white cardboard emblazoned with tendrils of flame. "Save our town," it said in block letters. "Put *out* the Mine fire Before it puts us *Out*!!" Behind Catharene traipsed Rachel Lamb, grinning and giggling with Trish. Rachel's family had recently moved into a state-sponsored trailer, but her trials on the Hill, coexisting with mine fire gases, remained fresh. Her sign, bedecked with a black cloud of smoke and a mass of red flames, bore a hand-lettered message saying "Why Put Out the People. Put Out the Fire."

A handful of teenagers sporting jeans and sneakers, ski jackets and down vests, followed Rachel, squealing and laughing. One of them was Trish Catizone, a Byrnesville resident who had attended North Schuylkill High School with Catharene. Like cheerleaders at a pep rally, they hoisted a sign from its wooden props. "Save Our Town! Put Out the Mine Fire," it said, in hand-painted capital letters atop a base of orange and red flames. Behind them, Tom hugged his placard to his belly, over his topcoat and jeans, like a horizontal sandwich board. Red satin streamers flittered from both his arms. In his wake trailed about two dozen men and women, walking two by two, and an elderly woman with a chiffon scarf knotted under her chin.

For Catharene, so endowed with energy that she was recharged after four hours of sleep, the gathering triggered an adrenaline release, like a party. She knew pro-life demonstrators rallied in Washington to publicize their cause; in fact, she drew the analogy for a local reporter. And this event, with its focus on families and children, had grabbed the media.

As the marchers sailed down Locust Avenue, reporters and photographers staked out turf along the parade route, training their cameras on the children and signage, snapping photos for the next day's front pages. One zoomed her lens on the boys near the helm, with Catharene's "Save Our Lives" placard poised in the background between them. A Wilkes-Barre-Scranton crew, capturing footage for the ABC affiliate, lingered on Katrina in her stroller, with the breeze buffeting her curls, and Rachel Lamb, already an evening news veteran, gazing into the camera and holding her sign aloft.

Tom Larkin, Centralia's prodigal ex-hippie, knew from personal experience the historical antecedents for the group's conduct, especially the recent ones. He knew the Reverend Dr. Martin Luther King, Jr., had invoked principles of nonviolence, including peaceful protests and children's marches, to dismantle segregation in the Jim Crow

South. He had read King's 1967 speech at Riverside Church in New York decrying the U.S. government as the world's greatest purveyor of violence, and embraced its message. With this march, Concerned Citizens showcased the plight of its youth, the girls and boys such as Katrina and Rachel who lived in the area affected by the mine fire. The imagery, in turn, resonated with the media, who crafted their narrative on the cracked asphalt: Centralia's people, taking it to the streets.

As a collective force, the march also harkened back to the coal region of Tom's ancestors, where miners swept from patch to patch, shutting collieries to assail workplace hazards and demand wage hikes. Almost eighty years had elapsed since Centralia breaker boys and striking miners rushed the Lehigh Valley depot, however, and in the interval, the sons and grandsons of the 1902 strikers had lost their jobs, their livelihoods, and their taste for dissent. Up and down Locust Avenue, row after row of front porches stood empty, bereft of supporters and even curious bystanders—as if Concerned Citizens had mounted a May Day tribute with Stalin portraits, Soviet tanks, and goose-stepping soldiers in knee-high boots. Down near Center Street, one spectator rushed into the road to salute the demonstrators, clapping as they passed.

Even Mary Lou, who rarely skipped a parade, whether celebrating Memorial Day or a championship baseball team, boycotted this one. At least, she refused to walk the two blocks down to Locust Avenue to watch in full view of the marchers. From her front porch, she saw enough: families from church, such as Charlie and Mary Theresa Gasperetti; the children of her friends, like Trish Catizone, whose mother she knew from Byrnesville; and Tommy Larkin, whose father had installed the electrical wiring in her house. All of them had sided against her.

Mary Lou even hated their name. She thought she and Tony were concerned citizens, scrapping to save Centralia. This crowd, with their banners and armbands—they were troublemakers, bent on hounding officials to acquire more properties and destroy the town. Once again, her home lay in the balance. Federal officials had targeted her and Tony for their million-dollar buyout, offering to purchase their house and resettle them elsewhere. She and Tony and Helen, no strangers to black damp, had declined to participate. After Tony's name and address landed in the local papers on a list of families who qualified for relocation, he had ordered Ed Narcavage to remove the carbon monoxide monitor from their furnace room.

As the protesters flowed toward the municipal building, the march buoyed Tom's spirits, like a wake for a friend who had anticipated—and bankrolled in advance—his mourners' thirst for Irish whiskey. Before today, no one had mustered the courage to air mine fire grievances in the borough's thoroughfares, where nonresidents might actually see and hear them. Perhaps their greatest accomplishment, however, arose from a basic fact: He and his compatriots had shattered two decades of silence.

OUTSIDE BOROUGH HALL, Mary Lou stared at the results. She had counted on victory, with a majority of Centralians voting, as she had, to reject relocation and excavation and remain in place. Instead, for the first time in twelve years—since the Birsters' canary expired and Dan Flood toured the dump—she realized she and Tony had carved their Maginot Line of defiance, jeopardizing their health and well-being, for nothing. All these years, she had thought they were defending Centralia's integrity and safeguarding the borough for generations to come, shielding the rest of the population from harm and dispossession. Now, she knew, they were alone in their quest, fighting for themselves. On the way home, she started crying. Tony spewed a torrent of epithets, cursing the goddamned sons of bitches for leaving Centralia.

Helen Womer managed to answer a few questions from the press. "I never thought it would go this way," she said. "We are going to suffer for years." Then, in the course of elaborating, she regained her composure. "To vote 'yes' means the politicians are going to work for the coal barons," she said. "In my opinion, Centralia committed suicide."

Tom Larkin, meanwhile, hailed the outcome. "I think everybody in Centralia is splendid right now," he said to an AP reporter. "I love everyone here."

In the privacy of the election booths, many Centralians expressed what they did not utter in the garment factory, at the post office, or outside church: their opinions, unfettered by self-censorship. When they filed into their polling places—from a beauty shop in the Swamp and a private home on West Park Street to an abandoned grocery store, where an American flag dangled over the counter and 7-Up T-shirts still lined the display case—they drew the curtains shut behind them. When a "no" vote would have ratified the status quo, wave after wave of voters picked up their pencils and pens and checked "yes": Either dig out the fire once and for all, or get us out of here.

After the polls closed at eight P.M., residents and borough council members congregated outside the municipal building, waiting for the results. A smattering of Concerned Citizens huddled nearby as well, on the sidewalk alongside Locust Avenue. Earlier in the day, members of the group had carpooled elderly voters to the polls and offered babysitting services so mothers could vote. Now, anticipating word of the upshot, Tom Larkin wore a button saying "Yes Means Help."

Around 8:30 P.M., election officials posted the tally on borough hall's front door, near the entrance Bootsie McGinley, the police chief, used for law enforcement business. The referendum passed with 68 percent of the vote, 434–204. Turnout had surpassed expectations, with 79 percent of the town's eight hundred registered voters casting ballots. The measure carried in three of Centralia's four election districts by the same ratio—regardless of proximity to the blaze—from the south, where some voters coexisted daily with gases and cave-ins or the threat of both, to the Swamp and the north, where the blaze did not imperil residents and, by many forecasts, likely never would. Only Byrnesville bucked the trend, trouncing the referendum 25–17, or 60 percent of the vote.

In the political universe beyond Centralia, however, the mandate barely registered. Neither the federal government nor the state appropriated any new funding to finance excavation or relocation. Few families, other than those eligible for the million-dollar buyout, enjoyed the option of selling their homes and bolting, even if they wished to. Few residents had a cushion of savings to underwrite a move, even to somewhere else in the coal region. The borough's housing market, stalled with the local economy after the collieries closed, had cratered under mine fire publicity. Who would buy a home in Centralia?

The day after the referendum, *The Village Voice* ran a Centralia cover story by Teresa Carpenter spotlighting the community's polarization. Carpenter, who had just nabbed a feature-writing Pulitzer, wove in color and commentary from a broad spectrum of sources. Tom Larkin posed for a photographer standing next to the milkshake machine in the Snyder's kitchen. Mary Lou posed near the Odd Fellows Cemetery, dressed in a pantsuit and white sandals. And in an interview before the election, Helen Womer denied the fire had flexed its tentacles under the borough, spurned suggestions that the vapors in her yard contained harmful emissions, and said she loved her home.

"If you have a *house* you can live anywhere," she said. "Some people, all they need is a television [and] a six-pack of beer . . . and they're happy no matter where they are. That's not the way I feel . . . and a lot of people feel in this town."

A FEW WEEKS after the referendum, Catharene sat down with Greg Walter, a reporter for *People* magazine. The ballot question had reignited media interest in Centralia, most recently from *Time* and *People,* and with assistance from Catharene and other members of Concerned Citizens, Tom Larkin intended to exploit the opportunity. When the phone rang, heralding word of another interview request, Catharene diverted her attention, shifting from Katrina, diapers, and vacuuming to answering questions. Like Tom, she wanted the story to remain in the news.

But Catharene, who had prided herself on her verbatim notes in high school, had begun to regard journalists with caution, surprised by how often they misspelled her name or misquoted her. The Concerned

Citizens' leadership, including Tom, told her not to worry. Any attention helped, he believed, and the group, which had few allies, could not afford to alienate the press by asking for corrections. On top of that, Catharene offered a unique perspective. As one of the few pregnant women on the Hill and the only one willing to submit to interviews on the record, she gave voice to the borough's young families and its children, born and unborn.

For Catharene, deep into her third trimester, safety considerations remained paramount—more than ever, as evidence of her baby's peril mushroomed. Just as she and Peacho settled back on Locust Avenue, a local paper ran an article saying fetal exposure to low-level carbon monoxide posed risks comparable to cigarette smoking by the mother, including low birth weight and stillbirths. At a public meeting after the protest march, a doctor urged women in her neighborhood to refrain from becoming pregnant, also raising the specter of premature delivery. When Catharene asked about her situation, two months shy of her due date, he told her it was too late; her fetus had already endured first-trimester exposure before she and Peacho escaped to the Jurgills' and third-trimester contact after they returned.

Inside her home, the gas monitor mapped incursions into her family's living quarters. Catharene deciphered the machine's paper printouts, spooling from the interior like cash register tape. During April and May alone, the sensor notched nine upticks in carbon monoxide, ranging from 6 to 22 parts per million, and the peak surge also lasted the longest, a full forty-five minutes. When carbon monoxide spiked, she loaded Katrina into the stroller and fled, opting for a walk, a visit with friends, or a series of errands.

Still, she did her best, as she had during her first pregnancy, to foster fetal health and development. She exercised almost every day, from walking and aerobics to swimming laps at North Schuylkill High School. She ate yogurt, lean meats, and fresh vegetables, shunned salt and alcohol, and restricted her exposure to secondhand smoke. Throughout her pregnancy, she prayed for a healthy baby.

When the *People* reporter asked, she said she felt like a guinea pig.

St. Ignatius Church, circa 1942. From the exterior, St. Ignatius conveyed a sense of humility and piety, presiding over Locust Mountain. Inside the sanctuary, the coal miners who built it had lavished attention on detail, as in a church in an Italian hill town bursting with Renaissance paintings.

PHOTO COURTESY TOM DEMPSEY.

Logan Colliery, circa 1884. Throughout Centralia and across the region, breakers and their effluvia dominated the landscape, from their covered ski-jump profiles and towering black spill banks to the coal dust that coated the miners' homes and seeped in through their windows.

PHOTO COURTESY GEORGE BRETZ COLLECTION, ALBIN O. KUHN LIBRARY, UNIVERSITY OF MARYLAND BALTIMORE COUNTY.

Breaker boys at North Ashland Colliery, about a mile outside Centralia, circa 1884. Pennsylvania law dating back to 1870 prohibited employment by children younger than twelve, but in miners' families, lurching between booms and busts, every paycheck mattered, even one earned by the smallest hands.

PHOTO COURTESY GEORGE BRETZ COLLECTION, ALBIN O. KUHN LIBRARY, UNIVERSITY OF MARYLAND BALTIMORE COUNTY.

Jim and Maggie Quigley and their seven children, circa 1890. Here, surrounded by his family, my great-grandfather projected an air of well-fed professionalism, like a Bloomsburg lawyer with a walrus mustache, attired for court. My grandfather James, then about eight or nine, is standing in the back row on the far right, with his hand on his brother Pat's shoulder.

PHOTO COURTESY THOMAS J. QUIGLEY.

The Quigley homestead in the Swamp, 120 East Center Street, circa 1984. The Quigley home is the first house on the left, on a double lot at the end of the row. From his front porch, my great-grandfather could chat with his next-door neighbor without leaving his property.

PHOTO COURTESY COLUMBIA COUNTY REDEVELOPMENT AUTHORITY.

My grandfather James Quigley, seated at his desk in Mount Carmel, circa 1936. As a state mine inspector during the Depression, my grandfather spent evenings at his desk, filling the lined pages of leather-bound notebooks with handwritten investigation reports. PHOTO COURTESY THOMAS J. QUIGLEY.

The cave-in that swallowed Todd Domboski, February 14, 1981. In the aftermath of Todd's rescue, the Shenandoah *Evening Herald* featured this close-up photo of the hole, with a visible root spanning the opening like a suspension bridge. PHOTO COURTESY TERRI COLEMAN.

United Centralia Area Mine Fire Task Force meeting at borough hall, 1983. In January, Helen Womer revived her plea for unity, spearheading this new coalition to salvage the town. Mary Lou Gaughan is second from left, and Elaine Jurgill is seated two chairs away, at far right, wearing a white hat. Helen Womer, in a light-colored turtleneck, stands behind Elaine.

PHOTO COURTESY MARY LOU GAUGHAN.

Mary Lou Gaughan on her Wood Street front porch, circa 1983. When she moved there after the war, Mary Lou relished her husband's neighborhood, with its hilltop setting four blocks from St. Ignatius Church. After years of exile in Byrnesville, whose residents hiked into Centralia for Mass, she had landed at the center of the local universe. She even felt closer to God.

PHOTO COURTESY STEPHEN PERLOFF.

Tom Larkin visiting his parents' graves in St. Ignatius Cemetery, Memorial Day, 2006. He believes his ancestors reside in the burial grounds emotionally and spiritually, like the dead in *Our Town* who scrutinize the living from their hardbacked chairs above the village.

PHOTO BY JOAN QUIGLEY.

Peacho Jurgill and Catharene (age seventeen) six weeks before their wedding.

PHOTO COURTESY CATHARENE GARULA.

Dave and Pat Lamb at their Christmas Eve 1988 wedding ceremony at borough hall, where a portrait of President John F. Kennedy hung from the cinder-block wall. Dave Lamb's first marriage disintegrated in part from the stress of coexisting with the mine fire.

PHOTO COURTESY DAVE LAMB.

Two passersby inspect steam from the mine fire in December 2000.
Not even the experts know how long the blaze will keep burning.

PHOTO BY JOAN QUIGLEY.

An American flag marks a veteran's grave at St. Ignatius Cemetery on Memorial Day, 2006. This holiday culminates Centralia's year-round culture of revering the dead.

PHOTO BY JOAN QUIGLEY.

"Nobody knows what the gases do to an unborn child," she said. "I guess I'm the test."

THE INSPIRATION for the image descended earlier in the week, when Tom huddled around Joan Girolami's kitchen table with the *People* reporter and photographer Leif Skoogfors. Over coffee and cigarettes, Tom and the *People* crew chatted about the mine fire. Skoogfors, whose craft had graced the pages of *Time, Life, Newsweek,* and *U.S. News & World Report* and who had once logged a shot of Jane Fonda at a Vietnam War protest rally with a young Navy lieutenant and veteran named John Kerry in the background, had been mulling how to convey the impact of the blaze. When he heard about Tom's profession, he had an idea for a photograph: the short-order cook frying eggs over the mine fire. Tom mentioned a void near the Odd Fellows Cemetery where he thought emissions from the blaze might generate enough heat.

Now, as Tom shook off a fog of sleep deprivation, he and the photographer homed in on their destination: a cavity in the topsoil, like a rabbit hole, about forty feet from the Protestant burial grounds. In the winter, when barometric pressure and underground air currents conspired to create an updraft, puffs of white steam snaked from the void, dissipating into the atmosphere about two feet above the surface. In the late spring and summer, when humidity levels plummeted and subterranean ventilation reversed to a downdraft, few tendrils of steam curled from the opening. Even without vapor trails, though, the stench of sulfur hung in the air, the mine fire's rotten-egg perfume.

Tom crouched down at the depression, measuring about two feet deep and a foot across. Around the clay perimeter, littered with pebbles the size of gumdrops, the earth felt warm—not burning with an open flame or blistering like the grill at Snyder's, but hot enough to melt snow. Tom placed a frying pan over the fissure, allowing the heat to seep into the aluminum. One by one, he cracked eggshells, pouring yolks and whites into the skillet. Within moments, he had amassed a pool of clear membrane dotted with six yellow globes. Then, with a two-pack-a-day habit and nothing left to do but wait, he stood and smoked a cigarette.

More than anything, Tom yearned to make a point. He wanted to prove that the ground underneath Centralia radiated enough heat to cook eggs, illustrating the dangers inherent in living there. He knew that this visual, if it worked, would reinforce the message, broadcasting it to the *People*-reading universe.

Of course, Tom and the photographer could have staged this demonstration at Coddington's or the Lambs', where steam and vapors from the mine fire also licked the surface. But Skoogfors, who had visited Centralia earlier that spring, cased several potential locations, returning at various times of day to gauge the lighting. Eventually, he settled on this one, near the Odd Fellows Cemetery, and finalized details for an early morning shoot. He bought a Teflon-coated pan at a hardware store in a nearby town, adding a coat of black spray paint to maximize the contrast between the cooking surface and the egg whites. He also asked Tom to bring his white cotton work apron.

The photographer's choice of location suited Tom, who would have cooperated even on Locust Avenue but did not object to a lower-profile venue. He knew this stunt, with its element of melodrama, might have attracted a crowd on Locust and probably a few hecklers. At worst, it would inflame the opposition. He steeled himself to the criticism, viewing it as inevitable, but, in the interim, he didn't want to jeopardize the shot. With relief, he repaired to the seclusion of the moonscape beyond the dump, out of range of Tony Gaughan's binoculars, where he and Skoogfors could toil in private.

On the makeshift grill, Tom checked for signs of progress. About thirty minutes had elapsed and the yolks still oozed moisture. Around the edges, the whites had solidified. The short-order cook and the photographer agreed: He and his concoction, reeking of sulfur, were ready.

Skoogfors crouched about six feet away, framing his photograph in silence. He worked with intensity and deliberation, recording the scene around him, the same tableau, over and over: *click, click, click.* Film clattered through his Nikon, several dozen black-and-white shots in all: *click, click, click.*

Tom, meanwhile, knelt atop a gravel plateau, facing the Odd Fellows Cemetery. To his right, well beyond the camera's range, the squat brick outline of St. Ignatius School presided over the baseball field, as if the nuns might intercede at any moment to call a runner out at home. Across Locust Avenue, the taller silhouettes of St. Ignatius church, convent, and rectory loomed over everything else, including the school and nearby houses. All five generations of his Larkin ancestors would have recognized the skyline.

In Tom's immediate vicinity, though, where Skoogfors focused his lens, a defoliated zone spanned the horizon. In the distant background, where bulldozers and fly-ash trucks had not disturbed the woods, a border of trees arose. To an untutored observer not oriented to the borough's landmarks and history of fire containment projects, Tom looked as if he had landed on Mars.

CATHARENE FLIPPED through *People*'s June 22 issue. On the cover, Lady Diana Spencer dipped her chin toward the neck of her ruffled white blouse and smiled, clenching a bouquet of irises and lilies; above her right shoulder, promotional copy teased a sneak preview of her upcoming Big Day, her impending nuptials to Britain's Prince Charles ("The wedding gowns: all 6 of them!"). On page 34, tucked amid features about designer jean rip-offs and the life of John Lennon's alleged killer, Mark David Chapman, lay a three-page piece about Centralia: "A Town with a Hot Problem Decides Not to Move Mountains but to Move Itself."

Catharene scanned the text. From the opening salvo, with its reference to Centralians having a "hot time in the old town tonight," the story did not inspire confidence. Some houses "tilt crazily out of line," it reported, which, even if true, had more to do with coal region geography and row home construction than with the mine fire. In the borough's cemeteries, it continued, graves were believed to have plunged into the "abyss of fire" raging beneath them. As far as Catharene knew, no such doom had befallen the borough's decedents, even before Father Suknaic halted plot sales at St. Ignatius.

The remainder of the piece hewed to the facts, exploring the travails of Chrissie Oakum, Agnes Owens, and Catharene, all of whom belonged to Concerned Citizens. For balance, the reporter quoted Helen Womer: "We're not afraid of the gases, and we're not going to become slaves to a machine," she said. "I'm not going to let the coal barons win." On the last page, amid photos of Helen Womer in her living room leafing through a scrapbook and Agnes Owens surveying East Park Street from her front porch, editors had injected a photograph of Catharene. She sat perched on a white metal chair in her backyard, cradling Katrina in her arms. The reporter spelled her name correctly, not transmuting it into Kathy, Cathy, or Catherine, as many journalists did, but honoring the combination engineered to commemorate both her grandmothers: Catharine and Irene.

Still, Catharene had not landed in *People* by virtue of her own merit or acclaim. She had not cured a disease or fostered world peace. She had become pregnant with her second child while living about half a block from the mine fire's trajectory. Worse still, the editors had allotted an entire page, one-third of their coverage, to a single image: a black-and-white photograph of Tom Larkin out near the Odd Fellows Cemetery, bedecked in his chef's apron and wielding a skillet with a half-dozen fried eggs.

Catharene knew Tom had devoted hours of his free time to Concerned Citizens. He fielded queries from journalists and shepherded them through the borough. He typed letters and placed often-unreturned phone calls to officials. *People,* with its national circulation, had trivialized him and the group, detracting, in her view, from the gravity of their condition. At the very least, she thought, the editors could have downsized his picture and probed health issues at greater length. Even the caption conveyed a tone of levity: "Chef Tom Larkin shows that the gases emitted by Centralia's underground fire are hot enough to cook breakfast," it said.

Down at the Acme supermarket in Ashland, near the checkout aisles, Tom plucked a copy of *People* from a magazine rack. In the front of the store, with a cart full of groceries, he scoured its contents. He didn't know when the Centralia article would run, but he thought it might land in this week's issue. Seconds later, he found himself gazing at his own likeness, reproduced across a full page.

Shoppers circled around him, pointing and marveling. He was in *People*. Wow.

Tom scooped up half a dozen copies, depleting the inventory.

MARY LOU SAW Tommy Larkin's picture, with his mine fire T-shirt peeking out from under his apron. She and Tony despised those shirts. "Centralia: the Hottest Town in Penna.," they read, superimposed over a foundation of orange and red flames. Now *People* magazine had plastered them and Concerned Citizens across its pages: Joan Girolami with her blond Farrah Fawcett tresses and Tommy Larkin with his skillet. She and Tony were trying to save Centralia, and here was Tommy out frying eggs for publicity. If we couldn't get help in the beginning, she wondered, why can they get help now?

Still, Mary Lou could not resist adding the magazine to her collection, preserving it for posterity. *People* had profiled her hometown. Even in Centralia, that didn't happen every day. Later, she snipped the article and cover and taped them into her scrapbook. "June 22, 1981," she scrawled across the top of the page with her red felt-tip pen.

Up and down the borough's thoroughfares, the *People* article, especially Tom Larkin's cameo, had sparked a consternation boomlet. Some residents accused him of grandstanding, a term he recalled from Maggie's vernacular, with its intimation of deprecation and disdain. Elaine and Leon Jurgill did not say anything to Catharene, but she knew it would not thrill them to spot their daughter-in-law and granddaughter just a few column inches and a page away from Tom Larkin and his antics. If they griped to Peacho, he protected his wife from the details. If he disapproved—and Catharene knew he did—he nursed his objections in silence. Catharene's mother, meanwhile, slid the *People* story under the glass top of her living room coffee table, opened to the photograph of her daughter and granddaughter.

ONE MONTH LATER, Catharene lay flat on her back with her feet lodged in metal stirrups. Overhead, in a round mirror, she could see the reflections of her obstetrician and a team of nurses ministering to her under the glare of overhead spotlights, checking her pulse, blood pressure, and heart rate and timing her contractions. Outside in the hallway, her parents tarried with Leon and Elaine Jurgill, awaiting word of her progress.

Catharene, a Lamaze devotee whose mother delivered six offspring without sedation, approached childbirth with the serenity of a long-distance runner, stoked on endorphins and impervious to pain. With Katrina, she had waddled from the labor room to the delivery room ten centimeters dilated. With both babies, she eschewed epidurals, preferring meditation, prayer, and breathing exercises, a series of quick yoga-like exhales. Even Tylenol posed too many risks. Women all over the world had delivered children for centuries without medication, in bedrooms and fields, and she would survive the short-term discomfort, just as they had, with her psyche channeled on the finish line.

Tonight, however, with a full moon shimmering over Shamokin Hospital, the labor and delivery rooms overflowed. Birthing mothers shrieked and moaned. Even Catharene's sense of smell had revved into overdrive. The odors she encountered, from antiseptics and mint chewing gum to the pork chops still clinging to someone's breath, left her roiled with nausea.

Whatever the outcome and prognosis, she had known throughout her pregnancy that she would love and nurture this baby. Still, she knew of no test to discern whether her fetus was normal or impaired. Sonograms were a rarity, reserved for life-and-death scenarios. For the past few weeks, reporters had called, trawling for tragedy, as if, in private, they rooted for the narrative heft of disfigurement or aberration.

Even a supermarket tabloid, the *National Examiner,* had tucked a Centralia article into its mix, amid coverage of robot housewives, Morgan Fairchild, and the mafia hit men who allegedly whacked JFK. The bulletin, which presaged babies with "hideous birth deformities" maimed by carbon monoxide exposure, led with a quote from Catharene. "I'm scared to death," she had said.

Still, as Catharene's pregnancy dragged into late July, one week past her due date, she endured a series of indignities, from the heat and humidity to her own enormousness. She had gained twenty-six pounds, nine more than with Katrina, and the baby pressed against her internal organs. Throughout the week, she tried in vain, through walks and bumpy rides, to coax it along, only to resign herself to its schedule. Just hours earlier, at a barbecue with some of Peacho's colleagues, guests had handicapped the onset of her labor, amassing wagers like an NCAA basketball pool.

Around one A.M. she awoke with contractions, clocking them at less than ten-minute intervals. Her lower back throbbed. She and Peacho called a relative to stay with Katrina and left.

Now, at seven A.M. on July 26, after six hours of chemical-free labor, Catharene delivered. Glancing down, she saw a pink baby girl with brown fuzz matted to her head. The nurses clucked and cooed, marveling at all her hair. The obstetrician clamped the umbilical cord. Moments later—no more than a minute had elapsed—the pediatric nurse whisked the newborn away to a separate room with an incubator and testing equipment. Catharene lay in the gynecological bed, shaking as though with a fever, still racked by contractions.

This is it, she thought.

Peacho, her Lamaze coach, hovered nearby as he had throughout her labor, massaging her back and uttering reassurances. Her in-laws and parents popped in and said hello. But Catharene, who had excelled at delivery, dissolved in its aftermath. With the exertion of childbirth behind her, she plunged into uncharted depths, a postpartum netherworld she had not navigated after Katrina.

From what Catharene had glimpsed and heard, her baby seemed

fine. In an adjacent chamber out of her sight, though, Katrina's pediatrician and a cast of medical professionals who knew that this mother hailed from Centralia—and lived in a home equipped with a carbon monoxide monitor—were inspecting her minutes-old daughter. She knew they had braced for the worst. She knew what they were looking for, and the possibilities only exacerbated her symptoms. Her chest tightened. Her heart raced. Her lungs felt as if they had ceased functioning, as if something had crushed her sternum, and she could barely breathe.

Then, above the din of clanking instruments, above the racket of doors opening and slamming and medical staff and family members roaming the hallway, Catharene heard her baby cry. As a mother, she equated a newborn's wail with health. A few minutes later, the pediatric nurse edged back into the delivery room with her infant swaddled in a receiving blanket and a cap nudged onto her head.

She's fine, the nurse said, tendering baby to mother.

Catharene peppered her with questions.

Her Apgar scores were fine, the nurse said, referring to a postdelivery evaluation of a newborn's physical condition. Her heart rate, breathing, and color are normal. We drew blood and we'll give you the results later. You should nurse her. She's probably starving.

Catharene nestled her baby against her chest. She didn't think her newborn would want to nurse right there on the delivery table, but she knew the medical profession viewed it as a bonding ritual. She unwrapped the receiving blanket and tugged off the hat. By instinct, she counted her daughter's toes and fingers; she admired her pink skin, her round head and dark hair. She looked just like a baby from her family, like her younger sisters when they were born. As a newborn, Katrina—though just as wondrous—had resembled Peacho.

She's so beautiful, she thought. *Maybe she'll look like me.*

CHAPTER SEVEN

Inside the Beltway

THE BABY FELL ASLEEP midmorning. She had arrived on the feast day of Saint Anne, the Virgin Mary's mother and the patron saint of grandmothers, so before they left the hospital, Catharene and Peacho named her Angelique. For everyday purposes, they called her Angel, and for the rest of the summer Catharene dodged interview requests. Over the past few days, though, events in Washington, D.C., had conspired against her self-imposed hiatus. A delegation from Concerned Citizens had descended on the capital to lobby lawmakers and federal officials. Producers and crew from *Nightline* had landed in the borough, scouting a location and guests for a program to air that evening, October 20—her third wedding anniversary.

In her bedroom overlooking Locust Avenue, Catharene unzipped a plastic garment bag. Each year on their anniversary, when Peacho returned from work, she greeted him at the door in her bridal gown. But three years ago she had weighed 108 pounds and looked good in a paper bag, let alone a fitted bodice and ten-foot train. Now, three months postpartum and still nursing, she wondered if she could wedge herself inside. Somehow, perhaps from chasing after her children, the dress fit. She threw it on the bed and hurled herself into her next task, finding a coat to wear on *Nightline*. If she appeared in an outdoor stand-up shot, she wanted to project an aura of credibility and gravitas, not Everymom plodding about town in maternity garb.

Catharene admired *Nightline* and its host, Ted Koppel. Unlike the evening news anchors, who sandwiched two- and three-minute mine fire bulletins in between exposés about serial killers, corporate mergers, and the Mount Saint Helens disaster, Koppel explored issues in depth, quizzing guests about a single topic throughout his thirty-minute program. For Concerned Citizens, whose media scrutiny had spanned the print and broadcast spectra from tabloid to *Time, Nightline* offered an unprecedented opportunity: analysis of its message and goals, beamed live to living rooms and bedrooms across the country.

For Catharene, however, *Nightline* renewed tension she had been massaging since Angel's birth, including about her role in Concerned Citizens. When she told Peacho about the broadcast, he snapped, asking her, for the first time since she had allied herself with the activists, not to participate. He wanted her at home, he said, under the covers with him, marking their anniversary. But she understood the real basis for his protest: He didn't want to antagonize his parents. Local press was one thing, but *Nightline* might strain relations to the breaking point.

Still, Peacho's stance only stiffened her resolve. Her own mother would not forgo a chance such as this simply because her father disapproved—and their marriage, a union of independent and coequal partners, had thrived. Catharene had agreed to submit to an interview and would not back out now, regardless of her husband's misgivings.

By now, of course, Catharene knew she and Peacho differed in outlook and temperament, even more so than her bipartisan parents. Peacho, who did not vote, scorned politics as a thicket of self-interest and ineffectiveness. Her mother and father rarely missed an election, and ever since turning eighteen, neither had she. After the Three Mile Island disaster, when radiation leaked from a nuclear reactor outside Harrisburg, she had panicked. But Peacho, a budding management star, backed the nuclear power industry. Peacho guarded his emotions behind a scrim of reserve and shyness; Catharene bubbled with passion and enthusiasm. In the end, she thought, it didn't matter. They were young and in love, with a pair of beautiful babies. If he smiled, her spirits soared.

Even if Catharene finessed the *Nightline* controversy, though, the onset of autumn filled her with uneasiness. Bottom line: When they shut the windows against late autumn's chill, their carbon monoxide measurements spiked. The previous winter, before they fled across town, Katrina battled a series of colds and infections. Catharene suspected mine fire gases of causing her daughter's illnesses, even if Peacho did not. Now, with two children, she dreaded the prospect of another winter with his parents, who blamed Catharene's activist colleagues for the government's million-dollar buyout. The *News-Item,* the *Evening Herald,* and *The Catholic Witness* had just published letters to the editor from her father-in-law, blasting the news media and Concerned Citizens for hyping the mine fire, traumatizing elderly residents, and faking carbon monoxide readings so they could sell their homes. "Give me PROOF that there is fire under the town, then I'll THINK about relocation," he said. "Any other nonsense, we can do without."

As soon as she and Peacho could manage the financing, Catharene knew, they would leave Centralia. For months, she had economized, clipping coupons and shopping grocery store sales, building a down payment reserve from his twenty-thousand-dollar-a-year salary so they could stretch and buy a larger home somewhere else. More recently, since Angel's birth, she had scoured real estate ads, hoping to spot a listing in a nearby town, close to Peacho's plant. Until they decamped for safer terrain, though, Catharene had decided: no more children. She knew Peacho hoped for a son, and she had always assumed their brood would keep expanding, like the families in which they both grew up. At her age, she enjoyed the luxury of time, even if they waited.

Later that afternoon, a *Nightline* crew reinterviewed Catharene at home. She didn't know whom they were vetting for the broadcast and she didn't fish for clues. By her calculations, the odds favored her rejection. She had not emerged as an organizer or a leader, a galvanizing force behind Concerned Citizens or its detractors. Plus, she offered only one story, not an overview born of age, wisdom, or tenure from plying the borough's political trenches or dwelling in the mine fire's backyard. When the staffers left, she thought they had eliminated her from contention.

PEACHO BURST THROUGH the door around five P.M., right on time. Catharene, still scrambling to finish dinner, sped upstairs to change into her wedding dress. Normally, they dined in the kitchen, with Katrina ensconced nearby at a plastic table and chair. For tonight, Catharene had set the dining room table with a white lace tablecloth and Peacho's favorite china, the blue and white willow-patterned porcelain her grandmother had given them as a wedding gift. In honor of the occasion, she had also prepared a feast: prime rib and baked potatoes, corn, green beans, and a green-leaf lettuce salad with Seven Seas vinaigrette.

The call came before they sliced the cake.

Catharene grasped the receiver, still enrobed in her bridal gown. On the other end, she heard a *Nightline* staffer saying they had selected her as a guest. She needed to report to John Coddington's gas station an hour before the show, at 10:30 P.M.

Of all the places they could have picked, why there?

Catharene grilled the caller, telegraphing, she hoped, the extent of her reservations. Did they know officials had closed the station because the area was too dangerous? And the station sat across the street from the cave-in where Todd Domboski fell? And a vent pipe there spewed gas from the mine fire? She couldn't imagine any other reason for venturing to that destination in the middle of the night, but from what she gathered, the decision had already been made.

Catharene hung up the phone. She couldn't give Katrina a bath in her wedding dress. She had to find her coat and put the girls to bed. And she couldn't shake the suspicion that *Nightline,* with its location, might be angling to sensationalize. Why else would they send her there?

After she hung up, Peacho quizzed her: Was she going and did she really want to do this?

Yes. She was certain.

Don't go, he said.

But she rebuffed him, saying she wouldn't be gone long.

She wasn't about to call *Nightline* back and say no, my husband won't let me.

UP IN HIS BATHROOM at the Washington Hilton, the modernist structure where John W. Hinckley, Jr., had attempted to assassinate President Reagan, Tom Larkin splashed warm water on his face. He had endured a series of setbacks over the past two days, an immersion course in politics and expedience, Washington-style. Now, before a limousine whisked him to the ABC studio, he needed to relax.

They had arrived in the capital yesterday, Tom and Dave Lamb, after carpooling down from the coal region, clad in suits and toting briefcases. A handful of other Concerned Citizens had joined them, including Joan Girolami, Eva Moran, and Eva's husband, Joe. As a group, they geared the trip, the first ever by Centralia residents to lobby Washington officials, toward a single goal: nudging Pennsylvania's congressional delegation to authorize an $850,000 borehole study, a drilling and mapping initiative to pinpoint the fire and erase any doubts about its location. To help finance the journey, they peddled bumper stickers for a dollar, with black and red text on a white background reading "Centralia, Pa. Mine Fire: Hell on Earth!"

Their itinerary opened with lunch at the Watergate, with its Nixon-era iconography, where they dined with lawyers from a public interest firm. Up on Capitol Hill, Senator H. John Heinz III, the Republican ketchup magnate from western Pennsylvania, scrubbed his appointment with Concerned Citizens at the last minute, sending staffers in his stead. Tom, who deemed the cancellation an affront motivated by party loyalty and White House deference, vowed never to trust Heinz again.

The next morning, Tom and his companions crammed into Congressman Nelligan's office while an ABC camera crew toiled in the background, shooting footage for *Nightline* that evening. When one of the Centralians inquired about relocating the community, Nelligan bristled, warning them not to seem greedy. His colleagues would laugh him off the floor of Congress, he said. Senator Arlen Specter, a freshman Republican and former prosecutor from Philadelphia, mollified them with his attention (they knew the cameras didn't hurt), his support for the borehole study, and his candor. "It may be necessary in the final analysis to move large numbers of people," he said.

Later, they braved the Interior Department, a Depression-era legacy of New Deal public works projects, with a neoclassical façade and bronze doors like an Italian Renaissance cathedral. Before the trip, Tom had typed a letter to Secretary Watt urging him to meet with them for fifteen minutes, hear their concerns about the community, and help them secure a permanent solution to the mine fire. He received no response. Eleanor and Fritz O'Hearn followed up with a telegram, prodding Watt to confer with their compatriots. "Centralia is worth saving," they said. "We are a small town with an enormous problem."

Their plea did not sway Interior, however, where the public relations team was squashing an insurgency from the left. On Monday, October 19, when the Centralians descended on Washington, a coalition of conservation groups, including the Sierra Club, staged a news conference on the Capitol steps, unveiling more than a million petition signatures demanding Watt's resignation. They also denounced his policies as radically out of step with the American people's wishes. Watt's spokesman, Douglas Baldwin, dismissed the affair as a fundraising and membership ploy. "I think this will help Secretary Watt, not hurt him," he said. "It strengthens the image of a man unfairly beaten upon by a small clique of opponents."

Still, Watt did not rush to clear his schedule for a delegation from

Centralia. The blaze had nabbed headlines again, at least locally, after state officials pronounced it the most serious of Pennsylvania's twelve abandoned mine fires—and perhaps the worst of the almost three hundred blazes consuming coal deposits nationwide. Instead, the meeting fell to Baldwin and Watt's deputy, Donald P. Hodel, who installed themselves around a conference table with Tom and his colleagues and hewed to their boss's vision.

Hodel, a lawyer, energy consultant, and former administrator of the Bonneville Power Administration, one of the Northwest's largest public power agencies, declined to say whether Interior backed the borehole project. Tom urged him to launch the study immediately. Hodel resisted, asking if it was feasible to drill in the winter. Baldwin asked Tom if he had developed a proposal for the postdrilling phase. "Do we have a *plan*?" Tom said, stunned by the implication that they, as amateurs, should dictate future containment strategy. "The Department of the Interior has the expertise to draw up the plan," he said. "We can only give advice."

Tom filed out of the building thinking they had achieved nothing. Later, the reservations staff at the Capital Hilton, where ABC News had arranged to shelter him for the evening, refused to check him in without a credit card. He buttonholed the manager, leveraging his *Nightline* appearance into an exception to the policy, but the two days had exacted a toll. Only in the hotel dining room did he happen upon a reprieve: two gin martinis and a steak, billed to his room, courtesy of ABC.

By this point, Tom had cultivated an appreciation for the network's expense account. Back in early August, after the mine fire ruptured the topsoil about a mile east of the borough and newscasts featured footage of the outburst, with tiny blue flames licking cherry-red rock, *Good Morning America* had booked Tom and Todd Domboski for an interview. The day before the show, ABC ferried them to New York in a chauffeured limousine equipped with a television and a bar and installed them at the St. Moritz, where Tom's room, with a bed the size of a station wagon, overlooked Central Park.

On the morning of their planned appearance, however, a strike by federal air traffic controllers dominated the news, bumping them to the next day. Tom, Todd, and Flo Domboski had romped through Manhattan, with excursions to Times Square, the Museum of Natural History, and the Dakota, so Todd could see the building where John Lennon had lived and died. After the broadcast, they motored back to Centralia in yet another limousine. The next day, Governor Thornburgh sent Watt a letter about the mine fire, his first statement since the borough hall press conference, saying responsibility for redressing the blaze rested with the federal government. He urged Watt to undertake the borehole project immediately, using existing federal funds.

Now, as Tom stroked a razor across his face in his Hilton bathroom, a downgrade from the St. Moritz, he harbored a mounting sense of unease. He knew, from watching *Nightline* several times a week, that Ted Koppel pounded his guests, especially if they tried to evade him. Before *Good Morning America,* someone from the staff had prepped him by phone, walking through his background, his role with Concerned Citizens, and his thoughts about the community. For the past two days, however, his Washington mission had consumed him. No one had primed him for this appearance, and Koppel was no Joan Lunden.

Under pressure, Tom knew, he stuttered, even without a camera trained on his face. Joan Lunden had soothed his preperformance jitters with her confidence and poise, encouraging him to relax as if he were seated in his living room, not a Manhattan studio set with potted plants and a wicker settee. With her in command, seated on a chair next to him, the interview unspooled like a conversation and he delivered a stutter-free performance. He indulged no such illusions about *Nightline*.

Around 10:15 P.M., the phone rang: a call from the lobby. The driver had arrived downstairs. Tom replaced the receiver in the cradle. A film of perspiration coated his palms. His heart pounded. Butterflies needled his stomach. He grabbed his coat, left his room, and stepped into the elevator, an experience that unnerved him under ordinary circumstances, with its sensation of hurtling between floors. When the doors glided open to reveal the lobby, his hands had started shaking.

CATHARENE EDGED OUT of bed. Down the hall, the children lay sleeping in their rooms. With 10:30 P.M. approaching, she needed to hustle. She pulled on a white blouse and black pants and freshened her makeup: brown eyeliner and eye shadow, copper lipstick.

Earlier, when she asked, Peacho said he'd stay up to watch, but he usually fell asleep by ten P.M., and they didn't have a television in the bedroom. She knew that in all likelihood he would miss the show altogether. Still, he had found her coat for her, hanging on a hook in the basement with his hunting regalia. Over the years and into the future, many more wedding anniversaries awaited, and they could honor all of them under the covers, just as he wished. How often would *Nightline* be in town?

At the front door, Peacho kissed her goodbye. Outside, the temperature had plummeted. When Catharene exhaled, she could see her breath. A block downhill, at Coddington's station, spotlights flooded the façade, like a high school stadium illuminated for a football game. Catharene strolled downhill along Locust Avenue, musing about October's unpredictability. Tonight, an aroma of crispness perfumed the air, with a hint of decay. Outside Dave Lamb's house, with its expanse of trees, her shoes crunched dry leaves on the sidewalk. Three years ago, when she and Peacho had said their vows, they'd basked in the warmth of Indian summer. She hadn't even needed a coat.

THE LANDSCAPE had shifted around Catharene and Peacho since their wedding, not just the weather. In the weeks before *Nightline*'s producers and crew landed in the borough, federal officials had settled with the twenty-seven participating property owners, offering between $7,500 and $31,000 for their homes, with relocation allowances ranging from $9,300 to $15,000. A handful of families had already moved, scattering to Mount Carmel, Bloomsburg, and Girardville. Catharene and Peacho, whose block officials had deemed safe and omitted from the buyout, did not qualify for inclusion. Dave and Eileen Lamb, who lived about a block away from Catharene, had been offered $27,000 for their home. With the Interior Department discounting appraisals as much as 45 percent, the Lambs fared well, almost doubling many of the other offers.

Still, in a dénouement Dave had prophesied after the governor's visit, he and Eileen had separated. Dave didn't blame the mine fire, at least not entirely, but the strain from living in its midst had accelerated their split. For several years, he and Eileen had suppressed recriminations and differences, sublimating them to uneasiness about Rachel's health. In the state-supplied trailer on the baseball field, their sanctuary from gases and cave-ins, they realized they couldn't live together anymore. Within a few months, their marriage dissolved, as if the mine fire had bound them together, like a centrifuge. Eileen was scouting houses in Mount Carmel for her and the children, and Dave, who had moved to Marion Heights, a few miles outside Mount Carmel, was renovating space above the Speed Spot for an apartment.

Even the neighborhood surrounding Catharene's block had transformed, with an abruptness that reverberated throughout the community. Underneath Dave's front porch, where a red ribbon still clung to a white support column, officials had spray-painted a red "2" next to the parlor window. An identical blaze flanked the Oakums' front window next door. Along Locust Avenue, from the Oakums' to Coddington's station to the O'Hearns', a column of structures bore the same branding.

Employees of the Columbia County Redevelopment Authority, the federal government's local partner in the million-dollar buyout, had roamed the neighborhood with spray paint. In official parlance, the acquisition constituted the second such initiative, after the demolition of several East Park Street homes earlier in the year. So workers tagged the houses of the participating families with crimson 2's, alerting demolition contractors which buildings to level.

FOR MARY LOU and Tony, the current project represented the third relocation, including the county's purchase of the Laughlin row in 1969. Either way, in late September, the government finalized its real estate deals and prepared for demolition. The neighborhood stretching downhill from St. Ignatius Church to Wood Street, the so-called 16-acre area, acquired a patina of blight, with plywood and plastic sheeting tacked over cavities where windows and doors once hung. As red 2's proliferated along the upper bounds of Locust Avenue, wrapping around the corner and spilling onto Wood Street, Tony dubbed the brandings blood numbers. That's what they looked like to him, with paint streaming from the digits' base in Day-Glo rivulets, like blood dripping from a knife in a horror movie.

Mary Lou had watched her neighbors raise their children, nurse their spouses through illnesses, and bury their husbands. She knew the rhythms and details of their lives, even their secrets, like who had survived breast cancer. When Carrie Wolfgang bounded up Flo's front steps in the evening, Mary Lou knew she carried a snack for Todd. When Jack Maloney died, Mary Lou watched the undertakers maneuver his corpse out the bedroom window. When the Birsters' canary expired, she and her neighbors had forged a compact, brothers and sisters of Wood Street, united to salvage their homes. If they had stuck together, like miners on strike, they could have saved the town. Now moving vans and borrowed trucks stalked Locust Avenue, carting furniture, appliances, and boxes from row homes and leaving behind vacant shells.

Pretty soon, she and Tony and Helen would have the entire street to themselves.

Still, Mary Lou tried not to brood; that's how depression took root. Instead, she clipped an *Evening Herald* advertisement sponsored by the

American Bible Society and taped it into her scrapbook, above her handwritten list of the twenty-seven families. At the top of the ad, a photo depicted a tree in a field, surrounded by lifeless trunks. Underneath, she bracketed the last of three paragraphs of text, erecting a red-ink barricade around them. "Most of our life is lived close to each other," it said. "But there are times when we find ourselves standing alone. In such lonely moments, God provides the faith and courage we need."

With her Magic Marker, she underlined the second half of the last sentence, tracing a red line from *God* to *need*.

CATHARENE STOOD OUTSIDE Coddington's with the proprietor and Tony Andrade. The station, a two-story wood frame building with a stone façade and a trio of windows upstairs, had long served as a gathering point for neighborhood men, and more recently, for out-of-town journalists. On the ground floor, two garage doors bisected the service bay, honeycombed with rows of side-by-side windowpanes. A one-story hub shaped like a hexagon flanked the main structure, creating space for the store, where children bought soda and candy and Coddington rang up their purchases on a manual cash register, acknowledging each transfer of coins with a *k'ching*. Outside the shop, a wooden bench faced downhill, overlooking Locust Avenue and Wood Street. A carport sheltering defunct gasoline pumps protruded from the front of the store, facing Locust. Now, as host, Coddington offered coffee, whiskey shots, and bathroom facilities to the *Nightline* staffers scurrying to ready the set.

A decade earlier, network executives would have waited hours, if not days, to screen the results from Centralia. In the late 1970s and early 1980s, however, video technology revolutionized broadcast news, liberating it from decades of dependence on film. Production crews armed with lightweight cameras and satellite uplinks began penetrating remote locations and beaming the imagery live into viewers' living rooms, unhampered by delays for developing and shipping reels to distant newsrooms. CNN, the Cable News Network, had launched its twenty-four-hour service in 1980. *Nightline,* inaugurated as a thirty-minute broadcast during the Iran hostage crisis, carved its niche by summoning guests from across the globe, from Washington, D.C., to Tehran, and linking them live to Ted Koppel.

Outside Coddington's station, technicians grappled with logistics, opening a line to WNEP, an ABC affiliate in Wilkes-Barre-Scranton, about fifty miles to the north. Across the pavement, they planted the hallmarks of their quest. A generator rumbled, churning power to feed the spotlights. Electrical wires crisscrossed the asphalt, fueling the sound and video equipment, and a panel van sat idling at the curb. Catharene, with her reverence for thrift, marveled at the waste of so much gasoline.

The *Nightline* staffers, meanwhile, groomed the three guests for their cameos, offering a crash course in broadcast technique. One brought Catharene a microphone, clipped it on, and showed her how to use it. Coddington and Tony had similar devices, and a sound person tested them, gauging their effectiveness, while a technician with earphones and a boom mike swept overhead. Another crew member explained how to perform on camera and handle questions from Ted Koppel, whom they would not see, even when he spoke to them: Gaze into the lens, not at each other. Catharene wondered how anyone would hear them over the generator.

As the prebroadcast countdown continued, Catharene, Coddington, and Andrade stood with their backs to the store, about twelve feet from a borehole drilled into the pavement. Officials had designed the opening, a two-inch pipe flush with the surface, as a release valve, to vent mine fire gases and reduce emissions inside nearby homes. On this night, with ventilation in the abandoned workings conspiring to create an updraft, steam trickled from the pipe. More than a dozen such voids dotted the asphalt along Locust Avenue and Wood Street, from the Laughlin row to Tony Andrade's. Catharene usually hastened through this sector to avoid them, speedwalking with the stroller until the air improved farther downhill. Tonight, however, with *Nightline* dictating the location of its live interview, she had little leeway. Fumes wafted into her face, damp with the scent of the underground blaze, and the mine fire's stench hung over the station like a tent.

Inside WNEP's studios, meanwhile, Ted Koppel hunkered over a manual typewriter in his shirtsleeves, revising the introductory script. A colleague labored nearby, burnishing page 6. Three assistants tackled five telephones, fielding calls from network executives in New York and Washington. Downstairs, a producer and a correspondent pored over new and old Centralia video, editing footage for the broadcast. "This small town has been . . . ," the tape said over and over. "This small town has been . . ."

At 11:23 P.M., Koppel strode onto the set, a sea of earth tones with mocha-colored walls, mustard-yellow trim, and the Channel 16 logo etched in brass, and slid his briefcase under the hexagonal brown Formica desk. Two minutes later, he requested a sound check with his guests scattered in Washington and Centralia.

In *Nightline*'s Washington studio, Tom Larkin perched atop a wooden stool with an earpiece lodged in his left ear. Overhead, several rows of spotlights trained their beams on his gray three-piece pinstripe suit, snagged on sale in Mount Carmel for his *Good Morning America* stint and pressed into duty without reprieve for the past two days. In the darkness beyond his knees, Tom perceived nothing, not even the cameraman: just a sea of blackness and his own trembling hands, bathed in the glow of track lighting. Congressman Nelligan, seated on a stool next to him, grabbed Tom's forearm, a few inches above his wrist.

Calm down, Nelligan said. It's going to be all right. It's only television.

On the set in Scranton, Koppel nudged two fingers against a receiver hidden behind his ear. The technicians hadn't perfected the audio link to Centralia. He couldn't hear one of the guests.

"I hope this clears up," he said. "If it doesn't, we can all switch over to Johnny Carson."

AT 11:30 P.M., viewers tuned to ABC saw a night-sky backdrop studded with white orbs. Against the black horizon, an image appeared in miniature, about the size of a postage stamp, expanding to fill more than half the screen: a pair of row houses engulfed in steam, as if a forest fire raged just off camera. In households across America, the voice of Ted Koppel pierced the silence. "Passing the buck," he said.

As the video clip lingered, Koppel continued his narration, still in voiceover. "Bureaucratic bumbling and mounting red tape," he said, "while Centralia, Pennsylvania, burns." As he spoke, a Centralia montage unfolded, from Todd Domboski's cave-in, twirling with vapors, and an aerial shot of St. Ignatius Church and School surrounded by autumn foliage, to a vent pipe in the middle of Locust Avenue belching steam. "Tonight, in a special edition of *Nightline* coming to you from northeastern Pennsylvania," he said, "we'll focus on an underground fire which is smothering a town because no one can decide who ought to pay for putting the fire out. It's a problem that's [been] building for almost twenty years."

Across the country, viewers saw their screens revert to black, like a theater after the houselights dim. Then, with a burst of drums rumbling through the bass register, programmers cued the overture. Trumpets blared, spanning the scale in four staccato bursts, *Nightline*'s audio hook. Across the screen, a credit rolled for ABC News, stamping blue and white capital letters onto the black backdrop. Underneath, a city skyline unfolded across the evening sky, transforming into the program's logo: the name of the broadcast, rendered in blue capital letters, with skyscrapers silhouetted across the base and horizontal lines spliced through the top like telegraph wires.

In Scranton, a camera trained on Ted Koppel, seated in the anchor chair in a gray pinstripe suit. With economy and verve, he condensed nineteen years into a paragraph, even using "Once upon a time": The mines closed, the dump ignited, and the blaze spread underground through the abandoned workings. "That, roughly, is how the story began," he said, transitioning to the focus piece, a taped bulletin designed to stake out a viewpoint and provoke debate among the evening's guests. "As George Strait reports, no one, however, seems to know how it will end."

Strait, a veteran reporter with degrees in biology and biochemical genetics, had already filed several evening news stories about Centralia, spanning topics from Todd Domboski to the referendum. For this broadcast, entitled "Raging Fire in Coal Country," he portrayed Centralia on the verge of another winter, beset with anxiety about gases and cave-ins and frustrated by governmental indifference and parsimony. Chrissie Oakum, who had relocated to Girardville, said she still found herself checking her boys at night to ensure they were breathing. Helen Womer, shown standing on her front porch in a scarlet suit with an apricot scarf knotted at her throat, said she declined the government's purchase offer because no one knew the fire's location. Strait, in his closing stand-up from a hillside above town, with a blue-sky backdrop and side-by-side houses spilling across the valley, hinted at the cost of further paralysis.

"Long range," he said, "if a way cannot soon be found to extinguish the fire, then, as it spreads, one by one people will be forced from their homes, leaving the town to the fire and the coal underneath here to whomever has enough money to come and dig it out."

On the set in Centralia, Catharene heard a voice from the crew saying they were next. For the first time, she deflected a bout of stage fright, a hint of preperformance butterflies. After the commercial break, Koppel framed the next segment.

"You are looking now at a live picture from Centralia, Pennsylvania," he said. On a screen behind him, visible to viewers at home, a camera swooped in on a borehole outside Coddington's station, showing a metal ring caked with rust and surrounded by cracked asphalt. A spurt of gray steam lofted skyward.

Next, Koppel introduced his guests. The screen at his back revealed a live image of Catharene, Coddington, and Andrade, arrayed shoulder to shoulder outside the station, with a garage door in the background. Catharene stood in her purple coat, buttoned down the front, with her hands tucked into her pockets and her shoulder-length brown hair layered and pouffed into a crown at the top of her head. Coddington and Andrade, bundled into winter jackets, shuffled their feet, rocking from side to side. A few feet away, a puff of steam rippled across the left side of the screen, as if from a fog machine.

Koppel spun in his chair, rotating 180 degrees and placing his back to the audience. From his perch, he faced a large screen near the anchor desk, where, thanks to the control room, viewers saw the projected images of his guests. To Koppel, who scrutinized his invitees on a television monitor located just beyond camera range, the surface before him looked blank. For the audience, though, the screen in front of the anchor filled with video from Coddington's station, locking on the three residents. Catharene fidgeted with her hands, easing one out of her pocket and resting it on her hip. Koppel pivoted to her, and with steam flowing from the borehole just a few feet away, teed up the question at the heart of his interview—and no doubt looming in the minds of many of his viewers.

"Mrs. Jurgill, let me begin by asking you, why do you stay?" Koppel asked.

Catharene's eyes darted, first toward Coddington and Andrade and then in the opposite direction, toward the Four Corners, as is she were plotting an escape.

In fact, she was wondering why Koppel had asked her that question. She had expected him to inquire about issues affecting the community, such as her hopes for a borough-wide relocation program. Instead, with his opening salvo, without realizing it, he had delved into her personal life, boring into the heart of her marriage. His query, though unintentionally, compelled her to expose her disagreement with Peacho—and she had no desire to do so, especially after consenting, against his wishes, to appear on this show. But she didn't know how to sidestep the question.

"Right now we have no way to get out of here," she said. "We're not financially able, and my husband really loves it here, so we're just gonna wait and see what happens." As she spoke, she shrugged her shoulders and flexed her elbows outward, a pantomime of resignation.

Koppel stayed with her for a follow-up.

"You know, I don't mean this to be an overly dramatic question, but those gases we see venting there—poisonous?" he said.

Catharene glanced at the fumes.

"Yes, I believe so," she said.

"And those are, what, all over town?" he said.

The camera zoomed in on Catharene, so close that viewers could make out the mother-of-pearl buttons on her blouse.

"They're in a large part of the town, from what we know," she said.

As Catharene spoke, wisps of steam swept across the screen.

"Well, what does that do to people?" Koppel said. "What does that do to young children? Do you have any idea? Have you ever talked to a doctor about it?"

Of course Catharene knew the effects of carbon monoxide exposure: Her trepidations about her children could have consumed the rest of the broadcast. She had, many times, consulted a doctor: her daughters' pediatrician, who drew blood from Katrina to inspect for carbon monoxide poisoning and examined Angel in the hospital just moments after delivery. Only someone who had grown up in Centralia, such as her husband, would behold this situation through a prism of normalcy.

"Well, it makes you drowsy at first, and gives you headaches and nausea," she said. At the base of the screen, yellow text identified her as "Catherene [*sic*] Jurgill, Centralia resident."

"It can also make you sick and pass out, and eventually, I guess, it could kill you—if you were in it long enough," she said.

Catharene's reply created a bridge to Coddington, with his first-hand knowledge about losing consciousness. Still, as the anchor drifted to him, Catharene couldn't fathom why Koppel hadn't posed the same questions as his subordinates earlier in the day. He hadn't even broached the subject of relocation or Concerned Citizens, the topics she hoped to discuss—and the reason she had climbed out of bed on her anniversary.

Catharene did not know, of course, that Koppel balked at delegating interview preparation to his staff. After *Nightline*'s first broadcast, a booker handed him a typed list of queries for a guest slated to appear the next evening. Koppel bristled. "Do not ever, *ever* give me questions," he said. Instead, as a matter of pride and professionalism, he approached interviews like a seminar, aiming for spontaneity, keying his follow-ups to his guests' responses and listening for a word, phrase, or remark warranting further exploration. Catharene, with her answer, had created just such an opening.

"Now, Mr. Coddington, that in fact—I mean obviously not the final thing, but I mean the sickness and the passing out—that happened to you," he said. "Why are you still there? Why are you still staying in that town?"

"Well, I'm actually not staying here anymore," said Coddington, who had just moved into a home a few miles away, purchased with his share of the million-dollar buyout. As for the past two years, he ducked the question. In late 1980, a year after officials closed his business, they urged him to evacuate. Rather than help him relocate by issuing emergency vouchers or finding him temporary housing, they told him to save receipts for his expenses and, if the government ever bought his building, they would deduct his expenditures from the purchase price. Coddington, who lost his livelihood to the mine fire, fled his apartment above the station only when the state offered him an emergency trailer on the baseball field. Now, with his family settled into permanent housing in another town, he had no reason to belabor the obvious: He could not have shouldered the cost of leaving earlier without government assistance. Rather, with the dexterity of an ex-mayor, he defused the inquiry with a joke, saying the air in his new home was a lot better than what they'd been putting up with in Centralia.

Koppel swung to Tony Andrade, who had relocated to Mount Carmel, and lobbed his query a third time.

"This fire has been going on now for, what, roughly nineteen, almost twenty years," Koppel said. "Why has it taken you this long to move out? I mean, I would think that those kinds of conditions would cause people to move out as quickly as possible."

Andrade, whose wife supported the family on her garment factory salary, also skirted the question. They had sunk eight thousand dollars into their home in the past three years, and without relocation aid from the government, they could not afford the expense of buying a new house, even after mine fire gases surged and the state declared their dwelling unsafe. Until recently, when officials offered him $14,500 for their home, the state's emergency trailer had remained their only option.

Still, Andrade and Centralians of his generation, who scraped for work after the mines closed, swelled with pride in their homes, their children, and their community. They volunteered their spare time at the church and the fire department, sipped draft beers at the Legion, and tended to elderly relatives and neighbors. They had a respect for family, place, stability, and tradition that defied translation to outsiders from higher income brackets, who did not know the reward of sleeping in the town, or perhaps even the bedroom, where their fathers and maybe their grandfathers were born, where they had landed after immigrating to this country and sought refuge after surviving another day in the mines. When reporters quarried, even obliquely, for details about their finances, they resisted, especially on national television.

For Tony, whose parents numbered among Centralia's few Portugese immigrants, relocating down the road had also created a sense of loss. He and Mary had treasured their Locust Avenue home, a sun-drenched corner unit hugging the hilltop along Wood Street. When mine fire emissions surged, tripping the alarm on their carbon monoxide monitor fifteen times in four months, they knew they had to flee. But their new house, sandwiched among neighbors in a row and bereft of daylight and memories, offered shelter and little more.

Andrade, instead of addressing Koppel's inquiry and divulging why he had stayed in his home, responded to his Centralia critics, who denounced him and the other twenty-six families for leaving. The federal government's million-dollar relocation initiative, he suggested, had deepened divisions in town, sparking remorse among those who qualified and resentment among those who did not, either because they inhabited safe terrain on the northern end of town, the government decreed their homes gas-free, or, like Helen and Mary Lou, they spurned the government's offer. "You can come in here and you'll see this is desolation and ruin of what was a proud and well-maintained community, close-knit, friends, relatives, and it's just a sad situation that people in Centralia weren't really in a frame of mind to have to do something like this," he said.

Koppel, sensing an impasse, veered back to Coddington, wondering aloud if this story had no villains. Coddington, whose earpiece malfunctioned, couldn't hear the question, even after Koppel repeated it. Koppel jammed his index finger into his temple and redirected the inquiry to Andrade, who said it was hard to pin responsibility on any one person. Once again, though, Andrade steered his response toward critics in the borough, describing the mine fire gases in his home.

With time running out, Koppel doubled back to Catharene.

"What do you think it'll take to convince your husband that you ought to move out of that town?" he said.

The camera pulled in for a close-up, homing in on her face.

Catharene inhaled, a quick breath, like a startle response.

"Umm—" she said, diverting her gaze.

To her, it was an unfair question. She couldn't speak for Peacho.

"I'm not really sure," she said. As she responded, her eyes again flitted left and right, as if she were parsing each word. "I guess that probably when he feels that there is danger for our particular family, that's when he'll leave."

Koppel pressed again.

"And he doesn't, and you don't?" he said.

Catharene's eyes welled with tears. She knew she and her daughters had to leave Centralia. Peacho hadn't told his parents he had even discussed the possibility of relocating. She had no interest in alienating her husband or blindsiding her in-laws by airing their conflict in public. Not on her anniversary.

"Well, I do a little more than he does," she said, acknowledging her understatement with a tight smile. "That's all I can say right now."

As the camera lingered, she sighed and swallowed, blinking back tears.

Koppel ended with a note of empathy, radiating humanity and grace.

"Mrs. Jurgill, Mr. Andrade, and Mr. Coddington, thank you all very much indeed, and get away from that gas, will you?"

ON CAMERA, Catharene grinned and laughed. After an hour on location outside Coddington's station, however, Koppel's parting comment rankled, especially since she had objected to the venue from the outset.

I'm here because you set me up here, she thought.

She had expected a news story, infused with analysis, context, and content. Instead, he had hammered her with personal questions, exploiting her youth and gender, the broadcast's token girl. On top of that, she had disappointed the group, failing to convey its message and fostering a perception that Centralia residents suffered from poverty and stupidity, lingering amid toxic gases when common sense dictated they should bolt. She had made a fool of herself in front of the entire country.

Moments after Catharene walked in the door, her mother called, assuring her she had done well. Catharene, whose head throbbed from inhaling fumes on the set, checked her irritation, not wanting to provoke a fight with her mom. She took two Tylenols and sipped mint tea, the only pain relievers she could risk while nursing.

TOM TRACKED the Centralia segment from his stool, on a television mounted atop a rotating stand. During the commercial break, a technician swiveled the TV around and lowered the volume. Moments later, Tom spotted a red light the size of a kidney bean atop a camera in front of him: They were live. In his earpiece, he heard Koppel's voice from Scranton, mentioning Concerned Citizens and their lobbying trip and introducing his Washington guests. Then he heard Koppel, who had once again whirled around from the audience, talking to him.

"When you met today with those folks at the Department of the Interior, did you get the impression that they were warm, compassionate, understanding, well plugged in?" Koppel said.

On the screen facing Koppel, viewers now saw Tom Larkin, silhouetted against a black backdrop. A red satin ribbon graced his lapel.

Actually, Tom had anticipated this question. Before the broadcast, Joan Girolami had called him from the Scranton studio, saying she had overhead someone say that Koppel would ask him about his meeting with Interior. Now, as Tom crafted his response to that very inquiry, he wielded language like a diplomat, indulging friends, snubbing enemies, and shoving animosities aside.

"Well, I think the reason that the undersecretary met with us today was out of courtesy to Congressman Nelligan and both of our senators, who had been helpful in arranging the meeting there," he said.

Tom used the phrase "our senators" on purpose, refusing to reward Senator Heinz, whose brush-off still smarted, by uttering his name on national television. Still, he knew that Hodel, whom he had tipped about *Nightline* before leaving the conference room, might be watching. He could not afford to alienate the Interior Department, so he continued to pirouette, muting his disdain with flattery but signaling his contempt.

"I really honestly must say that I don't think that Interior is sympathetic," he said, stifling a smile. "I did not get that impression today. The undersecretary listened; he listened well; but he was very, very noncommittal about anything at all."

Tom realized his nervousness had evaporated—and he was having fun.

Koppel angled for more, delving into the coalition's long-term goals.

"If you and your group could just kind of make a decision tomorrow and say, 'All right, let's get the money allocated,' what is it that you would do?" he said. "I mean, how—it sounds as though this fire is almost impossible to put out; it's been burning for almost twenty years."

Now Tom knew: Koppel wasn't being tough on him.

"Well, we don't know that the fire is impossible to put out," Tom said. "You ask what we would do with the money: We would drill the boreholes to find out where the fire is exactly located, so that we can begin to address the problem of the fire constructively. I personally believe that the fire can be excavated. Whether or not this is feasible remains to be seen. Until we find out exactly where it is and what is being affected by it, I really don't think that we can address the problem."

Koppel spun to Congressman Nelligan, with his silver mane and tab-collar shirt, like a corporate lawyer at a board of directors meeting.

"Congressman Nelligan, forgive me for sounding a little bit incredulous, but how is it possible that the location of the fire has not even been determined after what is now approaching two decades?" he said.

Tom suppressed a burst of glee.

Nelligan, however, did not flinch.

"Well, generally speaking, Ted, the central location of the fire is known," he said, staring straight into the camera. "But don't forget, this fire keeps burning and expanding, and has been doing so for twenty years. What is really needed, if we're talking about excavation, we have to know the area—in the broadest sense, the area that has to be excavated. To do this—because it has been progressive—we need a borehole study, and we now have, in the House version of a bill which I was responsible for getting through Congress, $850,000 for that borehole study. Once we determine the parameters of that fire, then we can determine the options available to put it out and, of course, the price tag—and the price tag is really the problem, when you get right down to it."

Koppel reached for one of his trademark phrases, a signal to his eight million viewers: This guy is trying to dodge me. If the *Nightline* anchor begged for indulgence, prefacing an inquiry with "Forgive me" or "Excuse me," savvy audience members braced. Koppel, in his role as their surrogate, had pounced.

"Congressman, excuse me, but you gave what sounded like two different answers to the same question," he said. "First, I said how come it's taken you twenty years to find out where the fire is; you said you know where it is."

Nelligan struggled to intervene.

"No, what I—" he said.

Koppel cut him off.

"But now we're talking about $850,000 to find out precisely where it is, right?" he said.

Nelligan, still unfazed, endeavored again.

"That's correct," he said. "In other words, we know where the heart of the fire is, but we don't know to what point it has been extended."

"Yeah, well, that was really my question," Koppel said. "Why has it taken twenty years to find out precisely where the fire is?"

Tom could barely contain himself.

Nelligan, who had served in Congress for only nine months, shifted to candor.

"Probably because nobody has paid the attention to it that should have been paid to it," he said.

Koppel pressed again.

"And why not?" he said.

Nelligan, who owed his election in part to Reagan's coattails, knew better than to blame the administration's fiscal policy or Interior's sagebrush rebels.

"I can't account for the people in the past," he said, "but I will say this, that this whole situation has been neglected."

Koppel swerved back to Tom, probing about the conspiracy theory.

Tom, who had answered this question dozens of times, recognized another softball.

"I adhere to that theory—the theory of the conspiracy," he said. "Until it is proven to me that there has been no conspiracy in the past to get at the vast coal reserves existing there, I'll continue to believe it. Many people believe that. The job could have been done years ago, but each time the fire, when they were excavating it and they got right to it and could have finished the job, they conveniently ran out of money. In 1962, for want of twenty thousand dollars, that fire could have been dug out; in 1965, for want of fifty thousand dollars, that fire could have [been] put out; and again in 1969—"

Tom had mustered conviction with each example, tapping reservoirs of indignation. Before his crescendo, the aborted 1969 trench, Koppel interrupted.

"All right, Mr. Larkin," he said. "I'm afraid we haven't run out of money, but we have run out of time."

Oh hell, Tom thought. *I was just getting started.*

CHAPTER EIGHT

Which Side Are You On?

ONE WEEK AFTER *Nightline,* a demolition crew descended on Wood Street. About four blocks west of Helen Womer's and Mary Lou's, where Hammey Chapman's hill punctuated the western skyline near St. Ignatius Cemetery, a bulldozer roamed, ramming the Chapman homestead into rubble. Within hours, workers had pulverized the wood frame duplex, altering the vista from Helen's and Mary Lou's front porches for the first time in more than a decade. At a borough council meeting on Election Day eve, Helen issued a plea for unity, urging Concerned Citizens and the rest of the borough to meet, without the news media, and swap views like adults. "United we stand, divided we stand still," she said. "We all started off on the wrong foot and we've been pulling farther apart. Unless we are unified, we'll never get anything accomplished."

Helen did not, however, soften her stance about her own predicament. Rather, she attacked the government, saying officials had violated her constitutional rights by seeking to evict her and seizing the twenty-seven homes. In an appeal to her Depression-baby counterparts, she harkened back to the 1940s, when the War Department staged anthracite production rallies and miners posed for publicity photographs with uniformed soldiers hundreds of feet underground. With the good-versus-evil patriotism of a newsreel, she cast herself as the Resistance, evoking the horrors of Nazi Germany. Officials must have derived some sinister satisfaction from spray-painting 2's on homes before demolishing them, she said, equating the numerals with Gestapo tactics. "We will be a fortress until we are forced out."

The following day, when Tom Larkin scored six write-in votes for mayor, one of the local newspapers drafted an editorial lauding Helen's overture. "The dissension in the community gives the bureaucrats a ready-made excuse for doing nothing to resolve the problem," the *News-Item* said. "When all is said and done, there is probably more agreement among Centralians than they all believe."

THE HOUSE APPROVED the borehole project in mid-November, earmarking $850,000 in the Interior Department's $7.5 billion appropriations bill for exploratory drilling and related work in Centralia. Federal officials, who had opposed the study from the outset, scurried behind the scenes to minimize their defeat. First, they proposed a more limited effort than drilling around the mine fire's perimeter, confining exploration to the borough's southern and western boundaries, where the fire jeopardized populated neighborhoods. A few days later, they floated a plan to cancel their gas surveillance program at the end of the year, removing carbon monoxide monitors from roughly twenty homes. By month's end, long-smoldering intramural friction spilled onto the pages of *The New York Times Magazine,* where an anonymous Bureau of Mines scientist said what Secretary Watt had strained to avoid acknowledging: The Centralia blaze ranked as the country's worst underground mine fire.

Two days later, a Harrisburg reporter approached Watt during a Republican governors' conference in New Orleans, quizzing him about Centralia. The mine fire posed "no threat to health and safety" of the borough's residents, Watt said. He predicted the blaze would eventually burn itself out. In the meantime, the fire remained the state's problem, with federal liability confined to the million-dollar buyout and the relocation of the twenty-seven families. For days,

Watt's remarks ricocheted across the wires and radio airwaves, sparking a spate of reactions and editorials, from Shamokin to Harrisburg and Philadelphia. Governor Thornburgh, whose reelection prospects pivoted on his fidelity to Reagan administration policy, declined to comment.

Tom Larkin, who toiled under no such burden, unleashed in an interview with a local reporter, challenging Watt to venture to the coal region and inspect the blaze himself. "Let him put his money where his mouth is and come here and prove the fire is so deep it will never harm us," Larkin said. "Let him come here and say that when somebody dies." As for Thornburgh, Larkin decried the governor's silence. "Where's his backbone?" Larkin said. "It's about time the governor of Pennsylvania stops letting Jimmy Watt push him around."

The next day, Thornburgh's office released the text of a letter to Watt, casting the secretary's gaffe as a misunderstanding.

FOUR WEEKS after *Nightline,* the carbon monoxide monitor in Catharene and Peacho's living room registered 100 parts per million, almost three times the government's safety threshold. It rated as her highest reading ever, eclipsing her previous record, 70 parts per million, attained only a few weeks earlier. Still, gas emissions ranked as only one of her concerns.

About a block away, where demolition crews had razed the houses in which the Lambs, Oakums, and Andrades once lived, a 16-acre grassland beckoned, riddled with cave-ins and the potential for more. Katrina, a three-year-old toddler, could wander down there, across the street from the yard where Todd Domboski fell. If Catharene's attention wavered for an instant, she might not notice in time to stop her. When Catharene pestered officials to enclose the 16-acre area behind a fence, however, Mary Lou and Helen objected, fearing a perimeter would only attract photographers and video crews trawling for sensationalism.

Even worse, when cold weather descended and Catharene and Peacho shut the windows, Katrina and Angel started battling a string of illnesses, from colds and coughs to vomiting, watery eyes, and runny noses. Catharene knew from babysitting her younger siblings that most infants rebounded from similar ailments in a matter of days. Her daughters, however, did not. Their symptoms lingered without improvement, like chronic maladies. At night, Catharene lay sleepless. Still, on one front she consoled herself: Their bedrooms, upstairs at the back of the house, remained gas-free.

ON DECEMBER 7, 1981, Tom Larkin emerged from a bus at the intersection of State and North Third streets in Harrisburg. Ahead, atop five flights of stairs, loomed the Pennsylvania Capitol, a five-story Renaissance edifice chiseled from Vermont granite with a 272-foot dome blanketed in avocado-green tiles. President Theodore Roosevelt, who dedicated the structure in 1906, pronounced it the handsomest building he had ever seen. Locally, where the statehouse dominated the skyline, presiding over a thicket of government office buildings and the state library and archives, citizens regarded it as a citadel of graft: Construction costs consumed only $4 million of the $13 million project, with much of the remainder siphoned into furnishings, such as mahogany desks from Belize and a $278 filing cabinet purchased for $2,470.

From the sidewalk along North Third Street, Tom embarked on his journey, trudging uphill in his *Good Morning America* suit. Back at the turn of the century, planners and architects had interspersed a series of plazas among the steps leading up to the statehouse, with granite benches grouped along the edges like modular sofas. For inspiration and context, the seating nooks bore inscribed quotations from Pennsylvania patriots and luminaries, from Benjamin Franklin and Benjamin Rush, signers of the Declaration of Independence, to Lucretia Mott, a Quaker abolitionist and suffragette. On the plaza between the first and second flight of stairs, about twenty feet above street level, one perch featured a reflection saying, "There is a time to pray and a time to fight."

At Tom's back, receding from view, lay State Street's Victorian brick façades, where lobbyists and trade associations housed their offices, like a Mount Everest base camp for professional influence peddlers. Two blocks closer to the Susquehanna River, at the corner of Church Street, the Romanesque cupolas and copper-topped dome of St. Patrick's Cathedral towered over the neighborhood. Here, Tom knew, the Harrisburg diocese housed its operations, from AA and CCD to public relations and social justice, an amalgam of the secular and the sectarian that resonated with subtext. A few days earlier, the Most Reverend Bishop Joseph T. Daley, a Girardville native who headed the Harrisburg diocese, had routed a letter to Thornburgh urging him to dispatch his lieutenant governor to confer with Concerned Citizens. In a snub evoking their treatment at the Interior Department, however, Tom and his colleagues scored an appointment only with one of Thornburgh's surrogates, the director of the Pennsylvania Emergency Management Agency.

At the summit, Tom filed through the visitors' entrance, two massive bronze doors topped by a bust of William Penn. On the left door, beneath carvings devoted to the Declaration of Independence and state history, a mining tableau showed five miners in an underground chute loading coal chunks into a wooden buggy. Inside, the rotunda unfolded before him, an array of gilt, marble, and Corinthian columns inspired by the U.S. Capitol and St. Peter's Basilica in Rome.

Straight ahead, a double staircase dominated the space, an expanse of polished white marble. The stairway, patterned after a similar structure in the Paris Opéra, swept toward the governor's second-floor office, where visitors tarried in a wood-paneled reception area designed to evoke an English manor. Overhead, at the base of the dome, turn-of-the-century artists had painted murals honoring Enlightenment themes, from religious liberty and science to the spirit of light, with draped figures rendered in medieval-manuscript jewel tones. High overhead, the rotunda soared more than twenty-five stories, dotted with alternating bands of red and blue, carved eagles and flower inlays, dusted with gold trim. Even the crimson terrazzo floor added ornamentation, with more than three hundred mosaic tile inserts depicting state iconography and fauna, from Native Americans, covered wagons, and ironworkers to bats, bears, and squirrels.

Just after ten A.M., Tom stepped up to a lectern at the base of the staircase, flanked by brass art nouveau lanterns, recessed statuary nooks, and a white marble railing. Behind him, off to the side, hovered a few of his colleagues, including Dave and Joan Girolami, who had again donned suits and clipped red ribbons onto their lapels. Eleanor O'Hearn huddled with them, brandishing one of the group's "Hell on Earth" bumper stickers, holding it over her head for the cameras. About half a dozen reporters, representing local news outlets and wire services, stood a few feet in front of him. State government workers and tourists milled in the background near the entrance, pausing to watch and listen. Across the rotunda, one mural depicted the Spirit of Vulcan while another traced the arc of Tom's past and present, from seminary to Concerned Citizens, with an inscription saying, "For religion, pure religion, I say standeth not in wearing of a monk's cowl but in righteousness, justice and well doing."

But Tom, who learned about the press conference during the bus ride from Centralia, did not pillage his surroundings for inspiration. Instead, he riffed on a thought that had popped into his head as he approached the lectern: *All this Republican clout, and still nothing*. As a thesis, it squared with his goal for the day: goading Thornburgh into standing up to Watt. It also echoed his belief that the time for nuance, including the dance he had performed on *Nightline,* had ended. Centralia had a Republican governor, two Republican senators, and a Republican congressman, he said. A Republican president occupied the White House. Still, Pennsylvania had not persuaded the Interior Department, headed by a Republican appointee, to extinguish the mine fire.

"The state and federal government have made a Ping-Pong ball out of Centralia," he said. "There are people's lives at stake here."

A FEW DAYS after Christmas, a mine inspector found low-level carbon monoxide, between 8 and 12 parts per million, in the nursery where Angel slept. This time, the pediatrician did not equivocate: He instructed Catharene to leave the house. She told Peacho, insisting they flee, and he agreed, but they hadn't saved enough money to purchase a larger home somewhere else. They still couldn't afford to abandon their investment on Locust Avenue. So once again they sought refuge with his parents until spring, moving back into the home where Peacho was raised and his father was born.

Meanwhile, Thornburgh, Watt, and their agents squabbled about Centralia, from the scope of the borehole project to who would shoulder future mine fire containment costs. Watt, who sat on the president's fiscal accountability commission, said his agency would gauge the most prudent expenditure of the $850,000 appropriation, from exploratory drilling to related work. In a letter to Thornburgh, who embraced Reagan's "new federalism," he dismissed the controversy over his New Orleans remarks, calling the tumult an "unfortunate misunderstanding."

Thornburgh responded with a counteroffer, like a lawyer posturing before settlement. Five years after federal lawmakers created the AML fund, compelling coal operators to underwrite the industry's environmental cleanup costs by taxing their revenues, he proposed reviving the pre-1977 statutory scheme. Under his proposal, the state would assume 25 percent of the tab and the federal government would finance the rest.

Federal officials, however, did not need to commission an $850,000 study to divine the fire's location. The answer lay in the interoffice mail. Throughout the winter, federal technicians tramped across Locust Mountain with thermometers and gas detection equipment, probing underground voids installed years earlier to monitor the fly-ash barrier. Months before the new study began, their routine surveillance yielded the prognosis. On the highway between Centralia and Byrnesville, a 140-foot expanse of dry pavement had emerged, where elevated underground temperatures melted snow at the surface. Temperatures spiked at 32 of the 144 sites they canvassed, almost 25 percent. Still, in public, officials minimized the evidence, saying cave-ins and steam along the highway near Byrnesville bore no relation to the mine fire.

In Centralia, federal technicians routed copies of their reports and analysis to the new borough council president, John Koschoff, the twenty-five-year-old son of a former councilman. But Koschoff, who instructed federal officials to funnel all correspondence through him, relished the trappings of power, not the paperwork. Moments after assuming office, he dismissed the borough solicitor, a Mount Carmel lawyer who had finessed Centralia's legal matters for ten years, and replaced him with his brother-in-law, Wayne Rapkin, a workmen's compensation lawyer. And Koschoff, who hailed from the basin, beyond the reach of the mine fire and its emissions, failed to disclose the borehole data to the voters who elected him.

On February 14, 1982, while Concerned Citizens staged a rally marking the first anniversary of Todd Domboski's rescue, Watt released a report to the president, entitled "A Year of Change," chronicling his first twelve months at Interior. In a letter summarizing his tenure, he touted his success at nudging the agency's land and resource management policies from "far left field," where he had found them, deemphasizing conservation and boosting domestic energy production. "As we move the pendulum to the center of the mainstream of the environmental movement, we will find the balance that is necessary for a strong and vibrant America," he said.

A few weeks later, in early March, Interior backed the state's version of the borehole project, agreeing to drill around the perimeter and chart the fire's coordinates. Thornburgh issued a press release heralding the compromise as a first step in the battle against the blaze. Watt opted not to comment. His agency had barred officials from speaking to reporters, particularly about the mine fire, and ceased issuing news releases, citing budgetary constraints.

In a separate development, though, the Environmental Protection Agency canceled a twenty-thousand-dollar research grant to measure carbon monoxide levels in Centralia residents' blood. The inquiry, designed by University of Pittsburgh scientists who pioneered public health research near Three Mile Island, had received preliminary approval a few months earlier. Still, the EPA, headed by Watt's fellow Coors protégée Ann Gorusch, said the proposal exceeded the agency's jurisdiction: If tests revealed elevated carbon monoxide levels among Centralia residents, the EPA lacked regulatory power to assist them.

During an interview with a local reporter, Tom Larkin scoffed at the agency's rationale. "I wonder if James Watt got to EPA," he said.

AS THE SPRING of 1982 progressed, the outlook in Centralia deteriorated. One of the federal technicians developed symptoms of carbon monoxide poisoning after a day of uncapping boreholes and taking gas and temperature measurements. Outside Mary Lou's house, where the M-2 borehole sat about a hundred feet from her front porch, gases a hundred feet underground hovered at 196 degrees. In May, the temperature inside the void rocketed past 500 degrees, a 300 degree hike in one month. Near Byrnesville, the temperature inside one borehole, the X-31, soared by 494 degrees in one month, from 190 to 684 degrees, liquefying three 500 degree thermometers and notching a sevenfold increase in one year.

The data suggested the mine fire had splintered and strengthened, like a thunderstorm spawning mini-tornadoes. On the Buck vein's south dip, the blaze was barreling down the mountain toward Mary Lou's hometown. Along the north dip, the fire had continued its assault on Wood Street and Locust Avenue, coursing into borough limits, despite Helen's protestations to the contrary, just outside and underneath Mary Lou's house. Secretary Watt, meanwhile, reconfigured the Interior Department's seal, realigning the American buffalo, whose head had faced to the left for 133 years, and flipping it to the right.

Helen and Mary Lou, of course, learned of the mine fire's encroachment anyway. Mary Lou, who still crept around her neighborhood with a thermometer and a notepad, recorded measurements mirroring the federal results. Helen, who notched her own daily gas logs, had long ago cultivated a friendship with the technician who culled the borehole intelligence. Before long, she began hectoring officials, urging them to reinforce the fly-ash barrier.

When officials converged on borough hall to explain the borehole project, Helen sat up straight in her chair, flanked by Mary Lou and Elaine Jurgill, and said the study, with its two-year timetable, would not protect them. "We still have to wait one or two years before they do a thing, and in the meantime we are agonizing," she said in an on-camera interview after the meeting. "The fire still burns unabated."

Three days later, at 7:55 A.M., she phoned the Office of Surface Mining about a depression in her backyard where, she said, steam had spewed for the past three years. She asked if she could fill the cavity and bill the federal government. The staffer who fielded her query, dutifully logging the call, told her the agency did not operate that way.

Still, temperatures and carbon monoxide levels in the boreholes dotting Locust Mountain continued to skyrocket. By July, the M-2 outside Mary Lou's house climbed to 522 degrees, the borough's highest recorded temperature, and the X-31 in Byrnesville soared to 810 degrees, the area's peak reading. Meanwhile, the AML fund, at least on paper, groaned with cash.

Since its inception in 1978, the fund had snared approximately $900 million in revenues from coal producers, including $102 million from Pennsylvania operators alone. In 1982, while Watt and Thornburgh negotiated the $850,000 borehole project, the Office of Surface Mining authorized almost $100 million for emergency and high-priority abatement projects nationwide, including $34 million in grants and outright assistance for Pennsylvania. Other than the one million dollars for relocating the twenty-seven families, however, the largesse did not trickle down to Centralia. In the interim, Watt had stalled, biding his time before endorsing Pennsylvania's long-foundering abandoned-mine reclamation plan. When he did, and the state achieved what the surface mining act called primacy—eligibility to tap into an estimated $40-million share of accumulated AML revenues—Interior could transfer all future Centralia costs to the state.

In mid-July, Watt presided over a ceremony marking his approval of Pennsylvania's abandoned-mine reclamation program, the twenty-first of twenty-four states to qualify. Five years after the surface mining act's passage, one of the country's most prolific coal-producing states—and one of a handful most in need of cleanup benefits—stood to realize its promise. Thornburgh's office, closing in on the final months of his bid for a second term, lauded the milestone as another victory for Reagan-era federalism, even though the underlying legislation dated back to the Carter presidency. With the governor running for reelection during a recession, and statewide and national unemployment rates approaching 10 percent—the highest since the Depression—the mine fire plummeted into obscurity. Pennsylvania slotted its initial windfall, approximately $11 million, for subsidence control and exploratory drilling projects near Scranton and Pittsburgh. Centralia, with its eight hundred predominantly Democratic votes, received nothing.

SIX WEEKS LATER, Mary Lou flipped through *The Catholic Witness,* a weekly tabloid from the Harrisburg diocese. On Fridays, when she and scores of other St. Ignatius parishioners ambled into the post office to collect their mail, they retrieved a copy, the *Time* or *Newsweek* of the capital-area faithful. Elaine Jurgill consulted the *Witness* for its lists of banned movies and books, enforcing the prohibitions in her home. Mary Lou tended to skim the broadsheet, glancing at car ads, novenas, and announcements, from first communions, confirmations, and weddings to priests and nuns celebrating jubilees, the twenty-fifth and fiftieth anniversaries of their vows. She didn't digest and memorize the contents so much as patrol them, on guard for something she didn't like.

This week, on August 27, Mary Lou's gaze settled on an article about the Campaign for Human Development, the church's nationwide antipoverty and social justice program headquartered in Washington, D.C. There, next to a photograph of a vent pipe near the Odd Fellows Cemetery, with the profile of St. Ignatius Church in the background, the third paragraph dealt a blow: Concerned Citizens, one of only twelve organizations in a seven-state region, had received a thirty-thousand-dollar grant. Her own church had turned on her, showering riches on the group that wanted to obliterate Centralia. Now they had everything.

Mary Lou, of course, needed no primer on the Campaign for Human Development, whose promotional literature said, "If you want peace, work for justice." In November, parishes across the country sponsored a special CHD collection, with 25 percent slated to remain in the diocese for local initiatives and the remainder funneled to the U.S. Conference for Catholic Bishops to underwrite projects by low-income groups, from economic development to education and housing. Since the program's creation in 1970, when bishops embraced the ethos of the 1960s and the antipoverty cause, it had collected almost $97 million from American Catholics, making it the hierarchy's primary funding vehicle. Mary Lou, who dropped a few extra bills into the CHD collection plate, from twenty to twenty-five dollars, had assumed her contribution helped relieve suffering among the poor: inner-city dwellers locked into public housing projects. She had not envisioned her pledge dollars boomeranging back to Centralia, let alone endorsing Concerned Citizens.

Until now, Catholic officialdom had maintained a façade of neutrality about the mine fire, at least in St. Ignatius parish. Father Suknaic, who curated his own scrapbook of mine fire articles, knew his flock had splintered. He had provoked outrage simply by announcing from the pulpit one Sunday his decision to stop selling cemetery plots.

In private, he confided to parishioners, including Tom Larkin, that he could not afford to take sides.

By 1982, of course, Father Hayes had receded into memory, as had his sermons during the 1902 strike urging miners to denounce the union and return to work. Father McDermott's stance against the Mollys still resonated, in part because residents had revived and retooled the legend of his curse, saying he had condemned the town itself, not just two parishioners, to burn. In the Reagan era, long after the collieries closed, St. Ignatius's pastor ducked the most compelling issues his parishioners confronted: the future of their homes and parish. His flock, with few exceptions, internalized the message, equating dissent and activism with heresy, on a par with divorce, failing to baptize a newborn baby, or eating meat on a Lenten Friday. In the year and a half since Todd Domboski's near fatality, residents who griped about Concerned Citizens had taken solace in the pastor's silence. When *The Catholic Witness* trumpeted the grant, the wall of separation between church and mine fire collapsed.

ABOUT A WEEK LATER, Tom's phone rang, rousting him from slumber.

His second-floor bedroom, nestled at the back of the house, overlooked an alley. Light filtered in through the window, the blue-gray glare of a streetlight. He knew, without switching on the lamp or checking a clock, that he had awakened before sunrise, somewhere between two and three A.M.

Tom rolled over and reached toward the nightstand, a mahogany-colored table with a wood-and-brass lamp and an olive-green rotary dial phone from his parents' bedroom arranged across the surface. Most evenings, after he finished reading and flipped off the light, he slept straight through to morning. Even the sirens of fire trucks summoned to douse a nearby blaze failed to rouse him. At this number, 875-2999, callers had a way of jarring him from sleep by accident when their fingers slipped a digit and misdialed the exchange for Ashland Hospital, 875-2000. Often they requested the nurses' station. Once he fielded two calls from the same guy, asking for a hospital room. When the caller phoned a third time, requesting the same patient, Tom said, Oh, him—he was discharged.

Since *Nightline,* however, Tom had heard from a different class of dialers: those who hung up after he answered. Once or twice a week this happened, as if by script. The phone rang somewhere between midnight and dawn. When he answered, he heard a click and a dial tone.

Tom plucked the receiver from the cradle and cupped it to his ear.

From the recesses of the earpiece, he heard a raspy voice, one he didn't recognize, as if whoever had phoned him was masking his or her identity.

That grant you're getting, the caller said. You'll never live to spend it.

Tom slammed the receiver back onto the phone.

TWO WEEKS LATER, Tom drove to Harrisburg to collect a $7,500 check payable to Concerned Citizens: the grant's first installment. A photographer tarried nearby snapping photographs as Tom conferred with a diocesan official. In an effort to stem criticism in Centralia, including protest letters that had streamed into the bishop's office, *The Catholic Witness* ran another story a few days later, with Tom defending the group's motives and intentions as well as his own. "The money will be used for a good purpose," he said. "I want to see the town survive."

For Tom, who had devoted much of the past eighteen months to Concerned Citizens, investing his energy, intellect, and hours of his spare time, this recognition should have capped his activism career. He knew the Catholic Church shrouded its decisions in secrecy, like the Central Intelligence Agency and the National Security Administration. Priests cycled in and out. Schools closed, including St. Ignatius. If parishioners disliked their pastor, they hoped for better luck the next time. If they objected to a decision or policy, from the elimination of Latin Mass to allowing nuns to don street clothes in lieu of habits, they resigned themselves to living within its dictates. In a regime centered on the Vatican, with orders flowing from the pope, few expected transparency. With this grant, however, the bishops had broken cover, stamping a seal of approval on Concerned Citizens.

Tom had suspected all along that the grant would spark controversy: Thirty thousand dollars represented a windfall in Centralia, three times the median income of its residents and roughly four times borough council's monthly tax revenues and spending budget. Bootsie McGinley, Centralia's chief of police, netted about $700 a month for his services, after taxes, and Peacho's father, the borough's maintenance worker, pocketed about $600. Still, residents did not think they lived in poverty, especially with the borough's high homeownership rates conferring the aura of middle-class stability. More than 90 percent of Centralia families owned their homes.

Even Tom balked at admitting, during the grant application process, that his minimum-wage earnings of $3.35 per hour fell below poverty guidelines. He didn't feel poor; his lifestyle just didn't require a lot of disposable income. He paid $115 every month for rent and divided the rest among utilities, gas, groceries, the collection plate, an occasional movie, and twenty-cent draft beers at Mary Wolchansky's bar, across the street from his apartment.

The late-night phone call had spooked him, of course, sending him downstairs in the dark for a cigarette. After mulling the threat, he vowed not to buckle, because he knew he was right. Throughout the borough, however, he sensed a hardening of positions, as if someone had painted a line down Locust Avenue, asking, like the 1930s anthem from Harlan County, Kentucky, "Which Side Are You On?" John Koschoff, borough council president, cornered a delegation from the diocese and barred Concerned Citizens from convening in the municipal building, forcing them into exile in the St. Ignatius School basement, at a rental cost of twenty-five dollars per meeting. Helen Womer hosted a handful of evening gatherings at her house, by invitation only, with guests including Mary Lou and Tony.

But even Helen Womer, with her arsenal of telephone numbers, could not derail the Campaign for Human Development. Father Suknaic reported to the bishop, who reported to the cardinal, and in this case the hierarchy endorsed Concerned Citizens. Bishop Daley, who had heard from several St. Ignatius parishioners about the church's failure to respond to the mine fire, had investigated Centralia for himself. More than a year earlier, before deciding to shutter St. Ignatius School, he had attended a meeting at borough hall and conferred with Ed Narcavage, the mine inspector, who knelt and kissed his ring. The bishop had even dispatched a community organizer from the Harrisburg diocese to work with Concerned Citizens, coaching them about lobbying Washington and Harrisburg politicians.

Still, Helen could shatter the grantee's credibility in the borough. In late September, she scoured her scrapbooks for newspaper articles quoting Tom, Dave Lamb, and Joan Girolami, plucking comments suggesting they favored relocation. Two days later, on September 28, 1982, she marshaled her evidence into a two-page dossier of transgressions, arranged on legal-sized paper. At the top, in capital letters, she typed and underlined a heading: "Profile of Centralia Concerned Citizens." Underneath, she unspooled the remarks, in chronological order: a handful of demands Tom Larkin penned for the Harrisburg trip, Dave telling a *Catholic Witness* reporter he thought the town was doomed and should be sold to a foreign country, a quotation from Joan Girolami saying she thought the government would eventually have to relocate everyone.

"And that's the kind of talk that infuriates the other side in the dispute," Helen typed. "The other side is not organized, but its adherents agree that talk of relocation is PREMATURE AND DESTRUCTIVE. They do not deny the fire, but they don't think it's wise to make hasty decisions."

LATER THAT EVENING, Tom Larkin knew he had lost control. From his seat at a banquet table in the St. Ignatius School basement, usually host to fish fries, wedding receptions, and funeral dinners, he beheld the opposition: about two dozen residents, including Helen Womer, Mary Lou Gaughan, and John Koschoff. They had packed into metal folding chairs arranged in rows before him, like witnesses to a hanging.

Up front, seated with Tom and his fellow officers, emissaries from the diocese and the Campaign for Human Development had converged for a public relations blitz. The guests, with their backgrounds in community organizing and consensus building, assumed Centralians could, with some prodding, bury their differences and unite around Tom. Unbeknownst to the visitors, however, Helen Womer had distributed her profile to a handful of allies before the meeting. Several minutes into the meeting, she appealed to Father Francis Kumontis, the diocese's vicar for social welfare.

"Father, the overwhelming mistrust that the people have of the Concerned Citizens is to me the reason for our division in the community," she said, sounding as if she were reading a statement. "Please believe me, I am not trying to cause more divisiveness. I am just presenting *facts*."

Helen was, of course, seeking to sow dissension. Her profile alone enumerated almost two dozen reasons to revile Tom, who, as she pointed out, had only returned to Centralia in 1980. But to preserve her aura of statesmanship, at least among the outside dignitaries, she deferred to John Koschoff, who had no such reputation to uphold. Koschoff, a near look-alike for *Animal House*'s Kent Dorfman, with aviator glasses and a face still padded by baby fat, picked up where Helen left off, reading from a copy of her profile and demanding to see a copy of the grant application. Tom, who knew the paperwork would inflame Koschoff, with its references to borough council's ineffectiveness, offered instead to share the grant objectives. Father Kumontis praised the compromise, touting Tom's effort to foster trust. Koschoff rebuffed the overture.

"Father, we're the council of this community," said Koschoff. "I think you should build up the trust in us, too." His voice, with its flat affect, did not command respect. Nor did it convey deference. The priest hedged, musing out loud about whether the Church was accountable to civil authorities.

"Civil authorities?" said Koschoff. "They should be accountable to all the people in our town."

IN EARLY OCTOBER, local newspapers broke the news to area residents, five months after federal technicians notified their superiors: The mine fire had surged toward Byrnesville and triggered 500 degree temperatures outside Mary Lou's house. Catharene walked to the government trailer, asked for the borehole data, and studied it herself. There, sprinkled across the handwritten charts and columns, lay the proof. Koschoff, who should have served the entire community, had blundered on a scale she couldn't fathom. Either he neglected to read the intelligence that officials routed to him, misread it, or failed to heed its import. Whatever the explanation, she blamed laziness, an affront to her work ethic.

At the next borough council meeting, on October 4, Catharene demanded Koschoff's resignation. Helen Womer leaped to his defense, saying borough council was running better than ever. His fellow council members, who directed officials to route them all future mine fire data, did not share her assessment. Koschoff had concealed the reports from them, too.

Koschoff retaliated at the next meeting, ordering his colleagues to read the borough's incoming and outgoing correspondence out loud, word for word, including a recent *Philadelphia Inquirer* article about the mine fire. One of the councilmen erupted, decrying the spectacle, and several fled the room to caucus in private. Koschoff's brother-in-law, Wayne Rapkin, stormed out, too, followed by members of Concerned Citizens. When the three-and-a-half-hour session adjourned, leaving only a handful of council members and local reporters in borough hall, Koschoff lingered to apologize to the media. He had devoted so much time to this job, he said, and the activists were attacking him and accusing him falsely of withholding information.

A LITTLE MORE than twenty-four hours later, Dave Lamb heard pounding: *Thwack. Thwack. Thwack.*

Inside his bedroom, fronting Locust Avenue, he glanced at the clock. The time, etched in digital orange, was 4:41 A.M.

Thwack. Thwack. Thwack.

Dave slid out of bed, pulled on jeans and a T-shirt, and ran down the hallway, his bare feet padding across the shag carpeting. At the end of the hall, where visitors entered through the mudroom, a flight of wooden stairs angled up from the parking lot, on the outside of the building. In the kitchen, just before the mudroom, he lifted a gold damask curtain—lined, so customers couldn't see if he was home and pester him after hours. He peered outside. One flight down, across Center Street, he spotted a parked car. In the darkness at the top of the steps, he discerned the figure of a man rapping on the locked screen door. He thought it might be a cop.

Dave opened the door.

Your place is on fire, the visitor said.

What?

Your place is on fire, he repeated. There's flames in the showroom.

Dave flew down the steps. He yanked open the door to the shop and a wall of white smoke, stretching from the floor to the ceiling, rushed toward him. The stench of combustion hung in the air, thick and acrid. He slammed the door and raced upstairs, down the hallway, and into the bedroom where his eleven-year-old son lay sleeping, and told him to get dressed. There's a fire downstairs, Dave said. Wait here and I'll be right back.

Dave, who spent his Vietnam tour as a Marine aviation base fireman in South Carolina, responded almost without thinking, as if it were 1968 and a fighter jet had crashed at the end of the runway. He slipped on his shoes, grabbed a flashlight, and ran. Downstairs, he pulled open the door to the shop and pointed a beam of light toward the interior, but still, with the smoke, he couldn't see beyond the threshold. He plunged inside, with fumes searing his eyes, and carved his path from memory.

About ten feet inside the showroom, where a plate-glass window overlooked Center Street, he spotted four clusters of flames, like campfires, leaping about two feet high. Just inside the window, a few feet from the blaze, six motorcycles sat in a row, facing the street, with gasoline pooled in their tanks. Cardboard cases of motor oil and transmission fluid lay interspersed among the motorcycles, stacked in pyramids: three at the base, two at the center, and one on top. Scattered across the display floor he had a few more motorcycles, with gasoline in their tanks, and an inventory of waxes and paints: a cauldron of volatility, about ten feet beneath the bedroom where he had left his son. Any second, the bikes could blow up.

In the Marines, Dave had braved aviation wreckage in a fireproof suit, boots, and helmet, hosed down the fuselage with chemical foam, and emerged unscathed. Now, clad in street clothes, he fended for himself, drawing on the same instincts. He lunged at the flames with a fire extinguisher and stomped them with his feet. He heaved motorcycles off to the side before the fuel tanks ignited, and shoved crates of motor oil out of the way. After an interval that felt like eons, a blur of impulse and adrenaline, he realized he had extinguished the blaze. He opened the doors onto Center Street and Locust to clear the smoke.

Then he remembered his son.

Dave sped upstairs and into the apartment. Dave Junior was standing in the bedroom in his coat, staring out the window onto Center Street. Dave ushered him out, nudging him onto the outside steps from the mudroom. As they climbed down the stairs, the Centralia fire truck pulled up, with its red lights flashing. Dave and his son edged around the store along Center Street, past the display window, where a hole the size of a softball had ruptured the glass about four feet above the sidewalk.

INSIDE THE SHOP later that morning, after the smoke dissipated, Dave sifted through the wreckage. About four feet from the Center Street window, where a row of racing trophies lined the windowsill, he found a two-inch shard of clear glass shaped like the bottom of a bottle. About three feet from the glass fragment, an archipelago of stains the diameter of a quarter stretched across the orange commercial-grade carpet where the edges had charred and peeled, exposing the plywood floor beneath. Piece by piece, Dave reconstructed the narrative, like the protagonists in the *Hardy Boys* mysteries he had devoured as a child: A sixteen-ounce Pepsi bottle filled with gasoline had landed under one of the motorcycles.

Outside, beyond the Four Corners, newspapers across the country and around the globe chronicled the happenings of November 1982, with Michigan convulsed by 16 percent unemployment and Moscow reporters speculating about Soviet president Leonid I. Brezhnev's health. Inside the Speed Spot, though, Dave had rocketed backward across the decades. Someone had tossed a Molotov cocktail into his showroom, harkening back to the reign of the Mollys, when incendiary devices detonated on scabs' front porches and breakers burst into flames in the middle of the night. Now, with class warfare turned on its head, the offense lay in speaking out and lobbying, not in crossing a picket line and reporting for duty during a strike. Dave had publicized the mine fire, agitated for accountability, and in the process earned the Catholic Church's imprimatur.

A week or two before, the phone had rung around seven P.M., when Dave stood alone at the counter after closing, tallying the day's receipts. On the other end, he heard a male voice, sounding as if the receiver was cloaked with a handkerchief. Mind your own business, the caller said. Stay out of other people's affairs. At the time, he had dismissed the episode as a prank. Now, in his display room, Dave linked the events: the phone call, the broken bottle, the gasoline splatters. Someone had sent him a message about Concerned Citizens, warning him to quit.

Whoever did this—and he had his suspicions—could have opted to hurl a cinder block through his window: an act of vandalism, pregnant with menace. Instead, they had tried to kill him, with his son sleeping right upstairs. By some combination of fate and luck, or perhaps even the bomb maker's incompetence, he had staved off disaster. Still, his entire store could have exploded into a fireball. He and his son could have slept right through it, perishing in the blaze, if a passing motorist hadn't pounded on his door, waking him and alerting him to his peril.

Dave chafed at the idea of quitting Concerned Citizens, a federation that had functioned as a family, a collection of outsiders in a town of insiders. He couldn't justify continuing, however, if his role jeopardized his safety and his children's lives. By any calculus, he couldn't afford the risk—not to defend a borough whose residents had shunned him since childhood, hadn't welcomed him on the Hill, and hadn't patronized his store, unless he counted their offspring who rode dirt bikes. Even the borough police and the volunteer fire department projected an air of detachment, a collective shrug of indifference, as if they had no idea how this had happened and no incentive to probe for clues.

He knew they wouldn't do anything about it. They didn't give a shit about him.

BOOTSIE MCGINLEY, the police chief, knew who did it: Mary Lou was certain of that. There's usually a squealer, someone who downs too many beers and blabs. In a town where residents knew what their neighbors ate for dinner, when they flushed the toilet, and when they dozed in front of the television, the Speed Spot firebombing proved no exception. Word of the culprit's identity rippled across the grapevine like gossip about an affair or an out-of-wedlock pregnancy. Still, insiders guarded the secret, especially from the state police, who packaged the bottle fragment as evidence and quizzed Dave about whether he had any enemies.

In private, Mary Lou knew many residents thought Dave, a loudmouth and a troublemaker, had gotten what he deserved. She tended to agree, although she didn't condone violence and would have renounced any group that did, including Helen's contingent. She and

Helen had enemies, too, and now, with the prospect of escalation, she wondered if her car or her house might be next. In the Speed Spot's display room, amid the singed carpeting and glass fragments, she deciphered the same message as Dave: an admonition to fold. If he and Tom Larkin disbanded their faction, so much the better.

CHAPTER NINE

This is Still America

CATHARENE SAT IN BED, balancing a notepad in her lap. Peacho snored quietly beside her. Katrina and Angel dozed in their rooms down the hall, where she had bedecked the carbon monoxide monitor with dinosaur figurines and dolls to make it look less scary. Catharene drew a line down the middle of the paper, fashioning two columns, one for pros and one for cons. Before dawn, when Peacho left for work and she plunged into the morning's activities, from mopping floors to feeding her daughters, she needed to make a decision.

A few hours earlier, at the first Concerned Citizens meeting since the firebombing, three of the five officers had resigned, including Joan Girolami and Eleanor O'Hearn, who cited circumstances beyond her control. Dave Lamb, who had holed up inside his store and apartment, didn't even attend. Tom Larkin, who had no advance knowledge of the announcements, struggled to project authority, thanking them for their service and calling for nominations to replace his colleagues. In the St. Ignatius School basement, after Tom adjourned the session, Joan Girolami burst into tears. Her resignation letter, typed on Concerned Citizens letterhead, said she had acted on her physician's advice.

After the meeting, Catharene huddled in the back of the room with her former schoolmate Trish Catizone, a twenty-year-old waitress just elected interim vice president. Catharene had anticipated Joan Girolami's bombshell; Joan had tipped her off. Neither she nor Trish had foreseen an officer-level exodus, and with the coalition spiraling into disarray, they grappled with the implications, as if they were White House interns and the president's cabinet had just departed en masse.

Marge Danner, the diocesan community organizer, approached Trish and Catharene, radiating gravity. She asked Catharene to assume a leadership role, as either president or treasurer. If a new management corps did not materialize, she said, the Campaign for Human Development would cancel the grant. Catharene asked Marge who else she was recruiting.

I don't have anyone else, she said.

Catharene, who had not envisioned herself in command, didn't know how to respond. She couldn't believe Marge had no other prospects. More than three hundred families still lived in Centralia; surely some other resident, even some other mother, could step forward now and save the grant. Catharene asked for time to mull the request. Marge agreed, but said she'd visit her at home the next day for her answer.

For almost two years, Catharene had toiled in the Concerned Citizens rank and file, a worker bee who skipped the Harrisburg and Washington, D.C., trips, opting to remain at home with her children. She had not crafted policy, issued directives, or participated in the grant application process. Tom, Joan, and Dave had, by their own admission, lived and breathed the mine fire, from collecting dues and tracking expenses to archiving correspondence and nurturing ties to the media and elected officials.

Catharene had, of course, injected creativity into the tasks she shouldered, from painting signs to carpooling neighbors. For borough hall meetings, she donned a mine fire T-shirt, a red chintz miniskirt, and red stiletto pumps and installed herself in the front row. Young men surfaced just to ogle; one even confessed he dreamed about her at night. Officials who spotted her, with her ankles crossed, called on her and answered her questions. She served, by design, as the antidote to Helen Womer's business suits, and since she had whittled away her pregnancy weight, she had no compunction about flaunting her physique, especially if it helped the cause.

Now, with the grant hanging in the balance, the diocese had asked her to salvage its Centralia mission, boosting her commitment, accountability, and profile, catapulting her from the back bench to the front office. In the current climate, of course, her confidence in her family's safety arose as an advantage. Even in a town brimming with hotheads, where brawls erupted at wedding receptions and Legion dances and Bootsie McGinley patrolled his beat with a pit bull, few had the temerity to risk inciting Peacho, whose recreation pivoted around target practice and bench presses. Nor did she feel intimidated by the so-called coal barons, some of whom counted among her parents' Ringtown neighbors, and she had long dismissed speculation about the industry's designs on Centralia's mineral rights. Strip-mining the basin, beset by the mine fire, struck her as a losing investment.

Still, as Catharene weighed her options, she realized she couldn't identify any other candidates for the post. Even before the firebombing, Concerned Citizens had consisted of Tom, Dave, Joan, Eleanor, and a handful of elderly residents and young mothers. Now, with the core disintegrating, she couldn't imagine anyone else wading into the maelstrom. She didn't want the federation to forfeit the grant, jeopardizing everything they had accomplished, especially when a cash infusion might, in the coming months, help shift momentum toward relocation.

The grant, she knew, could transform the activists, lending professionalism to their operations. They could open an office, hire a full-time staffer, and underwrite expenses, such as photocopying and phone calls and research. Until now, members had largely financed these costs on their own. Meanwhile, she could devote herself to her specialty, canvassing residents about their needs. When she switched off the reading lamp next to her bed, she had resolved to accept Marge's entreaty.

THE MORNING after his doctor's appointment, Tom Larkin sat down at his kitchen table with a mug of coffee at his elbow. Around his apartment, scattered amid his collection of elephant figurines, lay souvenirs of his stint with Concerned Citizens. His *People* magazine photograph, in a frame from the five-and-dime, sat on the dresser in his bedroom. In the living room, a Wilkes-Barre documentary filmmaker had interviewed him on the yellow and brown floral-patterned sofa. On his front porch railing, a hand-painted sign, recently photographed for a *Washington Post* article, bore the message "U.S. Dept. of Interior Plays Nero While Mine Fire Burns!"

A week ago, Tom had vomited blood. After his physician diagnosed a bleeding ulcer, Tom knew he had to resign. A new contingent of leaders had emerged to administer the grant, including Catharene Jurgill and Sam Garula, the Russian Orthodox priest. They had their own ideas and agenda, from helping residents cope with stress to building support for relocation, within and outside the community. They had even renamed Concerned Citizens, dubbing it the Centralia Committee for Human Development, reflecting their goal of focusing on the mine fire's psychic toll—and distancing themselves from their predecessors. Now, with the newcomers shunting him to the margins and stripping him of the camaraderie he had enjoyed with the original officers, he had to relinquish control.

Tom rolled a sheet of plain white paper into his Underwood. At the top, slightly off center, he typed his address. Underneath, he added the date: December 13, 1982.

"It is with deep regret," he typed, "and acting on the advice of a physician, that I offer my resignation as President of the Concernce [*sic*] Citizens." Tom, who had excelled in Miss Gillespie's typing class at Con-Cen High and typed the weekly bulletins in seminary, rarely made mistakes, especially in executing the coalition's name. As he composed this letter in his head and tapped it out on the keys, his eyes welled with tears. "It has been a great honor for me to serve as President of this fine Organization, and I feel a deep sense of personal loss, but circumstances prevent me from continuing," he wrote.

Tom's role with the activists had informed his existence for almost two years, lending him purpose he had not experienced since dropping out of seminary. Within the alliance, he had functioned as the parish priest, the center of the community. He had dedicated himself to the struggle, saving his hometown from the mine fire, like a second calling. Still, he saw no reason, in this missive, to belabor his medical condition, especially when he hadn't even confided the details to his brother. At least he could deprive his foes of the satisfaction of gleaning the extent to which their efforts had compromised his health.

Midway down the page, he started a new paragraph, his benedictory salvo. "Be assured that the organization will have my continued support," he typed, with tears rolling down his cheeks, "and I shall pray for the success of the organization."

TWO WEEKS LATER, Dave Lamb also wrote a resignation letter—a formality, since he had severed his ties to Concerned Citizens after the firebombing. In the interim, he barricaded himself inside his store and apartment with his gun collection, vowing—at least to himself—to hunker down in Centralia, proving that no one could force him out. Like Tom, though, he exited with grace, part apology and part pep talk.

"I will always feel that I did my best to help the residents of this community," he said. "Good luck to all and don't despair, help is just in sight."

WHEN CATHARENE heard the news, she couldn't breathe. Just outside of town, on the way to Byrnesville, a crack, measuring ten feet long had ruptured the highway. Twenty feet below the surface, where a natural gas pipeline coursed underneath Locust Avenue, temperatures had surged to 770 degrees. Borough officials had fretted about this contingency for years. Even Catharene, who knew the gas line ran about ten feet from her front porch, connecting to appliance hookups inside her home, had pondered the risk of cave-ins along the route. Until a local reporter phoned her in early January 1983, however, with word of the highway breach, she had not envisioned her home exploding with her and her daughters inside. When she did, she succumbed to a panic attack, just as she had in the delivery room moments after Angel's birth. One of her friends, another young mother, had walked over and slipped her a Valium.

Within days, the fissure widened, the pavement buckled, and the temperature in a nearby hole spiked from 140 to 770 degrees. Steam poured from the void and floated over Locust Mountain like a low-lying cloud, just beyond St. Ignatius Church. One of Catharene's neighbors said she couldn't see across Locust Avenue. State transportation officials closed the road, forcing Ashland-bound motorists to detour around Centralia. Penn Fuels, the pipeline's owner, said there was no risk of explosion, citing an emergency cutoff valve.

For Catharene, the incident shattered her last vestige of hope that officials somewhere might spring to her family's aid, as they had for the twenty-seven families. Now, with the state scurrying to reroute traffic and expedite road repairs, she reached a different conclusion: The bureaucracy reacted only to emergencies. As a corollary, she thought officials cared more about the highway than her well-being or her children's welfare. For months, Catharene had wondered whether Katrina and Angel might suffer long-term health consequences from fumes seeping into their home. Her daughters couldn't play in the yard, where the stench of smoke and sulfur hung in the air. With the pipeline at risk, she had no sense of safety inside her house or out. Relocation had arisen as an imperative, a feat to accomplish as soon as possible, especially since she and Peacho had saved enough money to tender a down payment on a home somewhere else—preferably not a coal town—and bolt.

Peacho agreed. He knew they had to flee, even if it meant starting over, writing off their Centralia real estate investment, and incurring a mortgage. In fact, he couldn't wait to leave. He even acquiesced to an interview together with Catharene, telling a reporter that the mental and physical health of his wife and children weren't worth all the money in the world.

At the end of January, Catharene and Peacho closed on a $34,000 four-bedroom Dutch Colonial in Frackville, across Broad Mountain, in a neighborhood that reminded her of Ringtown. Their house sat on a tree-lined street, flanked by brick single-family homes, with neighbors who made their living as lawyers, dentists, and doctors. Catharene's obstetrician lived down the block. Several of her high school friends also lived in the community, which teemed with young couples, children, and potential babysitters. She could stroll with Katrina and Angel to the town park, the town swimming pool, and the public library for story hour.

As soon as they moved, Catharene planned to quit the group.

HELEN WOMER, meanwhile, revived her plea for unity, spearheading a coalition, the United Centralia Area Mine Fire Task Force, in an attempt to salvage the town. About forty residents attended the first meeting at borough hall, cramming around conference tables to plot membership and mount a petition drive. With Concerned Citizens neutralized, Helen galvanized support from interest groups across the community, from the ambulance association and the American Legion to the senior citizen center and the teen club.

Within days, task force volunteers, including Mary Lou, had netted more than a thousand signatures on a petition to "Set Centralia Free in '83," calling for funds to combat the blaze. Helen mounted a press offensive, reaching out to reporters to publicize her efforts. She hoped to garner more than ten thousand signatures, from every state in the union, and deliver the petition to the president and Secretary Watt in Washington, she said in an interview.

On February 14, 1983, the second anniversary of Todd Domboski's plunge into his grandmother's backyard, the task force issued a press release touting its second initiative, Unity Day. The event, set to unfold on Sunday, March 6, heralded an ethos of cooperation unrivaled since the borough's centennial, with a fire engine parade, an interfaith service at St. Ignatius Church, and a cake-and-coffee social in the municipal building. "Centralia-Byrnesville will bloom again," the release said.

THREE WEEKS LATER, Mary Lou and Tony trekked over to the church from Wood Street. Gray skies hung over the basin, evoking November rather than early March, and at the top of town, fog and steam from the mine fire shrouded Locust Mountain. As Mary Lou approached St. Ignatius, scores of figures emerged into view, residents and officials milling in front of the parish, chatting and shaking hands. Sirens wailed from fire engines parked nearby. Church bells pealed, echoing across the mountaintop, to mark the commencement of an ecumenical service, the first of its kind at St. Ignatius, focused on reconciliation. Clusters of white balloons bracketed the entrance, where brides and first communicants, including Mary Lou, had filed in from the street over the decades, swathed in white gowns.

From the exterior, St. Ignatius conveyed a sense of humility and piety, with its stucco exterior and Romanesque silhouette, uncluttered by ornament or affectation. Inside the sanctuary, however, the coal miners who built it had lavished attention on detail, like a church in an Italian hill town bursting with Renaissance paintings. A red and white marble tile floor stretched from Locust Avenue to the altar in a pattern inlaid with alternating bands of opposites, like square bull's-eyes. Stained glass windows lined the perimeter of the nave, soaring almost from floor to ceiling, with intertwined borders and floral patterns wrought in red, blue, yellow, and green, like the Book of Kells. Corinthian columns supported the barrel-vaulted ceiling, and in the sacristy, under a gold leaf canopy, brass candlesticks gleamed against a moss-green backdrop, centered between side altars dedicated to the Sacred Heart and the Blessed Virgin. At the back, towering above the congregation, a rose window overlooked Locust Avenue, a kaleidoscope of patterns and primary hues.

Mary Lou settled into a pew, eyeing the dignitaries amassed up front, from local, county, and state officials to Congressman Frank Harrison, who had unseated Congressman Nelligan the previous fall. Even Tony, not one to gush in the presence of power, brightened a bit. Elaine Jurgill, whom Helen had drafted to coordinate the service, policed the aisles for infractions, counseling worshippers to leave their balloons outside. A typed program nestled inside a marigold-yellow cover listed the hymns and readings Elaine had selected, from "Faith of Our Fathers" and the first letter of Paul to the Corinthians, a paean to love's patience and kindness, to "God Bless America" and "Let There Be Peace on Earth," one of Mary Lou's favorites. When Father Suknaic stood to welcome the participants, he said he'd never seen the church so full.

FROM HIS SEAT in the middle of the nave, on the same side as the Blessed Virgin statue, Tom Larkin scanned the program. Helen and Elaine had tapped the borough's ministers to participate, from Catholic and Greek Catholic to Methodist. Only the Russian Orthodox priest, already disfavored for rescuing the grant and reviving the activists, had been denied a part. Tom, of course, noted his own absence from the roster. No one invited him to speak or sing, not even the Lord's Prayer, which he could have rendered with poignancy and solemnity befitting the occasion.

Tom knew his banishment had little to do with his vocal ability. He had been selected for a number of solos over the years, from his high school commencement ceremony to a few weddings and funerals. Helen and Elaine had rejected him, cut him out of the day's planning and execution, because of his affiliation with Concerned Citizens. They had consigned him to irrelevance, airbrushing him from the borough's history and ostracizing him in his own community. Inside the sanctuary where his family had worshipped for generations, he felt like an outsider. Forgive us our trespasses, indeed.

Mary Lou inched out of church after the recessional, an organ solo of "The Battle Hymn of the Republic" rendered by Elaine's daughter. Outside, a knot of people had formed, stretching up toward the rectory, where a shrine to the Blessed Virgin gazed out onto passersby. Volunteers fanned among the crowd, dispensing miniature American flags and Unity Day buttons and balloons emblazoned with the day's slogan, printed in red against a white background: "Set Centralia Free in '83." As Mary Lou hovered outside the church, mingling and chatting, mine fire vapors wafted into the crowd. She knew, with neighbors burying differences and politicians lending support, something would finally happen: The government would tackle the mine fire and she would be able stay in her home.

Around 2:30 P.M., the borough's police car launched the parade, rolling down Locust Avenue. The American Legion honor guard fell in behind, clustering around an American flag, with rifles slung across their shoulders and Unity Day buttons pinned to their lapels. A marching band from Mahanoy City's American Legion followed, bearing tubas and slide trombones. Senior citizens and middle-aged men and women surged forward alongside Cub Scouts from Mount Carmel, children pedaling bicycles, and teenagers in parkas. From sidewalk to sidewalk, a sea of bodies and balloons swamped Locust Avenue, from babies in strollers to garment workers, who brandished an American flag the size of a living room. About five hundred residents and civic leaders had materialized, some carrying signs inscribed with a range of messages, from "Centralia Needs More Than Lip Service" to "Burn Coal, Not People."

Mary Lou, clutching her balloon, landed somewhere in the midsection, behind the marching band and ahead of the fire truck and ambulance. As she swept downhill toward borough hall, American flags dangled from front porches along Locust Avenue. Red, white, and blue streamers fluttered from telephone poles. Elderly residents confined to home waved from their porches. If she marched down Fifth Avenue in the Saint Patrick's Day parade, she knew, it wouldn't be as nice as this.

CATHARENE JOINED the throngs inside and outside St. Ignatius, visiting with her old neighbors, greeting friends and acquaintances with hugs. Three weeks earlier, she and Peacho had decamped for Frackville, renting their semifurnished row home, with the living room sofa and Formica kitchen table, to a Penn State sociology professor who needed a Centralia beachhead while researching a book about the mine fire. Still, almost every day she found herself back in Centralia, where the successors to Concerned Citizens, CCHD, had set up an office in an abandoned store near the Four Corners and started lobbying the state to establish a mental health center in town.

For Catharene, who had already relocated, the sights and sounds of Unity Day validated her decision. All around her, from marchers spilling down Locust Avenue to the event's slogan, she saw a borough coalescing around a cause Helen Womer might not have anticipated: the need to flee, to escape homes the owners could not afford to relinquish and the prison, for some, of coexisting with toxic gases.

AFTER THE SERVICE, Tom Larkin visited his mother and father's grave site. Inside the gates of St. Ignatius Cemetery, about twenty feet from the entrance, Maggie's headstone occupied prime real estate, next to the paved walkway that sliced through the cemetery like a spine, shaded by a canopy of maples. Rows of headstones radiated outward from the path like side streets intersecting an avenue. Column after column, the gravestones bore Irish surnames such as McDonnell, McGinley, Rooney, and Ryan. Over and over, the miners' given names repeated: John, James, Michael, Thomas. In repose, they lay under blocks of gray and white granite, with adornment held to a minimum: a name, an engraved cross, a spray of flowers. In death, as in life, they lay next to their wives, whose names derived from a handful of saints, from Agnes and Catherine to Helen, Mary, and Margaret.

Tom pressed on, toward the northwest corner, about five rows from the back fence. His great-great-grandfather and great-grandfather lay closer to the southwest corner, with some of the oldest graves, weathered and worn by decades of exposure to rain, wind, and winter's near-permafrost. Five generations of Larkins had been interred here, including his sister, who died as an infant, and one of his brothers. On this hilltop, which resonated with their presence, he sensed he could hear them speaking, like the dead in Thornton Wilder's *Our Town,* scrutinizing the living from their hardbacked chairs above the village.

Reporters didn't badger Tom much anymore, but he had just confided in one about his connection to this cemetery, citing it as something he would miss if he ever left Centralia. This was his ancestors' home, where they endured emotionally and spiritually, and he called on them here at least once a week, tracing the practice to his Celtic roots. Legions of parishioners, he suggested, shared his outlook, an observation borne out in the parish burial grounds. Catharene's neighbor Clara Gallagher ambled down the path twice a day, pausing at her husband's graveside for a prayer. Others converged to pay tribute to a favorite grandparent, uncle, or aunt. Some just stopped by on their way somewhere else, to remember. Memorial Day, with its choreography of flower arrangements, proved the culmination of this practice, a year-round culture of revering the dead.

Today, Tom undertook his pilgrimage to commune with his parents: a Joycean quest for maternal love and an antidote to the cruelty of exclusion. While hundreds of Centralia residents streamed toward borough hall, Tom turned his back to Locust Avenue. At the grave where Gladys and Jack resided, marked by a gray granite headstone, he said hello.

Later, outside borough hall, Tom spoke to a *Catholic Witness* reporter, proffering an assessment infused with goodwill. "There is more cooperation now, and cooperation is the keynote of unity," he said. A photographer, homing in on his face, registered the dark circles rimming his eyes.

Federal officials finalized their review of the borehole project later that spring, saying the mine fire had consumed 140 acres: 70 acres near Centralia and another 70 near Byrnesville, where temperatures approached 1,000 degrees. Secretary Watt, meanwhile, burnished his reputation for political obtuseness. In April, he banned rock musicians from the annual July Fourth concert on the Washington mall, saying they attracted "the wrong element." In a bid to foster a family-oriented atmosphere, he proposed replacing the Beach Boys, known for endless-summer anthems such as "Surfer Girl" and "Help Me, Rhonda," with military bands and Wayne Newton, the Las Vegas–based casino balladeer. An avalanche of derision ensued, from disc jockeys, including one who dismissed Watt as the nation's chief nerd, to Capitol Hill and the White House, where President Reagan and the First Lady numbered among the Beach Boys' fans.

Two days later, Reagan tendered his interior secretary a gift: a plaster trophy shaped like a foot and pocked with a bullet hole. Underneath the choreographed façade, however, animosity festered, even after Watt reinstated the act as headliner, with White House officials carping under the cloak of confidentiality to the Associated Press and *The New York Times*. "Maybe we ought to invite Lawrence Welk and have him blow red, white, and blue bubbles," sniffed one. In Byrnesville, residents torched Watt in effigy during their annual July Fourth bonfire, placing a stuffed likeness of the interior secretary atop a pile of timber and tires, with a sign around his neck saying "Let It Burn Jim."

One week later, in mid-July 1983, the Office of Surface Mining's private consultants, hired by the Interior Department to analyze the borehole project data, issued their two-volume assessment, known as the GAI report. The cost of total excavation had skyrocketed to $663 million, they said. Instead of all-out containment, they recommended a compromise, an L-shaped $62 million trench across the heart of Centralia, measuring 3,900 feet long and up to 450 feet deep. If left untreated, they said, the blaze could encompass up to 3,700 acres and smolder for a century or more.

For two days in a row, the *News-Item* ran a front-page graphic of the proposed trench, a red wedge superimposed across Locust Avenue like a suture. Almost two hundred residents crammed into borough hall, where diagrams lined the walls, for a briefing on the report. The mine fire threatened all of Centralia and Byrnesville, the consultant's spokesman said. The trench would require demolition of about eighty structures, including three blocks of South Locust Avenue and most of Park Street—eliminating part of the community and disrupting almost everyone else, with no guarantee of success. In Washington and Harrisburg, the excavation proposal, with its eight-figure price tag, did not even warrant consideration, except as a bargaining chip. Relocation becomes something you've got to think about, said Congressman Harrison. Indeed, in the capitals, beset by recession, unemployment, and budget cutting, one issue emerged, the same conflict that had bedeviled mine fire containment since the early 1960s: Who would pay?

Governor Thornburgh, of course, sought to ratchet up pressure on the federal government, comparing Centralia to a community ravaged by natural disaster such as a flood or a hurricane. One of his cabinet secretaries invoked the example of Times Beach, Missouri, where the Environmental Protection Agency had announced a $33 million initiative to relocate more than two thousand residents from a town contaminated by dioxin—the debut buyout project under the 1980 Superfund law, a hazardous waste cleanup measure passed in response to Love Canal. The Office of Surface Mining, however, continued to insist that the mine fire, although serious, did not rise to the level of an emergency under the surface mining act and the state would have to underwrite any relocation project, in whole or in part, from its share of the AML fund.

In Centralia, Helen Womer redoubled her efforts to scuttle the trench, which, like previous incarnations, promised to obliterate her home. In mid-July, she flew to New York for a *Today* show appearance, telling Jane Pauley that officials still had not determined the fire's precise location. At a borough council meeting, she said she supported reinforcing the fly-ash barrier to save the town.

As much as Catharene loved her Frackville home, with its hardwood floors, pocket doors, and two-car garage, she rattled around inside with Katrina and Angel, fending off restlessness and boredom. Peacho, engrossed in an automation drive at work, shuttled between plants in Chicago and corporate headquarters in Seneca Falls, New York, training in new technology. To Catharene, it seemed he disappeared forever, traveling for weeks and even months at a stretch, as if by industry and ambition he could reverse the fate of his father, who once passed up a bus-driving job at Bloomsburg University because Elaine wanted him to toil nearby and return home for lunch in case she needed him.

Catharene, who had pined for a refuge from the mine fire, not the isolation of a stay-at-home mom, threw herself into her work. From Frackville, she dialed the CCHD office, asking what she could do, and made calls from home. In Centralia, she attended meetings, bearing crab dip and seven-layer Jell-O, and fanned out among her neighbors. Her dedication caught Peacho by surprise. He thought she had finished with her activism, cutting her ties when they moved. When he came home, she asked about his work and couched her Centralia activities in terms of visiting neighbors, a value he and his clan prized. When he traveled and they spoke on the phone at night, she chatted about Katrina and Angel, not about organizing strategies and the concerns of elderly Centralians.

Even after relocating, Catharene felt drawn back to Centralia, as if she were called to help her friends and neighbors who still lived there. If anything, she felt better equipped to mediate on their behalf since she had escaped the day-to-day angst of coexisting with the mine fire. No one had eased her family's path to relocation; she and Peacho had saved their way out, leveraging their nest egg into a new home. Still, in

Centralia, where she had forged a commitment to administering the grant, she felt needed.

FROM HER POST near the front of the room, Catharene surveyed the crowd. About two dozen residents sat in rows of folding chairs arranged in a semicircle and divided by a center aisle. A poster-sized pad of white newsprint rested nearby on a metal easel. Older men, including some ex-miners, sat and stood at the back. Off to the side, a table groaned with coffee and doughnuts.

The successors to Concerned Citizens and the thirty-thousand-dollar grant, the Centralia Committee for Human Development, had engineered this event, one in a handful of simultaneous meetings under way across town, from Byrnesville to K-9 Furniture World. In a community with a history of strife and interlopers, the group knew, residents unburdened themselves to their neighbors, the folks with whom they shared a wall, a back fence, or a row of homes. To encourage discussion, they convened small sessions in neighborhood settings, away from borough hall. And to foster candor, they barred the media.

Now, a Penn State biology professor with a hoop through one of his earlobes stood up front as the evening's moderator, an outsider and stranger recruited by the activists to enforce protocol, including a ban on interruptions and criticism. There's one question, he said. What do you want?

As the professor spoke, a volunteer transcribed his query at the top of the newsprint like a heading, etching each letter with a permanent marker. Squeaks from the pen's tip reverberated around the room. "What do you want?" the expanse of newsprint asked in five-inch black letters. In the silence that followed, Catharene sensed she could hear people thinking.

A few minutes later, after residents inscribed their answers on index cards, the moderator started calling on them, eliciting their views. Put out the fire, said one. I want to move. As the participants spoke, a volunteer at the front of the room transcribed their answers verbatim, like a handwritten transcript, onto sheets of newsprint.

Catharene circulated, collecting the cards and listening. Before the session, with weeks of planning at stake, she had wondered whether anyone would show up. Now, one voice at a time, residents shared their thoughts and desires, as if this were group therapy. As they spoke, tension in the room dissipated, as participants realized they had not stumbled onto another borough hall meeting, where citizens expressed opinions at their peril. Again and again, Catharene heard variations on the same refrain: relocation and fair market value; relocation and I want to stay with my neighbors; put out the fire and I want to move.

When the moderator canvassed the last resident, about 80 percent had named relocation as one of their choices. Afterward, as Catharene and the volunteers folded chairs and prodded people to take home the leftover doughnuts, several participants lingered, chatting with their neighbors. I didn't know you thought that, she heard one say.

For months, neighbors and friends had confided in Catharene in the privacy of their kitchens and living rooms, saying they wanted to leave. Now she had evidence, written across sheets of poster-sized paper: Their voices comprised the majority, not the dissent. Relocation opponents had hijacked the discourse, deploying volume to their advantage and earning respect for their efforts, with residual goodwill from Unity Day. They represented themselves, however, a minority at best. No one could convince her otherwise.

THE NEXT MORNING, Catharene stood atop a six-foot metal ladder in borough hall with rolls of masking tape dangling from her wrist like bracelets. Rows of empty chairs lined the floor in preparation for a town meeting set to unfold later that day. Dozens of newsprint pages lay stacked across a conference table, numbered and grouped by site. Together, they formed the "group memory," as she and the other volunteers dubbed it, the transcripts of the neighborhood meetings, like a spoken-word quilt. Piece by piece, she reassembled the previous evening's tapestry, starting in the corner near the fire station entrance. Page by page, she worked her way along the wall, affixing sheets to the cinder-block wall, one atop of another and side by side, with strips of masking tape anchoring the top and bottom of each.

When she had hung about three dozen pages, Mayor Wondoloski burst into the room. You can't do this, he said. Catharene and her counterparts had obtained permission to post their results in the municipal building, but borough officials had contemplated a page of data, not this: a swath of multicolored ink stretching halfway down the Locust Avenue side of the building, saying relocation, relocation, relocation.

Yes, I can, she said.

Catharene climbed down from the ladder and filed into the borough council chambers, a space dominated by filing cabinets with overhead fluorescent lighting and needle-shaped windows overlooking Locust Avenue. She reached into her purse and pulled out a list of emergency numbers, stashed next to the coupon envelope. While Mayor Wondoloski hovered in the doorway, she picked up the phone and dialed her colleagues, from Mary Theresa Gasperetti and Trish Catizone to Father Garula, who lived in Mount Carmel.

You're not going to believe this, she said. You better come down here.

Back in the meeting room, Catharene redoubled her efforts, realizing the more pages she hung, the harder it would be for borough officials to order their removal. Mary Theresa arrived on foot with her two children, who pitched in, smoothing masking tape onto the walls. Trish drove down from Byrnesville and took turns clambering up the ladder. A few residents even wandered in, diverted on their way to the post office by word of a commotion at borough hall.

Catharene stood in the middle of the room an hour later, surrounded by empty tables and chairs. Newsprint coated the perimeter. She strolled around the room and examined the pages up close, like paintings in a museum. A few more residents streamed in. When they saw the walls plastered with the group memory, they lapsed into silence, as if entering a church.

A FEW DAYS LATER, relocation gathered momentum again, this time with a nudge from Harrisburg. The state health department unveiled a study outlining the potential health effects of coexisting with trench construction, a catalogue of distress ranging from stress and anxiety to hearing loss, bronchitis, and cancer. Borough council scheduled another nonbinding referendum for August 11 and restricted the franchise to property owners, a condition that barred Centralia's tenants, including Tom Larkin, from participating. Twenty-one years after the dump ignited, voters would confront one question: Stay or relocate?

Helen and Elaine Jurgill swept across the borough with a petition to preserve Centralia intact, requesting the least disruptive option to contain the mine fire and limited relocation, at fair market value, for residents whose health and welfare the blaze legitimately threatened. Within days, they netted more than three hundred signatures. Helen, bolstered by the response, said the vast majority of Centralians did not want to move. A former borough councilman, Bob Lazarski, challenged her assessment, suggesting she had deployed high-pressure tactics, especially with elderly residents, who were afraid to alienate her.

Three days before the referendum, officials converged on borough hall for a thinly veiled effort to influence the vote, styled as a preballot education drive. No body of government, from federal authorities to the state, had authorized funding for any of the mine fire options, from trenching to relocation. Still, a health department official reiterated findings from his agency's report, saying the trench would expose residents to hazardous gases and stress-related illnesses. Another state official said residents could qualify for relocation payments ranging between $5,000 and $26,000 for a half-double and between $10,000 and $55,000 for a freestanding single home.

Helen, whose petition had carved out a middle ground, sought clarification.

"Are the only options a trench that will destroy our community or relocation?" she said. "Are two options all we'll have?"

"That's correct," said Robert Oberman, a spokesman for the state's Department of Environmental Resources.

After the meeting, as Mary Lou wended her way to the exit, she overheard two elderly women behind her saying they had changed their minds. That was enough to scare me, one said. Mary Lou glanced to her right, angling to eye the speakers, whom she did not know. If those two little old ladies backed relocation, she wondered, how many more were going to feel the same way?

MARY LOU and Tony voted in borough hall after her shift, around four P.M. Outside, gray skies and humidity sealed the basin in late summer torpor. Scores of journalists had again descended on Centralia, grappling for insight into why this town, with no stoplight or movie theater, no restaurant or grocery store, exercised such a hold over its residents. Earlier that morning, officials posted a handwritten sign on the borough hall door, barring the media. Reporters and cameramen loitered outside on the sidewalk, trolling for comments. In the privacy of their booths, Mary Lou and Tony both voted to remain, placing checks in the box marked "stay."

About four hours later, when the polls closed, Mary Lou and Tony drove back down to borough hall. Several dozen residents had gathered in the cool, damp air outside the entrance, knotted in groups, waiting for the results. Over the past few days, Mary Lou had talked to neighbors and coworkers, polling them about their preferences, and over and over, from the garment factory to the post office, she heard variations of the same theme: I don't want to leave; my mother doesn't want to leave. While election judges tallied the ballots, Mary Lou convinced herself the stayers would command a majority.

Just before nine P.M., Mayor Wondoloski emerged from the municipal building in his shirtsleeves, clutching a piece of paper. A swarm of journalists rushed toward him, armed with boom mikes and tape recorders. One reporter covered the results for *Nightline,* which had slotted the first half of its broadcast for the referendum.

The mayor stood in front of the municipal building entrance, bathed in the glow of television lights. Microphones bobbed at his throat. Relocation had won by 345 to 200, he said, or 63 percent of the vote. A few in the crowd gasped. Behind him, a cameraman logged reaction shots. One woman glared into the lens, expressionless, adjusting the sleeves of her pantsuit. Off camera, a younger woman frowned. Two middle-aged men with truckers' caps perched on their heads hunkered in the background, beyond interview range.

A reporter asked the mayor if he would like to see another Centralia, erected at a new location.

"Definitely," he said.

Later, Mary Lou and Helen huddled in the dark on the Gaughans' front porch. Helen had staked her reputation on the petition, and for her the outcome was personal. Mary Lou, who doubted the $62 million excavation would ever materialize, blamed government officials, with their scare tactics and health study, their doomsday scenarios. They had touted the trench like a bogeyman, whipping residents into a frenzy of judgment-clouding anxiety. As an added incentive, they had dangled the specter of five-figure payments for homes, even for half-doubles.

Then again, Mary Lou wondered—even if Helen did not—if she had misjudged the electorate. Maybe neighbors and friends had mollified her and Helen before the referendum, telling them what they knew they wanted to hear, not divulging their desire to flee. Perhaps they had added their names to Helen's petition out of respect. Behind the voting booth's curtain, with no one listening and watching, they had voted their consciences. And they had voted to go.

Still, Mary Lou's brain had adapted to processing mine fire news on two tracks, one telling her she would have to leave and the other insisting she could stay. She hadn't abandoned all hope. Officials in Harrisburg and Washington had not brokered an agreement about how to underwrite relocation. Without financing, she knew, the referendum meant nothing.

WITHIN WEEKS, relocation opponents regrouped and banded into a confederation, Residents to Save the Borough. By late September, they hosted weekly gatherings—closed to the news media—on the north side of town, in Anne Marie Devine's garage. Members such as Mary Lou, Helen, and Leon and Elaine Jurgill swapped intelligence and vowed never to leave. As one of their first priorities, they resolved to counter what they perceived as pro-relocation bias in the media, like Radio Free Europe during the Cold War, beaming prodemocracy news and analysis behind the Iron Curtain. With Helen serving as editor, correspondent, and typist, they cobbled together "fact sheets," four-page newsletters designed to inundate the borough with their views, from alleged referendum vote fraud to the need for full information about the trench. Virtually everyone else in town dubbed them the SOBs.

On Sunday afternoons, Mary Lou plied Tony with rump roast and mashed potatoes, grabbed a stack of fact sheets, and knocked on doors in the Swamp. If someone refused to accept one, she knew that family planned to leave. As for the others, those who accepted the missives, she thought the bulletins might sway them, appealing to values she and her compatriots cherished: independence, patriotism, and solidarity.

"This is still America," said one fact sheet, disseminated before the SOBs' September 20 gathering. "Our forefathers came to this area, built this town, and enjoyed peace and religious freedom. We still want these rights and privileges and under our democratic law we are entitled to them. We do not appreciate being harassed by the media and government officials trying to relocate people and use the land for their own gain. People should stop and think before they make any rash decisions. *Think positive!* This is a happy little town for many young and old alike."

The SOBs could not orchestrate events in Washington, however, where controversy again engulfed Watt. This time, he sparked a contretemps with his federal coal leasing program: a drive to unleash private mining operators on more than 17 billion tons of federally owned mineral deposits. Environmental groups decried his efforts, saying the initiative would threaten the integrity of several national parks, destroy ancient Anasazi archaeological sites, and overrun wildlife habitats. The General Accounting Office, Congress's investigative arm, uncovered oversight flaws, saying the agency's 1982 lease of 1.6 billion tons in the Powder River Basin in Montana, North Dakota, and Wyoming had yielded a hundred million dollars less than fair market value. In early August, a House committee imposed a moratorium through the end of the year. Watt declared the prohibition unconstitutional and auctioned eight tracts near the North Dakota–Montana border, prompting a federal judge to issue an emergency order blocking the sale.

On September 20, the day of the SOBs' meeting, the Republican-controlled Senate voted 63 to 33 to impose a six-month ban on federal coal leasing: a rebuke to Watt and his stewardship. The next morning, at a breakfast speech before the U.S. Chamber of Commerce, Watt blasted the news media for their obsession with sex, controversy, and scandal, and Congress for failing to endorse his energy development program. Stung by defeat, he said he fielded advice from a congressionally mandated coal leasing commission. Referring to the commissioners, he said: "We have every kind of mix you can have. I have a black, I have a woman, two Jews, and a cripple. And we have talent."

The remark provoked laughter. But during a question-and-answer session after the speech, an audience member inquired about its wisdom, given the administration's susceptibility to criticism from minorities. "If you can't joke about things, you shouldn't be in Washington," Watt said. At the White House, where aides were gearing up for Reagan's reelection bid, officials failed to see the humor. Within hours, Watt phoned one of the Jewish commissioners, who had a paralyzed arm, to apologize.

Still, Watt's contrition failed to derail Washington's version of blood sport: a countdown, like a deathwatch, surrounding a cabinet member's fall from grace. On Capitol Hill, veterans handicapped the interior secretary's tenure in days, not weeks. Watt, who once parsed the universe into "liberals and Americans," had scripted his own political obituary. And by engineering his own irrelevance, he accomplished more for Centralia than Todd Domboski, Concerned Citizens, and three decades of federal mine reclamation laws combined. Indeed, by removing himself as an impediment, he unsealed the one deep pocket—without litigation, without insurance company involvement—with the resources to relocate Centralians away from the mine fire: the AML fund.

Within hours of Watt's remark, congressional lawmakers, skilled in the art of manipulating power vacuums, sprang to Centralia's aid. A Republican congressman from Scranton, Joseph M. McDade, tucked an amendment into a supplemental appropriations bill, earmarking $42 million to relocate the borough's residents. Later that evening, as Watt battled to preserve his job, the House Appropriations Committee approved the measure. And, with Watt now powerless to object, legislators corrected the million-dollar buyout's inequities: They provided fair market value for Centralia homeowners, with no mine fire penalty, and charged 75 percent of the program's cost to the interior secretary's discretionary Abandoned Mine Lands budget. It was the outcome Thornburgh had pitched from the outset—with Pennsylvania contributing only 25 percent, from its share of the fund's proceeds—and one the Interior Department had rebuffed on *Nightline* only six weeks earlier, hours after the referendum.

Meanwhile, calls for Watt's departure resounded across the capital, from *The Washington Post*'s editorial pages to Republican stalwarts such as Senator Robert Dole, a disabled World War II veteran, who said the comment offended him. Watt conceded his mistake and asked Reagan's forgiveness. Off the record, White House officials signaled that the president would accept his interior secretary's decision to quit.

Still, for two more weeks, Watt clung to his post. With the Senate poised to approve a resolution urging his resignation, however, he holed up on a friend's ranch near Santa Barbara, California. Even his supporters in the Wyoming delegation, Congressman Richard B. Cheney and Senator Alan K. Simpson, had distanced themselves. At the end of the weekend, on Sunday, October 9, 1983, Watt phoned President Reagan at Camp David and resigned. The only way to deal with a lynch mob, Reagan said, is to get out of their road and move on, so you can live to fight another day.

Afterward, Watt and his wife, Leilani, rode out on horseback to a pasture where Texas longhorns grazed beneath an oak tree and a clutch of reporters waited. In the distance, on a mountain overlooking the Santa Ynez Valley, lay President Reagan's six-hundred-acre ranch. Watt dismounted, helped his wife off her horse, and clipped a microphone to his shirt. Leilani, a farmer's daughter who had sewn her own wedding and inaugural ball gowns, held the reins while he read his resignation letter, his voice quavering at times.

"The time has come," said Watt. "We confronted the neglect and the problems. We gave purpose and direction to management of our nation's natural resources. The restoration of our national parks, refuges and public lands is well under way. In fact, all the Department of Interior lands are better managed under our stewardship than they were when we inherited the responsibility. Our actions to reduce the nation's dependency on foreign sources of energy and strategic materials are working. The balance is being restored."

Then Watt came to the point of his missive. "It is time for a new phase of management, one to consolidate the gains we have made," he said. "It is my view that my usefulness to you in this Administration has come to an end. A different type of leadership at the Department of Interior will best serve you and the nation. I leave behind people and programs—a legacy that will aid America in the decades ahead. Our people and their dedication will keep America moving in the right direction."

Watt folded the letter and slipped it back into his pocket. He helped his wife back onto her horse, mounted his, and fielded a few questions.

When reporters quizzed him about his plans, he vowed to keep pressing his agenda. "We will continue our crusade and our efforts to establish spiritual freedom and political liberty in this country, for that is the real battleground," he said.

Back at the ranch, he grasped Leilani's hand and prayed.

SIX WEEKS LATER, Tom Larkin stood on the east steps of the U.S. Capitol. Behind him, Corinthian columns soared over the entrance at the base of the rotunda, the midpoint between the House and Senate chambers. At his back and high overhead, the legislature's neoclassical dome soared over Capitol Hill, dominating the Washington skyline.

A few feet in front of Tom, a handful of politicians were arrayed behind a red grosgrain ribbon. Congressman Harrison and Senators Heinz and Specter grasped the strand in the middle. Two former borough councilmen, Bob Burge and Bob Lazarksi, anchored the ends, a role befitting their return from retirement to head a coalition, dubbed the Centralia Homeowners Association, to coach families through relocation. Kevin Troup, Burge's seven-year-old grandson, nudged a pair of scissors toward the fabric band while the congressman cupped his hand over the handles. As onlookers beamed, the boy snipped the filament in half.

Tom had arrived in the capital by chartered bus earlier in the day with a contingent of thirty Centralians, drawn by the prospect of witnessing history. In the House gallery, where security officers imposed decorum, warning visitors not to stand or shout, they watched the last day of the 98th Congress's first session, as legislators voted on a $302 million catchall spending vehicle. Buried amid the arcana of omnibus appropriations, including an increased contribution to the International Monetary Fund, the bill contained Centralia's $42 million relocation package. When the measure passed, 226–186, a few of the borough's partisans clapped and cheered. The Centralia relief provision, already approved by the Senate and now awaiting the president's signature, had not even triggered debate.

For the ribbon-cutting ceremony after the vote, Tom hovered in the background, enveloped by neighbors, including some who, like him, could trace their Centralia roots back five generations. On this day, almost a year after he typed his resignation letter, he blended with them, evading the spotlight and savoring the affirmation, however belated, of his activism and Concerned Citizens. Others had stepped in where he faltered, administering the grant, shepherding residents through the referendum, and now presiding over relocation. Still, if it hadn't been for Concerned Citizens, with its determination to keep the mine fire in the news, Tom knew this celebration would not have materialized. Congress would not have funded the borehole study. The Campaign for Human Development would not have deemed Centralia worthy of attention. Half a dozen people might have perished by now, from fumes or cave-ins or both.

As a man of faith, though, whose strain of Irish Catholicism tempered pride with humility and superstition, Tom shared credit with the cosmos. This moment, for all its richness, transcended the physics of mortality, the nexus of money, media, influence, and ideology. Here on the steps of the Capitol, a temple of secular politics, he sensed a communion of the sacred and the profane, a civics lesson suffused with the hand of the divine, the Lord's intervention, reversing Father McDermott's curse.

God brought us here, he thought.

EPILOGUE

Home

Lines etch Mary Lou's face, furrows slicing into her cheeks and forehead. When she stands barefoot in her kitchen, fixing tea or toast with butter and homemade strawberry jam, bunions balloon from the sides of her feet. Her hair, curled, set, and sprayed by a former Centralia resident who grooms and coifs from an Aristes salon, glows the hue of copper.

Even in retirement, Mary Lou's days reverberate with frenzy. The kitchen phone, mounted on the wall next to the refrigerator, trills with inquiries from friends, grandchildren, and her son Joe, a trucker and recent husband and stepfather, who welcomed his own first child, a boy named Anthony, in March 2005. Mary Lou, her brogue intact even as she masters the Internet and e-mail, renders the baby's name as "Antnee." When Joe checks in by cell phone from Interstate 81, a stretch through the coal region renowned for fog, accidents, and speeding eighteen-wheelers, she tells him to slow down.

The mailman, a Centralia native who grew up with Bootsie McGinley's son and has earned a cult following among the elderly women on his route, drops by most mornings to hand Mary Lou her mail and chat at her kitchen table. When he leaves, she prods him to grab a piece of candy on the way out, a Bit-O-Honey or a York peppermint pattie from the dish in the living room, next to the scented candle. Her sister Rosie stops in with bulletins about swim aerobics, Weight Watchers, or a meeting at St. Joe's, Ashland's Catholic parish. During Lent, Mary Lou and Rosie and a handful of elderly volunteers stand on their feet for weeks, eight hours a day, fashioning chocolate Easter eggs with peanut butter, coconut, and buttercream fillings. The first year, when they hawked their confections at fifty cents each, they raised five thousand dollars for the parish. The priest tapped Mary Lou for a committee, and her picture landed in the local newspaper.

People have a way of finding Mary Lou when they need something: alterations to a school uniform; eyewitness accounts for a school project about the mine fire. Even the occasional reporter. She still has a hard time saying no.

Inside her home, now a freestanding midblock single atop an Ashland hillside, sun filters through the living room windows, photographs of her grandchildren line the walls, and greeting cards from friends meander across tabletops and the piano, from Valentine's Day to Christmas. A shrine to the Blessed Virgin presides over a corner of her backyard, gazing toward the porch. A painting of St. Ignatius Church hangs from the wall at the top of the stairs, near a framed cross-stitched sampler saying "Happiness is Contagious." The parlor window, looking out onto the front porch, heralds the seasons and holidays: green lights for Saint Patrick's Day, orange lights for Halloween, and red, white, and blue bunting for Memorial Day, the Fourth of July, and Labor Day.

On Saturday mornings, when Mary Lou drives to Aristes for her hair appointment, she passes through Centralia. St. Ignatius Church, razed in 1997, no longer graces the skyline at the top of Locust Mountain. Parishioners salvaged chunks of French marble from the altar—red stone flecked with white veins, like a steak. A private collector bought the bell. After the last Mass, a local newspaper featured a photograph of Helen seated in a pew with her head buried in Carl's shoulder.

On Locust Avenue, acres of grassland unfold where blocks of row homes once stood, like a prairie. Back in the mid-1980s, when relocation funds trickled into the borough, bulldozers leveled houses on both sides of the street, demolishing block after block, from St. Ignatius to borough hall and beyond. Joe Moyer's home stands alone at West Park Street now, with brick support columns propping the sides and half-closed venetian blinds in the second-floor windows. Tar paper peels off the roof of the pigeon shed in his backyard.

Just across Park Street from Joe's house, a stone fence along Locust Avenue marks where the American Legion once stood, and before that, Alexander Rea's home. Veterans still rotate through the cemeteries on Memorial Day, from Aristes to St. Ignatius. But these days, they pile into pickup trucks, SUVs, and minivans and fall into a convoy with the borough's fire truck and ambulance. Toward the end of their procession, they cluster around the flagpole at the site of their former headquarters, pausing for a prayer, a rifle salute, and taps. Just a few feet away, beneath a stone marker, the centennial time capsule lies buried underground, waiting to be unearthed in 2016, the town's 150th anniversary.

Afterward, the veterans retreat to their new post, a squat trailer-shaped building atop Aristes Mountain in Wilburton, where they hauled the framed copy of Kennedy's inaugural address and the Little League trophies and reconstructed the bar, with Genesee and Yuengling on tap. As a fund-raiser, one of the members peddles copies of his Centralia home movies, featuring clips from the borough centennial. In the basement, veterans and their spouses line up at a buffet table for Memorial Day refreshments, loading their plates with macaroni salad, pierogies, sausages, and slices of a sheet cake decorated with an American flag. A red heart-shaped sign hangs from the white tile wall with the hand-painted message "We Love Centralia."

Down at the Four Corners, St. Mary's still towers over the basin. A fire demolished the Speed Spot in late 2002. Most of the old-timers have vanished, too, prevented by death or infirmity from frittering away summer afternoons in an empty lot a few feet from the intersection, seated on a pair of orange benches under the shade of a maple tree. Tourists descend in the summer, armed with tales from the Web, pausing at the intersection or up near St. Ignatius Cemetery, on a quest for the town with the underground inferno.

Inside borough hall, where the fire truck and ambulance repose in the truck bay, mildew scents the air in council chambers, and a bucket captures water dripping from the ceiling. A photograph of President George W. Bush hangs from the cinder-block wall. Almost every resident serves on the council, Centralia's population having sunk to around a dozen, and they convene once a month around a conference table overlooking Locust Avenue.

Still, when Mary Lou rounds the bend from Ashland and glides downhill on Locust Avenue, past the cemetery entrance, she can't help swiveling her head to the right and glancing down Wood Street. It takes just a second: a strip of pavement, riddled with cracks and engulfed by trees. Helen's house, with its maroon and white shingled exterior, is the only structure left.

MARY LOU folded in 1993. Governor Robert P. Casey, the son of a Scranton miner, had invoked his eminent domain powers and threatened to evict the borough's remaining eighty-odd residents, the holdouts who hadn't scattered to nearby towns. From Aristes to Wilburton, many ex-residents could look up and down the streets of their new subdivisions and count the former Centralians among their neighbors. Mary Lou had seen eminent domain disputes unfold on television, owners who refused to yield to a highway project until bulldozers flattened their homes. She couldn't afford to lose everything.

So seven years after Tony died of heart failure, expiring in his parlor chair after heaving himself out of the bathtub, Mary Lou capitulated. And a decade after President Reagan inked his signature on Centralia's $42 million relief package—and officials announced that relocation would remain voluntary—she sold the home where she and Tony had raised their children, unloading it on the government for

$43,000, plus almost $45,000 for relocation costs. When she confided in Helen about her decision, Helen stopped speaking to her.

In October 1993, the same day the garment factory shuttered its doors, Mary Lou moved into a brick and siding split-level near Ashland, the first new home she had ever inhabited. Her neighbors drove into their garages at night and disappeared inside their Colonials and ranches, buffered by shrubbery and acres of grass. No one knocked on her door. No one popped in to visit. Chairs dotted front porches along the street, but in the summer, she didn't see anyone reclining in them. She took a second job, an evening shift waiting tables at Fountain Springs Country Club, just to stave off loneliness.

In November 1998, Mary Lou sent Helen a birthday card, wishing her well on her seventieth. Four months later, Helen responded with a Saint Patrick's Day card. Inside she tucked a two-page note, penned in green ink, on paper adorned with shamrocks and leprechauns. "I feel there has always been a bond between us that no one or nothing could ever destroy and that is why I wanted to reach out and heal the wounds as best I could," Helen said. "So glad you accepted," she added, converting Mary Lou's gesture into her own and claiming credit for an apology.

Mary Lou picked up the phone and dialed Helen's number. They chatted for a few minutes, trading news about their children and grandchildren, as if six years had not intervened since their last conversation and they had just bumped into each other at the grocery store. When Mary Lou hung up, she started crying.

The last time they saw each other, in August 2001, Mary Lou's forty-one-year-old son Tony had just died, of complications stemming from obesity. Helen came to the wake and funeral, radiating health. I always liked your Tony, she said. It was their first conversation since Mary Lou called her about the Saint Patrick's Day card—and their last.

Helen died in November 2001, a few days after her seventy-third birthday. Several months earlier, physicians had diagnosed a cancerous brain tumor, pronouncing it inoperable. At home on Wood Street, as her health failed, she huddled under a baby afghan Mary Lou had crocheted for one of Helen's grandchildren.

When bulldozers leveled Catharene and Peacho's row home in December 1984, they had already separated. Even with their family's health assured, they could not bridge a fundamental difference in outlook and expectations, once sublimated to long-term planning and dreams about the future. Catharene, inspired by her Centralia experience, yearned for work and fulfillment outside the house, building on her volunteer activism career or pursuing her education while she raised her daughters, who remained her first priority. Peacho insisted she stay at home with the children full-time.

Catharene moved to Harrisburg with Katrina and Angel, rented a two-bedroom apartment, landed a job as a clerk-typist, joined the ranks of state government employees, and finalized her divorce. In May 1987, she married Sam Garula, the former Russian Orthodox priest from the Centralia Committee for Human Development, who had divorced his wife and left the clergy. Together, Catharene and Sam raised their four children and engaged in part-time consulting, counseling communities beset with environmental disasters about government-financed relocation. In 1995, Catharene spoke at a workshop sponsored by the Tulane Environmental Law Clinic. "They move whole communities to make way for airports and highways," she said. "We tell everybody you have an even bigger stake: your life."

Katrina graduated from Dickinson University in 2000 and received a master's degree in theology from Emory in 2006. Angel graduated from New York University in 2002 with a 4.0 grade point average and works in New York. In September 2002, at age forty-one, Catharene gave birth to a son, Jonathan Garula. Sam stays at home with Jonathan, managing their ten-acre farm and his own computer consulting practice. Catharene commutes to Harrisburg, where she works in sales for an online advertising company, generating leads for business-to-consumer products and services.

Tom Larkin moved from Centralia to Ashland in 1984. As a tenant, he pocketed about five thousand dollars in relocation benefits. In 1995, he helped launch an Irish American newspaper, *An Scathan,* Gaelic for "the mirror," covering politics, news, arts, and entertainment. Three years later, after a dispute with his partners, the business folded and he moved to Philadelphia, where he sold advertisements for a free weekly newspaper. He retired in January 2005, after his sixty-fifth birthday. He still adheres to the conspiracy theory.

Dave Lamb remarried at borough hall on Christmas Eve 1988. Anne Marie Devine, a former SOB who won election as the borough's first female mayor, presided over the ceremony. Dave sold the Speed Spot to the redevelopment authority in 2000, eighteen years after the firebombing, and moved to Bloomsburg, where he lives with his wife, Pat.

Helen Womer lies in St. Ignatius Cemetery, just a few feet from Tony Gaughan. Her husband and daughter still live in her Wood Street home, where peonies bloom along the porch in the spring and snow melts in the winter, exposing a smudge of grass in the backyard. On Memorial Day, Helen's family members convene to pay tribute to her memory, depositing roses, impatiens, and red, white, and blue carnations at her grave.

FORMER GOVERNOR Richard J. Thornburgh served as U.S. attorney general during the last five months of the Reagan administration, a post he retained for almost three years under President George H. W. Bush. In 2004, CBS News tapped him for a panel charged with investigating a flawed report, first broadcast on *60 Minutes,* raising questions about President George W. Bush's service in the Texas Air National Guard. Thornburgh is an attorney in private practice in Washington, D.C.

In 1995, a federal grand jury indicted James Watt on twenty-five felony counts of perjury and obstruction of justice, stemming from an independent counsel's investigation of influence peddling at the Department of Housing and Urban Development during the 1980s. The charges accused Watt of lying about the extent of his dealings with top HUD officials and withholding documents potentially relevant to his work as a private consultant seeking federal HUD aid after he resigned as interior secretary. Watt, who originally maintained his innocence, pleaded guilty to a single misdemeanor charge of trying to influence a federal grand jury; a federal district judge ordered him to pay a $5,000 fine and perform five hundred hours of community service, and placed him on five years' probation. In a brief statement, Watt said he had made a "serious mistake" in his conduct during the investigation. "I didn't take it seriously enough," he said.

The mine fire, meanwhile, has fractured into four fronts, spreading in each direction. Even the federal government's Centralia expert, housed in a Wilkes-Barre office, balks at predicting how long it will smolder: No one knows. Decades at least, maybe a century. Thousands of tons of anthracite still lie wedged in seams underneath Centralia and the hills that surround it, rolling through the Western Middle Field. When a mine fire ignites in the region, federal officials launch into overdrive, combating the blaze around the clock, exceeding their budgets if necessary. Forty-four years after the dump caught fire, no one wants another Centralia.

INSIDE HER ASHLAND HOME, where she moved after selling the split-level in 2001, Mary Lou does not grieve. Some do, she knows, former Centralians haunted by loss. Not Mary Lou. She survived—cancer, the Depression, the mine fire, suburbia. Now, about a mile downhill from where her grandfather Michael Dougherty sank roots after fleeing the potato famine, she has what she thought she'd never find outside Centralia: a home.

At night in her bedroom, Mary Lou hears the echo of truck traffic grinding into gear for the steep grade up Locust Mountain and into Centralia. Three of her former neighbors wait tables across the street at Snyder's, dishing out curly fries, rice pudding, and BLTs. Former Centralians number among the customers, too, seated in the Naugahyde booths or at the counter near the ice cream freezer, overlooking Center Street. When Mary Lou sees them, they swap greetings and tidbits of news, like neighbors bumping into each other at the post office. After she eats, she leaves a 25 percent tip.

AUTHOR'S NOTE

THIS IS A WORK OF NONFICTION. The characters and scenes depicted in this book are real. For events I did not observe, I drew on my own reporting, including close to two hundred interviews with current and former Centralians, government officials, journalists, and other witnesses to the incidents described.

Whenever possible, I supplemented my interviews with information gathered from thousands of pages of documentary evidence culled from a variety of sources, including state and federal archives, the Library of Congress, private collections, the news media, and government agencies. I delved into the Office of Surface Mining's Centralia records, housed in several file cabinets in Wilkes-Barre, and filed a Freedom of Information Act request, the largest in the staff's memory. I obtained extensive records from the state agency that monitored mine fire gases for years, including mine maps and daily and weekly reports from carbon monoxide testing and monitors. I pored over contemporaneous newspaper accounts, photographs, news broadcasts, and, where available, film, videotape, cassette tapes, and meeting transcripts and minutes. I also relied extensively on collections maintained by former residents, including scrapbooks, newspaper clippings, photographs, videotapes, home movies, cassette tapes, correspondence, gas readings, and still more government documents. When I could not locate documentary evidence to corroborate my interviews, I was usually able to confirm events with at least two persons.

I have tried, wherever possible, to confirm the substance of conversations with both parties, if they were still alive. Some persons I contacted, of course, did not agree to be interviewed, including Helen Womer, before she died in 2001. If speech or dialogue appears in quotation marks in the text, I pulled the remarks verbatim from contemporaneous sources, such as news broadcasts, newspaper and magazine articles, meeting transcripts, videotapes, cassette tapes, letters, or letters to the editor. If dialogue or internal dialogue springs from a source's memory, it does not appear in quotation marks.

My narrative of how and when the mine fire started is based on multiple sources, including interviews with volunteer firemen, the former fire chief, borough officials, and several eyewitnesses, as well as contemporaneous borough council minutes. My account differs slightly from an earlier version published in a 1986 book by David DeKok, a former reporter for the Shamokin *News-Item,* who concluded that the fire started on May 27, 1962, when the volunteer fire department ignited a controlled burn at the dump. Evidence I unearthed from eyewitnesses, however, as well as the written record, supports the approach I have taken.

Over and over, during the course of researching this book, residents and former residents offered a similar explanation of how the fire started: Someone hurled hot ashes onto the dump. A few said the landfills caught on fire all the time, so frequently that volunteer firemen wearied of heeding the alarm. Still others, including some former borough officials, said the blaze started decades earlier in the Bast colliery, a long-defunct mine on the outskirts of town. The Bast theory, however, has been discredited over the years, mainly because a fault in the coal seam would have blocked the fire from traveling between the colliery and the dump. Still, the cash-strapped borough had an incentive to float this version. Several weeks after the dump ignited, the borough solicitor said Centralia officials could seek reimbursement for their expenses if they were fighting an old fire. As the Bast had been shuttered since the Depression, any blaze spreading from its confines clearly qualified as old.

When I interviewed the former fire chief, who has since died, and several other former firefighters, they said the fire company did torch the dump for Memorial Day 1962—but their efforts did not trigger the mine fire. Much, if not all, of the documentary and eyewitness evidence buttresses this conclusion. One eyewitness, to whom I granted confidentiality because this person feared reprisal in the community, tracked down a fireman at the dump, either the day the fire started or the next day, and asked what had happened. The fireman said, Curly was just up here and he dumped a lot of hot ashes.

The borough had two commercial haulers, Curly Stasulevich and Sam Devine, and two approved dumping days, Wednesday and Saturday. By Sunday, May 27, when Mary Lou Gaughan arrived at the dump, she heard a variation of the same account: Someone had heaved hot ashes onto the dump, but the firefighters thought they had extinguished the blaze. Of course, in the dump fire's initial hours and days, few foresaw that it would expand into a mine fire, let alone *the* mine fire. None of these eyewitnesses had an incentive to lie about what happened or how. It was just another dump fire.

Still, more than four decades after the mine fire ignited, even the ex–fire chief, then an elderly man battling ill health, balked at discussing how the blaze ignited, hinting he would fear for his life if he did. I expressed disbelief. You don't know Centralia, he said.

His answer resonated, probably in more ways than he realized.

THE FIRST TIME I visited Centralia, at fifteen, I attended a funeral. My ninety-four-year-old grandmother had just died in a Harrisburg nursing home, disrupting our annual August vacation on Martha's Vineyard. We traded the whaling captains' homes and yachts of Edgartown for a coal region wake and burial, flying off-island in a chartered plane—my father, who had ended his piloting career after the war, eyed the instruments warily. After the funeral Mass in Mount Carmel, we drove four miles east, across a massive black moonscape laid bare by strip mining, toward St. Ignatius Cemetery. In any other town—even any other hamlet in the coal region—the graveyard would have offered a serene setting, with its hilltop views and breezes. But in my grandparents' hometown, seventeen years after the blaze ignited, ribbons of sulfur-laden steam wafted from vent pipes in the ground, and the stench of rotten eggs blanketed the hillside.

On the way back to Mount Carmel, I pressed my father for an explanation. An abandoned underground mine had ignited, he said, and no one had extinguished the blaze. Even for me, a native Clevelander who had weathered years of jokes about my birthplace, from Lake Erie's polluted depths to a fire that once raged in the Cuyahoga River, his answer defied comprehension.

Eight years later, on a July afternoon in 1987, my parents and I returned to Centralia to visit my grandparents' grave. Vacant, boarded-up houses lined Locust Avenue, as in East Cleveland in the 1970s, decimated by riots. In St. Ignatius Cemetery, columns of sulfurous steam poured from cracks in the ground. After a hasty graveside Hail Mary, we retreated to the safety of the car, where my parents lamented the cemetery's plight—and how its condition would have devastated my grandmother. I sat in the backseat, imagining the entire graveyard plunging into the underground fire.

I rarely thought about Centralia until twelve years later, right after my thirty-fifth birthday. I had followed in my father's footsteps, and the grind of law school, billable hours, litigation, and investigations had left me depleted. In July 1999, though, I sat in my parents' kitchen one weekend afternoon, listening as their discussion turned to Centralia—and whether anyone would ever tell the mine fire story. For the next week, I trawled through newspaper articles and surfed the Internet, poring over a site devoted to the town. The more I read, the more I understood—or thought I did—why a dozen or so holdouts had refused to leave, even after the federal government offered to relocate them. That's when I decided to write this book.

Still, some of the story's personal threads defied traditional reporting and research, including the circumstances surrounding my great-great-grandfather's departure from Ireland. My father and his older brother have labored over the years to marshal evidence about Patrick Quigley and his flight, details of which remain murky across the generations. I based my narrative on interviews with them and their contemporaneous written records of their undertakings, as well as on my own additional research. To the extent that the oral and written history contains gaps or omissions, I have pointed them out in the text.

ACKNOWLEDGMENTS

SEVEN YEARS AGO, when I decided to write this book, I hoped to answer one question: Why did so many residents want to stay in Centralia, even as toxic fumes and cave-ins beset part of the community they loved? If I have done my job, this book addresses that issue, from both sides of the divide that fractured the borough. If not, the responsibility rests with me, not with the scores of Centralians who welcomed me into their homes, plied me with cake and soda, and shared their keepsakes, scrapbooks, and family photographs, their wedding albums and home movies, and, most precious of all, their time.

I owe a special debt to a handful of stalwarts whose cooperation proved essential to my labors: Catharene and Sam Garula, Mary Lou Gaughan, Dave Lamb, and Tom Larkin. They endured marathon interviews—sometimes as often as once a week—with patience and good humor. They fielded my phone calls and e-mails when I needed to double-check facts, opened their personal files, and trusted me with their stories. I could not have written this without them, and they have my everlasting appreciation.

Tom Dempsey, Centralia's former postmaster and most knowledgeable historian, gave generously of his time and expertise, from countless hours responding to my queries in person, by e-mail, and at the

Historical Society of Schuylkill County, where he is a volunteer, to helping me unlock the mystery of my family's ties to Crow Hollow, opening his vast holdings of vintage Centralia photographs, and guiding me on a tour of Centralia Colliery's crumbling remains. He is an invaluable resource, a civic-minded encyclopedia, infused with the ethos and spirit of the coal region—and he has my enduring gratitude.

For their assistance and insights along the way, I also thank Tony and Mary Andrade, Tom Beck, Harry Beierschmitt, Jake Betz, William J. Birster, Stella Brosakas, Bob and Nina Burge, Jack Carling, Trish Catizone, Mary Chapman, Cindy Chower, James Cleary, Ronald and Terri Coleman, John Comarnisky, Stephen R. Couch, H. T. Crown, Margaret Danner, Molly Darrah, David DeKok, Anne Marie Devine, Flo Domboski, Todd Domboski, Robert A. Dunkelberger, Doris Dysinger, Mary Anne Laughlin Dyson, Emil Ermert, Pat Flynn, George Fogel, Carl Frankel, Mary Theresa Gasperetti, Joan Girolami, Francis Goncalves, Mary Janet Gosdock, Virginia Green, Roland Harper, Julie Hartenstein, Richard Hill, Paul Hubbel, Bonnie Hynoski, Mary Anna Hynoski, Carolyn Johnson, Barbara Jurgill, Elaine Jurgill, Francis Jurgill, Sr., Joseph Jurgill, Leon Jurgill, Sr., Leon Jurgill, Jr., Mrs. Michael Jurgill, Kathleen Kenney, Bill Klink, George Klischer, Jane Konmath, John Koschoff, Deb Lokitis Kranzel, Dorothy and Steve Kranzel, Steve Kroll-Smith, Pat Lamb, Rachel Lamb, Joe Larish, Jody Lasecki, James Lavelle, Eddie Lawler, Bob and Mary Lazarski, Richard Lesser, Greg Lindner, Joe Liptock, John Lokitis, Jr., Rita Reilley Long, Mary Ann Lubinsky, Peter Lynn, Joe Maczka, Boris Maksymuk, the Reverend Anthony J. McGinley, Joe McGinley, Kate Birster McGinley, Owen and Mary McGinley, Lamar Mervine, Bob Miller, Red Miscavage, Sandy Mitchell, Joe Moyer, Tony Mussari, Duke Narcavage, Bill Nork, Sister M. Patrizia O'Connor, Eleanor and Fritz O'Hearn, Mary Teresa Pepper, Stephen Perloff, David R. Philbin, Stephen E. Phillips, Ed Polites, Jeanne Purcell, Mary Quigley (Doylestown, Pa.), Tom Quigley (Moorestown, N.J.), Ray Reilley, Leonard Rogers, Eddie Rooney, Karen Russo, Sara Saunders, Mali Schminkey, Mike Sherbon, Leif Skoogfors, George Strait, Joe Stutz,

Helen Tanis, Kathy Tanney, Clement Thatcher, Eleanor Johnson Tilmont, Tom Trauger, Al Visintainer, and Carl F. Womer.

I logged many hours at the following institutions, rummaging through the collections, hounding the staff, and hogging the photocopiers and microfilm readers: Mount Carmel Public Library, Shamokin Public Library, Bloomsburg Public Library, Harvey A. Andruss Library at Bloomsburg University, Ellen Clarke Bertrand Library at Bucknell University, Schuylkill County Historical Society, Columbia County Historical Society, the Pennsylvania State Library, the Pennsylvania State Archives, the Pennsylvania Historical and Museum Commission (Scranton, Eckley, and Ashland), Pioneer Mine and Tunnel Tour in Ashland, St. Mary's Church in St. Clair, Our Lady of Mount Carmel in Mount Carmel, and St. Patrick's Church in Pottsville. Without them, the coal region's history would be far less well preserved.

The Lukas Prize Project, with its generosity in 2005, freed me to focus on writing and finishing the manuscript full-time, unfettered by part-time or freelance work.

Sam Freedman, whose lessons in craft shaped this project from the outset, persisted in finding a home for it long after I abandoned hope. He also had the grace to publish a book distilling his advice, *Letters to a Young Journalist,* at the precise moment when I needed a refresher.

Betsy Lerner, my agent, bolstered my efforts with her levelheadedness, editorial judgment, and sense of humor. I am lucky to have her on my side. Ileene Smith acquired the book for Random House, and Julia Cheiffetz shepherded the manuscript to completion with pluck and verve, improving it immeasurably in the process.

Many friends and family members helped me through the long slog of pulling this book together, and I am grateful to all of them. Several deserve a special mention. In 2000, my then colleagues at the Securities and Exchange Commission's Enforcement Division in Washington, D.C., graciously granted my request for a leave of absence so I could begin researching this book: Bill Baker, Joe Cella, Toni Chion, Charles Clark, Bob Hanson, Jessica Kline, Bob Leef, Tray Mitchell, and Andrew Snowdon. Two years later, *Miami Herald* colleagues taught me invaluable lessons about reporting, writing, tenacity, and fairness: Pat Andrews, Jerry Berrios, Ellie Brecher, Cara Buckley, Wanda De Marzo, Tom Fiedler, Gregg Fields, George Haj, Rick Hirsch, Brad Lehman, and Terrence Shepard.

More recently, Melanie Kaplan reviewed the first three chapters in their infancy, when they ran much longer than necessary. Dr. John T. Queenan read each chapter and made invaluable suggestions about the delivery room scene, his arena of expertise. Holley Bishop read the entire manuscript, spotting holes and saving me from all kinds of embarrassment.

My mother probably launched me on this track by introducing me to *Little House on the Prairie,* driving me to the library and paying my overdue fines. My father, who may not have known about the fines, did much of the rest, with his reverence for history, hard work, linguistic exactitude, and Irish wit, his genealogical pursuits, and his daily newspaper habit. My brothers, Tom and James, kept me motivated with their enthusiasm for all things coal region, from eBay finds to original songs. Uncle Jim helped flesh out the family portraiture and needled me—with good reason—about bogging down in research. Dylan and Emma Quigley, my niece and nephew, and Dylan Furst inspired simply by being themselves. My maternal grandmother, Mildred Holland Reifke, sadly did not live to see me complete this book, but her spirit—her intellect, compassion, and curiosity, her love of adventure and the written word—guided me every step of the way, as it did for the almost forty years I was lucky enough to know her.

And finally, of course, Robert, who lived with this project from the outset, and all it did—and did not—entail, including a year in New York, eighteen months of almost weekly coal region road trips, and a whole lot of stories about Jake. I couldn't have brought this to fruition without him.

FURTHER READING

More than five hundred government documents, the vast majority of which are unpublished, served as primary sources for this book, along with news-media reports, private correspondence, and archival records. The full bibliography and chapter notes are online at www.thedaytheearthcavedin.com. The following books, which served as secondary sources, may interest readers seeking more in-depth treatment of the anthracite region's rich history, Irish immigration, the Reagan era, or Centralia itself.

Blatz, Perry K. *Democratic Miners: Work and Labor Relations in the Anthracite Coal Industry, 1875–1925.* Albany: State University of New York Press, 1994.

Burrows, Edwin G., and Mike Wallace. *Gotham: A History of New York City to 1898.* New York: Oxford University Press, 1999.

Culin, Stewart. *A Trooper's Narrative of Service in the Anthracite Coal Strike, 1902.* Philadelphia: George W. Jacobs, 1903.

DeKok, David. *Unseen Danger: A Tragedy of People, Government, and the Centralia Mine Fire.* Philadelphia: University of Pennsylvania Press, 1986.

Dempsey, Thomas. *Centralia 125: Special Anniversary Edition (1866–1991).* Selinsgrove, Pa.: Meadowood Publications, 1991.

Dublin, Thomas. *When the Mines Closed: Stories of Struggles in Hard Times.* Ithaca, N.Y.: Cornell University Press, 1998.

Goodell, Jeff. *Big Coal: The Dirty Secret Behind America's Energy Future*. New York: Houghton Mifflin, 2006.

Historical and Biographical Annals of Columbia and Montour Counties, Penn.: Containing a Concise History of the Two Counties and a Genealogical and Biographical Record of Representative Families. Chicago: J. H. Beers, 1915.

Jacobs, Renee. *Slow Burn: A Photodocument of Centralia, Pennsylvania*. Philadelphia: University of Pennsylvania Press, 1986.

Johnson, Deryl B. *Images of America: Centralia*. Charleston, S.C.: Arcadia, 2004.

Jones, Eliot. *The Anthracite Coal Combination in the United States*. Cambridge, Mass.: Harvard University Press, 1914.

Kenny, Kevin. *Making Sense of the Molly Maguires*. New York: Oxford University Press, 1998.

Koppel, Ted, and Kyle Gibson. *Nightline: History in the Making and the Making of Television*. New York: Random House, 1996.

Korson, George. *Minstrels of the Mine Patch: Songs and Stories of the Anthracite Industry*. Hatboro, Pa.: Folklore Associates, 1964.

Kroll-Smith, J. Stephen, and Stephen R. Couch. *The Real Disaster Is Above Ground: A Mine Fire and Social Conflict*. Lexington: The University Press of Kentucky, 1990.

Mauchline, Robert. *The Mine Foreman's Handbook*. Philadelphia: Henry Carey Baird, 1893.

Mead, Richard R. "An Analysis of the Decline of the Anthracite Industry Since 1921." Ph.D. diss., University of Pennsylvania, 1935.

Miller, Donald L., and Richard E. Sharpless. *The Kingdom of Coal: Work, Enterprise, and Ethnic Communities in the Mine Fields*. Philadelphia: University of Pennsylvania Press, 1985.

Miller, Kerby A. *Emigrants and Exiles: Ireland and the Irish Exodus to North America*. New York: Oxford University Press, 1985.

Morris, Edmund. *Theodore Rex*. New York: Random House, 2001.

Pendley, William Perry. *Warriors for the West: Fighting Bureaucrats, Radical Groups, and Liberal Judges on America's Frontier*. Washington, D.C.: Regnery, 2006.

Poliniak, Louis. *When Coal Was King: Mining Pennsylvania's Anthracite*. Lebanon, Pa.: Applied Arts Publishers, 1996.

Poor, H. V., and H. W. Poor. *Poor's Manual of the Railroads of the United States*. New York: American Bank Note Co., 1902.

Schuylkill County, Pennsylvania: Genealogy, Family History, Biography, Containing Historical Sketches of Old Families and of Representative and Prominent Citizens Past and Present. Chicago: J. H. Beers, 1916.

Strouse, Jean. *Morgan: American Financier.* New York: Random House, 1999.

Thornburgh, Dick. *Where the Evidence Leads: An Autobiography*. Pittsburgh: University of Pittsburgh Press, 2003.

Wallace, Anthony F. C. *St. Clair: A Nineteenth-Century Coal Town's Experience with a Disaster-Prone Industry*. New York: Knopf, 1987.

Watt, Leilani, with Al Janssen. *Caught in the Conflict: My Life with James Watt*. Eugene, Ore.: Harvest House, 1984.

ABOUT THE AUTHOR

Joan Quigley, the granddaughter and great-granddaughter of Centralia miners, first glimpsed the mine fire at age fifteen, during her grandmother's funeral at St. Ignatius Cemetery. A former *Miami Herald* business reporter, she is a graduate of Princeton and of Columbia University's School of Journalism. She won the 2005 J. Anthony Lukas Work-in-Progress Award for her efforts on this book. She lives outside Washington, D.C.

ABOUT THE TYPE

This book was set in Bembo, a typeface based on an oldstyle Roman face that was used for Cardinal Bembo's tract *De Aetna* in 1495. Bembo was cut by Francisco Griffo in the early sixteenth century. The Lanston Monotype Company of Philadelphia brought the well-proportioned letterforms of Bembo to the United States in the 1930s.

363.37 QUI
Quigley, Joan
The day the earth caved in
: an American mining
tragedy